Object-Oriented

Programming in Kotlin:

A Practical Guide to Clean and Efficient Code for Scalable,
Maintainable, and Robust Software

Matthew D.Passmore

1

Table Of Content"

Chapter 1
Introduction to Kotlin and Object-Oriented Programming (OOP)

Chapter 2
Getting Started with Kotlin Basics

Chapter 3
Core Principles of Object-Oriented Programming

Chapter 13
Case Studies and Real-World Applications

Chapter 1
Introduction to Kotlin and Object-Oriented Programming (OOP)

Kotlin is a modern, statically typed programming language developed by JetBrains. It is designed to be concise, expressive, and fully interoperable with Java, making it a popular choice for Android development, backend services, and even cross-platform applications. Kotlin's syntax is more readable and less verbose than Java, reducing boilerplate code while maintaining strong type safety.

Why Kotlin for Object-Oriented Programming?

Kotlin follows the principles of Object-Oriented Programming (OOP), allowing developers to structure their code efficiently using classes, objects, and interfaces. OOP helps in designing scalable and maintainable software by encapsulating data, promoting code reuse, and enabling flexibility through polymorphism and inheritance.

Key OOP Features in Kotlin:

Classes and Objects – Fundamental building blocks for organizing code.

Encapsulation – Restricting access to data and ensuring controlled modifications.

Inheritance – Promoting code reuse by extending existing classes.

Polymorphism – Allowing different classes to be used interchangeably through a common interface.

By combining Kotlin's concise syntax with OOP principles, developers can write cleaner, more efficient, and more maintainable code. This guide will explore these concepts in depth, providing practical examples and best practices for leveraging OOP in Kotlin.

1.1 What is Kotlin?

Kotlin is a modern, statically typed programming language developed by JetBrains and officially supported by Google for Android development. It is designed to be concise, expressive, and safe, offering improved syntax and features compared to Java while maintaining full interoperability with it.

Key Features of Kotlin:

Concise and Readable – Reduces boilerplate code compared to Java.

Null Safety – Eliminates null pointer exceptions (NPEs) by enforcing null checks.

Interoperability with Java – Works seamlessly with existing Java codebases.

Object-Oriented and Functional – Supports both OOP and functional programming paradigms.

Coroutines for Asynchronous Programming – Simplifies multithreading and background tasks.

Cross-Platform Development – Supports Kotlin Multiplatform for writing shared code across Android, iOS, Web, and Desktop applications.

Kotlin is widely used in Android app development, backend services (Spring Boot, Ktor), and cross-platform applications. Its growing adoption and developer-friendly features make it a powerful choice for modern software development.

1.2 Key Features of Kotlin for OOP

Kotlin is designed with modern programming paradigms in mind, and its support for Object-Oriented Programming (OOP) makes it a powerful language for building scalable and maintainable applications. Below are the key OOP features of Kotlin:

1. Classes and Objects

Kotlin follows a class-based OOP model, allowing developers to define classes and create objects to represent real-world entities.
It provides primary and secondary constructors for flexible object initialization.

Example:

kotlin
Copy code
```kotlin
class Car(val brand: String, val model: String) {
    fun drive() {
        println("$brand $model is driving")
    }
}

val myCar = Car("Toyota", "Camry")
myCar.drive()
```

2. Encapsulation and Visibility Modifiers

Kotlin supports encapsulation by using visibility modifiers (private, protected, internal, public) to restrict access to class members.

This ensures data security and controlled access to properties and methods.

Example:

kotlin
Copy code

```kotlin
class BankAccount(private var balance: Double) {
  fun deposit(amount: Double) {
    balance += amount
  }

  fun getBalance(): Double {
    return balance
  }
}

val account = BankAccount(1000.0)
account.deposit(500.0)
println(account.getBalance()) // Output: 1500.0
```

3. Inheritance and Abstract Classes

Kotlin allows classes to inherit properties and behavior from a parent class using the open keyword.
It also supports abstract classes, which provide a blueprint for subclasses

Example:

```kotlin
Copy code
open class Animal(val name: String) {
    open fun makeSound() {
        println("$name makes a sound")
    }
}

class Dog(name: String) : Animal(name) {
    override fun makeSound() {
        println("$name barks")
    }
}

val myDog = Dog("Buddy")
myDog.makeSound() // Output: Buddy barks
```

4. Polymorphism (Method Overriding & Overloading)

Method Overriding allows a subclass to provide a specific implementation of a method from its parent class.
Method Overloading allows multiple functions with the same name but different parameters.

Example:

```kotlin
Copy code
open class Shape {
    open fun draw() {
        println("Drawing a shape")
    }
}

class Circle : Shape() {
    override fun draw() {
        println("Drawing a circle")
    }
}

fun main() {
    val shape: Shape = Circle()
    shape.draw() // Output: Drawing a circle
}
```

5. Interfaces for Multiple Inheritance

Kotlin supports multiple inheritance through interfaces.
An interface can define methods that multiple classes can implement.

Example:

kotlin
Copy code

```kotlin
interface Flyable {
    fun fly()
}

class Bird : Flyable {
    override fun fly() {
        println("Bird is flying")
    }
}

val bird = Bird()
bird.fly() // Output: Bird is flying
```

6. Data Classes for Immutable Objects

Data classes automatically generate toString(), equals(), and hashCode() methods, making them ideal for data storage and manipulation.

Example:

kotlin

Copy code
data class User(val name: String, val age: Int)

val user1 = User("Alice", 25)
println(user1) // Output: User(name=Alice, age=25)

7. Sealed Classes for Restricted Inheritance

Sealed classes allow restricted class hierarchies, making them useful for defining state-based logic.

Example:

kotlin
Copy code
```
sealed class Response
class Success(val data: String) : Response()
class Error(val message: String) : Response()

fun handleResponse(response: Response) {
    when (response) {
        is Success -> println("Success: ${response.data}")
        is Error -> println("Error: ${response.message}")
    }
}
```

Conclusion

Kotlin provides a powerful, concise, and expressive approach to Object-Oriented Programming. With features like data classes, interfaces, encapsulation, and sealed classes, Kotlin ensures clean, efficient, and maintainable code. By leveraging these OOP principles, developers can build scalable and robust applications effortlessly.

1.3 Benefits of Using Kotlin for Clean Code

Kotlin is designed to enhance readability, maintainability, and efficiency, making it an excellent choice for writing clean code. Its concise syntax, strong type safety, and modern programming features help developers write scalable and bug-free applications. Below are the key benefits of using Kotlin for clean code:

1. Concise and Readable Syntax

Kotlin eliminates boilerplate code, making programs shorter and easier to read.
Features like type inference, data classes, and extension functions reduce unnecessary verbosity.

Example (Java vs Kotlin Comparison):

Java:

```java
Copy code
public class Person {
    private String name;

    public Person(String name) {
        this.name = name;
    }

    public String getName() {
        return name;
    }
}
```

Kotlin:

```kotlin
Copy code
class Person(val name: String)
```

Kotlin achieves the same functionality in just one line, improving readability and reducing errors.

2. Null Safety (Prevents NullPointerException)

Kotlin has built-in null safety, reducing runtime crashes due to NullPointerException (NPE).
It uses nullable (?) and non-nullable types to enforce safer code.

Example:

kotlin
Copy code
var name: String? = null // Nullable type
println(name?.length) // Safe call, avoids crashes

The safe call (?.) operator prevents null-related crashes, making the code more robust.

3. Type Inference and Immutability

Type inference eliminates the need for explicit type declarations, making the code cleaner.
Immutability (val) ensures variables cannot be changed unexpectedly, leading to safer and predictable code.

Example:

kotlin
Copy code

val age = 30 // Kotlin infers 'age' as Int without explicit declaration

This reduces redundancy and enhances readability.

4. Functional Programming for Cleaner Code

Kotlin supports functional programming features like higher-order functions, lambda expressions, and collections operations to simplify complex logic.

Example:

kotlin
Copy code
```
val numbers = listOf(1, 2, 3, 4, 5)
val doubled = numbers.map { it * 2 }   // Functional approach
println(doubled) // Output: [2, 4, 6, 8, 10]
```

This approach is more concise and expressive than traditional loops.

5. Extension Functions for Improved Modularity

Kotlin allows adding new functionalities to existing classes without modifying their source code using extension functions.

Example:

```kotlin
Copy code
fun String.reverse(): String = this.reversed()

val message = "Kotlin"
println(message.reverse()) // Output: "niltok"
```

This improves code reusability and modularity, making the code cleaner and more maintainable.

6. Default and Named Arguments for Readability

Kotlin allows default values for function parameters, reducing method overloading.
Named arguments make function calls more readable.

Example:

```kotlin
Copy code
fun greet(name: String = "Guest") {
    println("Hello, $name!")
}
```

21

greet()   // Output: Hello, Guest!
greet("Alice")   // Output: Hello, Alice!

This eliminates unnecessary function overloads and enhances code clarity.

7. Data Classes for Simplified Object Representation

Data classes automatically generate methods like toString(), equals(), and hashCode(), making them ideal for clean, structured data handling.

Example:

kotlin
Copy code
data class User(val name: String, val age: Int)

val user = User("Alice", 25)
println(user) // Output: User(name=Alice, age=25)

This reduces boilerplate code and improves code maintainability.

8. Coroutines for Efficient Asynchronous Programming

Kotlin coroutines simplify background operations, making asynchronous code more readable and efficient compared to traditional thread management.
Example:

kotlin
Copy code
```kotlin
import kotlinx.coroutines.*

fun main() = runBlocking {
    launch {
        delay(1000L)
        println("Hello, Kotlin Coroutines!")
    }
    println("Start")
}
```

Unlike callbacks, coroutines provide a cleaner and structured way to handle asynchronous tasks.

9. Sealed Classes for Safer State Management

Sealed classes restrict class hierarchies, ensuring type safety and exhaustive when-expressions.
This is useful for state-based programming, improving code robustness.

Example:

```kotlin
Copy code
sealed class Result
class Success(val data: String) : Result()
class Error(val message: String) : Result()

fun handleResult(result: Result) {
  when (result) {
    is Success -> println("Success: ${result.data}")
    is Error -> println("Error: ${result.message}")
  }
}
```

This makes error handling and state management more predictable.

Conclusion

Kotlin promotes clean, maintainable, and efficient code by reducing boilerplate, enforcing safety, and providing expressive features like null safety, functional programming, extension functions, and coroutines. These features help developers write bug-free, readable, and scalable applications effortlessly.

Chapter 2
Getting Started with Kotlin Basics

Kotlin is a modern, concise, and statically typed language that simplifies development while ensuring type safety. Whether you're new to programming or transitioning from Java, Kotlin offers a smooth learning curve and clean syntax.

1. Setting Up Kotlin

You can start coding in Kotlin using:

Kotlin Playground (online editor) – play.kotlinlang.org
JetBrains IntelliJ IDEA (Recommended IDE)
Android Studio (For Android Development)
Command Line with Kotlin Compiler

2. Kotlin Syntax Overview

A simple "Hello, World!" program in Kotlin:

```kotlin
Copy code
fun main() {
    println("Hello, World!")
}
```

fun defines a function.
main() is the entry point of a Kotlin application.
println() prints output to the console.

3. Kotlin Variables and Data Types

Kotlin has two types of variables:

Immutable (val) – Read-only (cannot be changed).
Mutable (var) – Can be reassigned.

Example:

```kotlin
Copy code
val name: String = "Alice"  // Immutable
var age: Int = 25        // Mutable
```

age = 26 // Allowed since 'age' is declared with 'var'

4. Control Flow: Conditions and Loops

Conditional Statements:

kotlin
Copy code
```
val number = 10
if (number > 0) {
    println("Positive number")
} else {
    println("Negative number")
}
```

Loops:

kotlin
Copy code
```
for (i in 1..5) {
    println(i) // Prints numbers from 1 to 5
}

var x = 1
while (x <= 3) {
    println(x)
    x++
```

}

5. Functions in Kotlin

Functions make code reusable and modular.

kotlin
Copy code
```kotlin
fun greet(name: String): String {
    return "Hello, $name!"
}

println(greet("Alice")) // Output: Hello, Alice!
```

Kotlin also supports single-expression functions:

kotlin
Copy code
```kotlin
fun square(n: Int) = n * n
println(square(4)) // Output: 16
```

Conclusion

These basics provide a foundation for learning Kotlin. With its simple syntax, null safety, and concise structure, Kotlin makes coding efficient and enjoyable. Next, we'll explore

Object-Oriented Programming (OOP) in Kotlin to build structured applications.

2.1 Setting Up Your Kotlin Development Environment

Before you start coding in Kotlin, you need to set up a development environment. Kotlin offers multiple ways to write and run code, whether you're working on a simple script, an Android app, or a backend application.

1. Using Kotlin Playground (Online Editor) [Beginner-Friendly]

If you want to experiment with Kotlin without installing anything, use Kotlin Playground:

Open play.kotlinlang.org in your browser.
Write and run Kotlin code directly in the browser.
Great for learning and testing simple Kotlin programs.

2. Installing Kotlin Locally

To write Kotlin code on your computer, you need an IDE (Integrated Development Environment) or a command-line setup.

A. Using IntelliJ IDEA (Recommended for Kotlin Development) JetBrains' IntelliJ IDEA is the official IDE for Kotlin development.

Steps to Install:

Download IntelliJ IDEA Community Edition (free) from JetBrains.

Install and launch IntelliJ IDEA.

Create a new Kotlin project (File → New Project → Select Kotlin).

Write your Kotlin code and run it inside the IDE.

Why IntelliJ IDEA?

✔ Built-in Kotlin support
✔ Advanced code completion and debugging
✔ Easy project setup

B. Using Android Studio (For Android Development)

If you're developing Android apps, Kotlin is the preferred language.

Steps to Install:

Download Android Studio from developer.android.com.
Install and launch it.
Create a new Android project and choose Kotlin as the primary language.
Start building Android apps with Kotlin!

C. Using Kotlin with the Command Line (For Lightweight Development)
If you prefer coding in a simple text editor and running Kotlin from the terminal:

Install Kotlin Compiler

Install Java Development Kit (JDK 8 or higher) from AdoptOpenJDK.

Install Kotlin via Kotlin Compiler:

On Windows: Download and install Kotlin Compiler.

On Mac/Linux: Use Homebrew:

sh

Copy code

brew install kotlin

Run Kotlin Code from the Terminal

Open a terminal or command prompt.
Create a Kotlin file:

sh

Copy code

touch hello.kt

Write a simple Kotlin program in hello.kt:

kotlin

Copy code

```kotlin
fun main() {
    println("Hello, Kotlin!")
}
```

Compile and run the program:

sh

Copy code

kotlinc hello.kt -include-runtime -d hello.jar

```
java -jar hello.jar
```

3. Using Kotlin with Build Tools (Gradle & Maven)

For larger projects, Kotlin integrates with build tools like:

Gradle (Android & Java projects)
Maven (Enterprise applications)

Setting Up Kotlin with Gradle (Kotlin DSL)

Install Gradle from gradle.org.
Add Kotlin plugin in build.gradle.kts:
kotlin
Copy code
```
plugins {
    kotlin("jvm") version "1.8.0"
}
```

Run the Kotlin project:
sh
Copy code
```
gradle run
```

Conclusion

Kotlin offers flexible setup options based on your development needs. Whether you're using Kotlin Playground for quick tests, IntelliJ IDEA for full-fledged development, or Android Studio for mobile apps, getting started is easy. Choose the right setup, and you're ready to write Kotlin code efficiently!

2.2 Kotlin Syntax Overview

Kotlin has a clean, concise, and expressive syntax that enhances readability and reduces boilerplate code. Whether you're coming from Java or starting fresh, Kotlin's syntax is designed to be easy to understand and efficient to use.

1. Hello World Program

Every Kotlin program starts with a main() function, which serves as the entry point.

kotlin
Copy code
```kotlin
fun main() {
    println("Hello, World!")
```

}

fun declares a function.

main() is the standard entry point.

println() prints text to the console.

2. Variables and Data Types

Kotlin supports two types of variables:

Immutable (val) – Read-only, cannot be reassigned.
Mutable (var) – Can be changed later.

kotlin

Copy code

```kotlin
val name: String = "Alice"  // Immutable variable
var age: Int = 25        // Mutable variable
age = 26  // Allowed, because 'age' is a var
```

Kotlin also infers types automatically, so you can write:

kotlin

Copy code

```kotlin
val city = "New York"  // Type inferred as String
var temperature = 20   // Type inferred as Int
```

3. Functions in Kotlin

Functions help reuse code and improve modularity.

A. Basic Function

kotlin

Copy code

```kotlin
fun greet(name: String): String {
    return "Hello, $name!"
}
println(greet("Alice"))  // Output: Hello, Alice!
```

B. Single-Expression Function

Kotlin allows concise functions using = for single-line expressions.

kotlin

Copy code

```kotlin
fun square(n: Int) = n * n
println(square(4)) // Output: 16
```

C. Default and Named Arguments

kotlin

Copy code

```kotlin
fun greetUser(name: String = "Guest") {
    println("Hello, $name!")
}
```

greetUser()   // Output: Hello, Guest!
greetUser("Alice")   // Output: Hello, Alice!

4. Conditional Statements

Kotlin supports if-else conditions for decision-making.

kotlin
Copy code
val number = 10
if (number > 0) {
   println("Positive number")
} else if (number < 0) {
   println("Negative number")
} else {
   println("Zero")
}

Using if as an Expression

kotlin
Copy code
val max = if (10 > 5) 10 else 5
println(max) // Output: 10

5. Loops in Kotlin

A. for Loop

```kotlin
for (i in 1..5) {
    println(i)  // Prints numbers 1 to 5
}
```

B. while and do-while Loops

```kotlin
var x = 1
while (x <= 3) {
    println(x)
    x++
}
```

```kotlin
var y = 1
do {
    println(y)
    y++
} while (y <= 3)
```

6. Null Safety in Kotlin

Kotlin prevents NullPointerExceptions (NPEs) with built-in null safety.

kotlin
Copy code
```
var name: String? = null  // Nullable type
println(name?.length)  // Safe call, avoids crashes
```

? makes the variable nullable.
?. safely accesses properties without throwing exceptions.

7. Collections in Kotlin

Kotlin provides lists, sets, and maps for handling data collections.

A. Lists (Ordered, allows duplicates)

kotlin
Copy code
```
val fruits = listOf("Apple", "Banana", "Cherry")
println(fruits[0]) // Output: Apple
```

Mutable lists:

```kotlin
Copy code
val numbers = mutableListOf(1, 2, 3)
numbers.add(4)
println(numbers) // Output: [1, 2, 3, 4]
```

B. Sets (Unordered, no duplicates)

```kotlin
Copy code
val uniqueNumbers = setOf(1, 2, 3, 3, 4)
println(uniqueNumbers) // Output: [1, 2, 3, 4]
```

C. Maps (Key-Value pairs)

```kotlin
Copy code
val capitals = mapOf("USA" to "Washington", "UK" to "London")
println(capitals["USA"]) // Output: Washington
```

8. Classes and Objects

Kotlin is an object-oriented language, and classes help structure code.

kotlin
Copy code

```kotlin
class Person(val name: String, var age: Int) {
    fun introduce() {
        println("Hi, I'm $name and I'm $age years old.")
    }
}

val person = Person("Alice", 25)
person.introduce()   // Output: Hi, I'm Alice and I'm 25 years old.
```

9. Extension Functions

Kotlin allows adding new functions to existing classes without modifying them.

kotlin
Copy code

```kotlin
fun String.reverse(): String = this.reversed()

val message = "Kotlin"
println(message.reverse()) // Output: niltoK
```

10. Coroutines for Asynchronous Programming

Kotlin coroutines handle background tasks more efficiently.

```kotlin
Copy code
import kotlinx.coroutines.*

fun main() = runBlocking {
    launch {
        delay(1000L)
        println("Hello, Kotlin Coroutines!")
    }
    println("Start")
}
```

Coroutines simplify asynchronous operations without blocking threads.

Conclusion

Kotlin's syntax is clean, concise, and expressive, making it easy to write and maintain code. With null safety, functional programming, extension functions, and coroutines, Kotlin offers a modern programming experience for Android, backend, and multiplatform development.

2.3 Understanding Kotlin Data Types and Variables

Kotlin is a statically typed language, meaning every variable has a specific data type that is known at compile time. Kotlin's type system helps improve safety, readability, and performance.

1. Declaring Variables in Kotlin

Kotlin provides two keywords to declare variables:

val (Immutable) → Read-only, cannot be reassigned.
var (Mutable) → Can be reassigned.

kotlin
Copy code
```
val name: String = "Alice"   // Immutable (cannot be changed)
var age: Int = 25       // Mutable (can be reassigned)
age = 26 // Allowed since 'age' is declared with 'var'
```

Type Inference

Kotlin automatically infers types, so explicit type declaration is optional:

kotlin
Copy code
val city = "New York" // Inferred as String
var temperature = 30 // Inferred as Int

2. Kotlin Data Types

Kotlin provides various built-in data types grouped into Numbers, Characters, Boolean, Strings, and Collections.

A. Numeric Data Types

Kotlin supports different types of numbers:

Data Type	Size (bits)	Example
Byte	8	val b: Byte = 127
Short	16	val s: Short = 32000
Int	32	val i: Int =

		1000000
Long	64	val l: Long = 10000000000L
Float	32 (Decimal)	val f: Float = 3.14F
Double	64 (Decimal)	val d: Double = 3.1415926535

Example:

kotlin
Copy code
val num1: Int = 100
val num2 = 200L // Inferred as Long
val pi: Double = 3.14
val percentage: Float = 99.9F

Use L for Long and F for Float.

B. Boolean Type

Booleans hold either true or false:

kotlin
Copy code
val isKotlinFun: Boolean = true

C. Character Type

A Char represents a single character enclosed in single quotes:

kotlin
Copy code
val letter: Char = 'K'

D. String Type

A String represents a sequence of characters:

kotlin
Copy code
val greeting: String = "Hello, Kotlin!"

Multiline Strings use triple quotes (""""):

kotlin

Copy code
val multiLine = """"This is
a multiline
string.""""

String Interpolation:

kotlin
Copy code
val name = "Alice"
val age = 25
println("My name is $name and I am $age years old.")

3. Null Safety in Kotlin

Kotlin prevents NullPointerException by making variables non-nullable by default.

kotlin
Copy code
var name: String = "Kotlin"
// name = null // Compilation Error (non-nullable)

Nullable Variables (? Operator)

To allow null values, use ?:

kotlin
Copy code
var name: String? = null
println(name?.length) // Safe Call, avoids crashes

Elvis Operator (?:) provides a default value if null:

kotlin
Copy code
val length = name?.length ?: 0 // If 'name' is null, use 0

4. Type Conversion in Kotlin

Kotlin does not allow implicit type conversion (unlike Java). Use explicit conversion functions:

kotlin
Copy code
val number: Int = 10
val doubleValue: Double = number.toDouble() // Convert Int to Double
val stringValue: String = number.toString() //

Convert Int to String

Function	Purpose
toByte()	Converts to Byte

toShort()	Converts to Short
toInt()	Converts to Int
toLong()	Converts to Long
toFloat()	Converts to Float
toDouble()	Converts to Double
toString()	Converts to String

5. Constants in Kotlin (const and val)

For compile-time constants, use const val:

kotlin
Copy code
const val PI = 3.1416
const val must be top-level or inside an object/class.
Regular val can be initialized dynamically, but const val must be assigned at compile time.

Conclusion

Kotlin's type system ensures safety and efficiency by enforcing strict type checking, null safety, and concise syntax. By understanding variables, data types, and null safety, you can write robust, error-free Kotlin code!

Chapter 3
Core Principles of Object-Oriented Programming

Object-Oriented Programming (OOP) is a programming paradigm that structures code using objects and classes to improve modularity, reusability, and maintainability. Kotlin, as an OOP language, supports four fundamental principles of OOP: Encapsulation, Inheritance, Polymorphism, and Abstraction.

1. Encapsulation (Data Hiding)

Encapsulation ensures that an object's internal state is protected from direct modification. It is achieved using private properties and getter/setter methods.

Example:

kotlin
Copy code

```kotlin
class BankAccount(private var balance: Double) {
    fun deposit(amount: Double) {
        balance += amount
    }

    fun getBalance(): Double = balance  // Controlled access
}

val account = BankAccount(1000.0)
account.deposit(500.0)
println(account.getBalance()) // Output: 1500.0
```

The balance variable is private, preventing direct access from outside the class.

2. Inheritance (Code Reusability)

Inheritance allows a class to derive properties and behavior from another class, reducing code duplication.

Example:

kotlin
Copy code
```kotlin
open class Animal(val name: String) {  // Parent class
    fun eat() = println("$name is eating")
}
```

```kotlin
class Dog(name: String) : Animal(name) {  // Child class
    fun bark() = println("$name is barking")
}
```

```kotlin
val myDog = Dog("Buddy")
myDog.eat() // Inherited method
myDog.bark()
```

The Dog class inherits from Animal, reusing its properties and methods.

3. Polymorphism (Multiple Forms)

Polymorphism allows objects to be treated as instances of their parent class, enabling flexibility and scalability.

Example:

kotlin
Copy code
```kotlin
open class Shape {
    open fun draw() = println("Drawing a shape")
}
```

```kotlin
class Circle : Shape() {
    override fun draw() = println("Drawing a circle")
```

```
}

class Square : Shape() {
    override fun draw() = println("Drawing a square")
}

val shapes: List<Shape> = listOf(Circle(), Square())
for (shape in shapes) {
    shape.draw()  // Calls appropriate overridden method
}
```

The same draw() method behaves differently based on the object type.

4. Abstraction (Hiding Implementation Details)

Abstraction allows defining only essential details while hiding unnecessary implementation. It is achieved using abstract classes or interfaces.

Example:

```kotlin
Copy code
abstract class Vehicle {
    abstract fun start()
}
```

```kotlin
class Car : Vehicle() {
    override fun start() = println("Car is starting")
}

val myCar = Car()
myCar.start()
```

The Vehicle class provides a blueprint, while Car implements the specific behavior.

Conclusion

OOP in Kotlin enhances code organization, reusability, and maintainability. By applying Encapsulation, Inheritance, Polymorphism, and Abstraction, you can write scalable and clean Kotlin applications.

3.1 Abstraction: Simplifying Complexity

What is Abstraction?

Abstraction is an object-oriented programming (OOP) principle that simplifies complex systems by hiding unnecessary details and exposing only the relevant parts. It allows developers to focus on what an object does rather than how it does it.

Kotlin achieves abstraction using abstract classes and interfaces.

1. Abstraction with Abstract Classes

An abstract class serves as a blueprint for other classes. It can have both abstract methods (without implementation) and concrete methods (with implementation).

Example: Abstract Class in Kotlin

```kotlin
Copy code
abstract class Animal(val name: String) {
    abstract fun makeSound()  // Abstract method (no implementation)

  fun eat() {
    println("$name is eating")
  }
}
```

```kotlin
class Dog(name: String) : Animal(name) {
    override fun makeSound() {
        println("$name barks")
    }
}
```

```kotlin
val myDog = Dog("Buddy")
myDog.makeSound()  // Output: Buddy barks
myDog.eat()        // Output: Buddy is eating
```

Key Points:

✔ Cannot create objects of an abstract class
✔ Must override abstract methods in subclasses
✔ Can contain both abstract and concrete methods

2. Abstraction with Interfaces

An interface defines a contract that a class must follow. Unlike abstract classes, interfaces do not store state and support multiple inheritance.

Example: Interface in Kotlin

kotlin

Copy code
```
interface Vehicle {
   fun start()  // Abstract method (no implementation)
}

class Car : Vehicle {
   override fun start() {
      println("Car is starting")
   }
}

class Bike : Vehicle {
   override fun start() {
      println("Bike is starting")
   }
}

val myCar = Car()
myCar.start()  // Output: Car is starting
```

Key Points:

✔ Interfaces cannot store state (no instance variables)
✔ A class can implement multiple interfaces
✔ All interface methods must be implemented in the subclass

3. Difference Between Abstract Class and Interface

Feature	Abstract Class	Interface
State Storage	Can have variables	Cannot store state
Multiple Inheritance	Not supported	Supported
Function Implementation	Can have both abstract & concrete methods	Only abstract methods (before Kotlin 1.1)
Use Case	When objects share common behavior	When unrelated objects share functionality

Why Use Abstraction?

Reduces Complexity: Hides unnecessary implementation details.

Enhances Code Reusability: Common behavior is shared among multiple classes.

Improves Maintainability: Changes to the underlying implementation do not affect users of the class.

Supports Scalability: Helps in designing large, modular applications.

Conclusion

Abstraction in Kotlin helps simplify complex systems by exposing only essential details through abstract classes and interfaces. By using abstraction effectively, developers can write scalable, maintainable, and clean Kotlin code.

3.2 Encapsulation: Protecting Data

What is Encapsulation?

Encapsulation is a fundamental principle of Object-Oriented Programming (OOP) that hides the internal details of a class and restricts direct access to its data. It ensures that the internal state of an object is modified only through controlled access methods, improving data security, maintainability, and modularity.

In Kotlin, encapsulation is implemented using access modifiers (private, protected, internal, public) along with getter and setter functions.

1. Encapsulation Using Access Modifiers

Kotlin provides four access modifiers to control data visibility:

Modifier	Visibility Scope
private	Visible only within the same class
protected	Visible in the same class and subclasses
internal	Visible within the same module
public	Visible everywhere (default)

Example: Private Data Members

kotlin
Copy code
```kotlin
class BankAccount(private var balance: Double) {

    fun deposit(amount: Double) {
        if (amount > 0) balance += amount
    }

    fun withdraw(amount: Double) {
        if (amount > 0 && amount <= balance) balance -= amount
    }

    fun getBalance(): Double = balance
}

val account = BankAccount(1000.0)
account.deposit(500.0)
account.withdraw(200.0)
println(account.getBalance())  // Output: 1300.0
```

Key Points:

✔ The balance variable is private, preventing direct modification.

✔ The class provides controlled access via deposit(), withdraw(), and getBalance().

2. Encapsulation Using Getters and Setters

Kotlin provides custom getters and setters to control how data is accessed or modified.

Example: Custom Getters and Setters

```kotlin
Copy code
class Person {
    var age: Int = 0
        set(value) {
            if (value >= 0) field = value  // Ensuring valid age
        }
        get() = field  // Getter (default behavior)
}

val person = Person()
person.age = 25  // Valid assignment
println(person.age)  // Output: 25

person.age = -5  // Invalid assignment, ignored
println(person.age)  // Output: 25 (unchanged)
```

Key Points:

✔ field is used inside the setter to avoid recursive calls.
✔ The setter ensures age cannot be negative.

3. Benefits of Encapsulation

Data Security: Prevents unintended modifications to sensitive data.
Code Maintainability: Makes code more manageable by defining clear access rules.
Reusability: Encapsulated classes can be used as independent modules.
Flexibility: Allows controlled modification of class properties via getter/setter methods.

Conclusion

Encapsulation in Kotlin helps protect data by restricting direct access and allowing controlled modifications through private variables, access modifiers, and custom getter/setter functions. It ensures better security, maintainability, and modularity, making your code more robust and error-free.

3.3 Inheritance: Reusability of Code

What is Inheritance?

Inheritance is one of the core principles of Object-Oriented Programming (OOP) that allows a class to inherit properties and behaviors (methods) from another class. Inheritance facilitates code reusability and promotes a hierarchical relationship between classes. The class that inherits from another is called a subclass, while the class being inherited from is called the superclass.

In Kotlin, inheritance is achieved using the open keyword, which marks a class or method as inheritance-friendly. By default, all classes in Kotlin are final (cannot be inherited from) unless explicitly marked with open.

1. Basic Syntax of Inheritance in Kotlin

In Kotlin, to allow a class to be inherited, you need to use the open keyword. A subclass can then override methods or properties of its superclass.

Example: Simple Inheritance
kotlin
Copy code

```kotlin
open class Animal(val name: String) { // Superclass marked as 'open'
    fun eat() {
        println("$name is eating")
    }

    open fun sound() { // Open method to allow overriding
        println("$name makes a sound")
    }
}

class Dog(name: String) : Animal(name) { // Subclass
    fun bark() {
        println("$name is barking")
    }

    override fun sound() {  // Overriding method from superclass
        println("$name barks loudly")
    }
}

val dog = Dog("Buddy")
dog.eat()    // Inherited from Animal
dog.bark()   // Specific to Dog
dog.sound()  // Overridden method
```

Key Points:

The Animal class is open to be inherited by other classes.

The sound() method in Animal is open to be overridden in the subclass.

The Dog class inherits the eat() method from Animal and overrides the sound() method.

2. Constructor Inheritance

A subclass can call the constructor of the superclass using the super keyword. This ensures the proper initialization of the inherited properties.

Example: Constructor Inheritance

```kotlin
Copy code
open class Vehicle(val brand: String) {
    open fun start() {
        println("The $brand vehicle is starting.")
    }
}

class Car(brand: String, val model: String) : Vehicle(brand) {
    // Calling superclass constructor
```

```kotlin
  fun drive() {
    println("The $model car is driving.")
  }

  override fun start() {
    println("The $brand $model car is starting.")
  }
}

val car = Car("Toyota", "Corolla")
car.start() // Overridden start method
car.drive() // Car-specific method
```

Key Points:

The Car subclass calls the Vehicle constructor using Vehicle(brand).

The start() method is overridden in the Car class to provide a more specific implementation.

3. Accessing Superclass Methods and Properties

The super keyword in Kotlin allows a subclass to access methods or properties from its superclass that have been overridden.

Example: Using super to Access Superclass Methods

```kotlin
kotlin
Copy code
open class Animal {
    open fun sound() {
        println("Animal makes a sound")
    }
}

class Dog : Animal() {
    override fun sound() {
        println("Dog barks")
    }

    fun callSuperSound() {
        super.sound() // Accessing the superclass method
    }
}

val dog = Dog()
dog.sound()      // Output: Dog barks
dog.callSuperSound() // Output: Animal makes a sound
```

Key Points:

The callSuperSound() method in the Dog class calls the superclass (Animal) method using super.sound().

4. Benefits of Inheritance

Code Reusability: Inheritance allows the reuse of existing code, preventing duplication and simplifying maintenance.

Extensibility: Subclasses can extend and customize behavior without modifying the superclass.

Maintainability: Changes to the superclass propagate to all subclasses, making updates easier.

Improved Organization: Inheritance structures classes into a hierarchical relationship, enhancing code organization.

5. Inheritance and Overriding in Kotlin

In Kotlin, you can override a method or property from the superclass using the override keyword. Only methods or properties marked with open in the superclass can be overridden. If a method is not overridden, the subclass uses the method from the superclass.

Example: Overriding a Property

kotlin
Copy code

```kotlin
open class Person(val name: String) {
    open val role: String = "Employee"
}

class Manager(name: String) : Person(name) {
    override val role: String = "Manager"
}

val manager = Manager("John")
println(manager.role)  // Output: Manager
```

Key Points:

The role property is overridden in the Manager class to provide a more specific role.
override ensures that the subclass provides its own implementation.

Conclusion

Inheritance in Kotlin enables code reusability and allows developers to build on existing functionality without rewriting it. By using the open keyword for superclass methods and properties and the override keyword in subclasses, Kotlin ensures a clean, maintainable approach to inheritance. This hierarchical structure makes the codebase more organized, extensible, and easier to update.

3.4 Polymorphism: Flexibility in Design

What is Polymorphism?

Polymorphism is a core concept in Object-Oriented Programming (OOP) that allows a single interface to represent different underlying forms. It enables objects of different classes to be treated as instances of the same class through a shared interface or superclass. Polymorphism is achieved by overriding methods in subclasses and invoking them dynamically based on the object type at runtime.

In simpler terms, polymorphism allows different classes to be used interchangeably, providing flexibility in design while minimizing the need for rewriting code.

1. Types of Polymorphism in Kotlin

There are two main types of polymorphism in Kotlin:

Compile-time Polymorphism (Static Binding)
This is achieved via method overloading or operator overloading, where multiple methods with the same name but different parameters exist within the same class.

Runtime Polymorphism (Dynamic Binding)
This occurs when a method in a subclass overrides a method in the superclass. The method called is determined at runtime based on the object type.

Example: Runtime Polymorphism (Method Overriding)

kotlin
Copy code
```kotlin
open class Animal {
    open fun makeSound() {
        println("Animal makes a sound")
    }
}

class Dog : Animal() {
    override fun makeSound() {
        println("Dog barks")
    }
}

class Cat : Animal() {
```

```kotlin
    override fun makeSound() {
        println("Cat meows")
    }
}

fun main() {
    val animal: Animal = Dog()
    animal.makeSound()  // Output: Dog barks

    val anotherAnimal: Animal = Cat()
    anotherAnimal.makeSound()  // Output: Cat meows
}
```

Key Points:

The makeSound() method is overridden in both Dog and Cat.
The type of the object (Dog or Cat) determines which makeSound() method is called at runtime, even though both are treated as Animal references.
This is runtime polymorphism.

2. Compile-time Polymorphism (Method Overloading)

Method overloading is another form of polymorphism where multiple methods with the same name but different parameters can exist in the same class. The appropriate method is chosen at compile time based on the argument types passed to the method.

Example: Method Overloading

kotlin
Copy code
```kotlin
fun add(a: Int, b: Int): Int {
    return a + b
}

fun add(a: Double, b: Double): Double {
    return a + b
}

fun main() {
    println(add(3, 4))      // Output: 7 (Int version)
    println(add(3.5, 4.2))    // Output: 7.7 (Double version)
}
```

Key Points:

The add() method is overloaded to accept both Int and Double types.
The correct method is chosen at compile time based on the arguments passed.

3. Using Polymorphism with Interfaces

Polymorphism can also be implemented using interfaces. A single interface can be implemented by multiple classes, and objects of these classes can be treated as instances of the interface.

Example: Polymorphism with Interfaces

kotlin
Copy code
```kotlin
interface Drawable {
    fun draw()
}

class Circle : Drawable {
    override fun draw() {
        println("Drawing a circle")
    }
}

class Square : Drawable {
    override fun draw() {
        println("Drawing a square")
    }
}

fun main() {
    val shapes: List<Drawable> = listOf(Circle(), Square())
    for (shape in shapes) {
```

```
    shape.draw()  // Output: Drawing a circle, Drawing a
square
  }
}
```

Key Points:

Both Circle and Square classes implement the Drawable interface.
The draw() method is called polymorphically, depending on the
actual object type (Circle or Square).
This is runtime polymorphism using interfaces.

4. Benefits of Polymorphism

Code Reusability and Extensibility:

Polymorphism allows you to reuse code and extend it without
modifying the existing code. You can add new classes or methods
while keeping the existing code intact.

Reduced Complexity:

It simplifies the design by allowing a single interface to be used for
objects of different classes, making the system more flexible and
scalable.

Improved Maintainability:

By enabling a single interface for different objects, polymorphism helps in minimizing code duplication. Changes to common behavior can be applied in one place, ensuring consistency across multiple objects.

Dynamic Behavior:

Polymorphism allows objects to behave dynamically based on their actual type at runtime, making the system more adaptable and flexible in responding to changes.

5. Practical Example of Polymorphism in Kotlin

Consider a scenario where you have different types of payment methods, and you want to process each payment differently, but treat them using a common interface.

Example: Polymorphism in Payment Systems

```kotlin
Copy code
interface Payment {
    fun processPayment(amount: Double)
}

class CreditCard : Payment {
```

```kotlin
    override fun processPayment(amount: Double) {
        println("Processing credit card payment of $$amount")
    }
}

class PayPal : Payment {
    override fun processPayment(amount: Double) {
        println("Processing PayPal payment of $$amount")
    }
}

fun main() {
    val payments: List<Payment> = listOf(CreditCard(),
PayPal())
    for (payment in payments) {
        payment.processPayment(100.0)
    }
}
```

Key Points:

The Payment interface defines a common method processPayment().

Both CreditCard and PayPal classes implement this interface and provide their own behavior.

This allows flexibility in processing different payment methods using the same interface

Conclusion

Polymorphism in Kotlin provides flexibility and adaptability in your code, allowing objects of different types to be treated uniformly while enabling dynamic behavior at runtime. Whether through method overloading (compile-time polymorphism) or method overriding (runtime polymorphism), polymorphism simplifies code structure and improves maintainability and scalability. By utilizing interfaces and inheritance, polymorphism makes it easier to extend systems without breaking existing functionality.

Chapter 4
Classes and Objects in Kotlin

What is a Class?

A class in Kotlin is a blueprint for creating objects. It defines the properties (fields) and behaviors (methods) that the objects of that class will have. Classes in Kotlin can have a primary constructor, secondary constructors, properties, methods, and more.

Example: Defining a Class in Kotlin

kotlin
Copy code
```kotlin
class Person(val name: String, var age: Int) {
    fun introduce() {
        println("Hi, I'm $name and I am $age years old.")
    }
}
```

In this example:

Person is a class with two properties: name and age.
It has a method introduce() that prints a simple introduction.

What is an Object?

An object is an instance of a class. When a class is defined, no memory is allocated. When you create an object from that class, memory is allocated to hold the object's properties and methods.

Example: Creating an Object

kotlin
Copy code

```kotlin
fun main() {
    val person1 = Person("Alice", 30)  // Create an object of class Person
    person1.introduce() // Output: Hi, I'm Alice and I am 30 years old.
}
```

In this example:

person1 is an object of the Person class, created with the name "Alice" and age 30.
The introduce() method is called on person1.

Primary Constructor

In Kotlin, the primary constructor is part of the class header and is used to initialize properties when an object is created. It is declared directly after the class name.

Example: Primary Constructor

kotlin
Copy code
class Car(val make: String, val model: String, var year: Int)

Here:

make, model, and year are properties initialized via the primary constructor.

Secondary Constructor

A class in Kotlin can have one or more secondary constructors if the class needs to be initialized in multiple ways. These are declared using the constructor keyword.

Example: Secondary Constructor
kotlin
Copy code
class Car(val make: String, val model: String) {
    var year: Int = 0

```kotlin
constructor(make: String, model: String, year: Int) :
this(make, model) {
    this.year = year
  }
}
```

In this example:

The secondary constructor allows you to create a Car object with or without the year parameter.
Accessing Properties and Methods
Once an object is created, you can access its properties and call its methods using the dot (.) notation.

Example: Accessing Properties and Methods
kotlin
Copy code
```kotlin
fun main() {
    val car = Car("Toyota", "Corolla", 2020)
    println("Car: ${car.make} ${car.model}, Year: ${car.year}")
// Access properties
}
```

Conclusion

In Kotlin, classes are blueprints for creating objects. Classes can have a primary constructor to initialize properties, and optionally secondary constructors for additional ways of initializing the object. Objects are instances of these classes and hold the data defined by the class. With classes and objects, Kotlin supports the basic principles of object-oriented programming, enabling efficient and organized code design.

4.1 Defining and Using Classes

Defining a Class in Kotlin

A class in Kotlin is a blueprint for creating objects. It defines properties (variables) and methods (functions) that describe the behavior of objects created from the class. You can define a class in Kotlin using the class keyword.

Basic Syntax of a Class

kotlin

Copy code

```
class Person(val name: String, var age: Int) {
    fun introduce() {
        println("Hello, my name is $name and I am $age years old.")
```

```
    }
}
```

In this example:

Person is a class with two properties: name (immutable) and age (mutable).
introduce() is a method that prints a message introducing the person.

Key Components in a Class:

Properties: Defined within the class to hold data. Can be val (immutable) or var (mutable).
Methods: Functions defined within the class to perform operations using the class's properties.

Creating an Object from a Class

To use a class, you need to create an object. An object is an instance of the class, where the properties are initialized and methods can be called.

Creating an Object

kotlin
Copy code

```kotlin
fun main() {
    val person1 = Person("Alice", 25)  // Create an object of the Person class
    person1.introduce()  // Call the introduce() method
}
```

person1 is an object of the Person class. It has the properties name set to "Alice" and age set to 25.

The introduce() method is called on person1, which outputs "Hello, my name is Alice and I am 25 years old."

Primary Constructor

Kotlin classes can have a primary constructor, which is used to initialize properties directly when the object is created. The primary constructor is defined immediately after the class name.

Example: Primary Constructor

kotlin
Copy code
```kotlin
class Car(val make: String, val model: String, var year: Int) {
    fun displayInfo() {
        println("Car: $make $model, Year: $year")
    }
}
```

Here:

make, model, and year are properties initialized in the primary constructor.
The displayInfo() method prints the car's details.
Creating an Object with Primary Constructor

kotlin
Copy code
```kotlin
fun main() {
    val car1 = Car("Toyota", "Corolla", 2021)
    car1.displayInfo()  // Output: Car: Toyota Corolla, Year: 2021
}
```

Secondary Constructors

A class can also have secondary constructors. These are additional constructors that provide more ways to initialize an object. They are defined using the constructor keyword.

Example: Secondary Constructor
kotlin
Copy code
```kotlin
class Car(val make: String, val model: String) {
    var year: Int = 0
```

```kotlin
    // Secondary constructor
    constructor(make: String, model: String, year: Int) :
this(make, model) {
    this.year = year
  }

  fun displayInfo() {
    println("Car: $make $model, Year: $year")
  }
}
```

Here:

The secondary constructor allows creating a Car object with or without the year parameter.
The year property is set via the secondary constructor.

Creating an Object with Secondary Constructor

kotlin
Copy code
```kotlin
fun main() {
    val car2 = Car("Honda", "Civic")  // Using primary
constructor
    car2.displayInfo() // Output: Car: Honda Civic, Year: 0
```

```kotlin
    val car3 = Car("Ford", "Mustang", 2022)   // Using
secondary constructor
    car3.displayInfo() // Output: Car: Ford Mustang, Year:
2022
}
```

Accessing Class Properties and Methods

Once an object is created, you can access its properties and invoke its methods using the dot notation.

Example: Accessing Properties and Methods

kotlin

Copy code

```kotlin
class Person(val name: String, var age: Int) {
    fun introduce() {
        println("Hello, my name is $name and I am $age years old.")
    }
}

fun main() {
    val person = Person("Bob", 30)
    println(person.name) // Accessing the property 'name'
    person.introduce()   // Calling the method 'introduce'
}
```

Output:

```csharp
Bob
           Hello, my name is Bob and I am 30 years old.k my
```

Kotlin

Default and Named Arguments

allows default values for constructor parameters, as well as named arguments to make object creation more readable.

Example: Default Parameters and Named Arguments

```kotlin
class Car(val make: String, val model: String, var year: Int =
2020) {
    fun displayInfo() {
        println("Car: $make $model, Year: $year")
    }
}

fun main() {
    val car = Car(make = "Tesla", model = "Model S")
```

car.displayInfo() // Output: Car: Tesla Model S, Year: 2020
}

year has a default value of 2020. It is optional when creating a Car object.

Named arguments (make = "Tesla", model = "Model S") make the object creation more readable.

Conclusion

In Kotlin, classes define the structure and behavior of objects, while objects are instances of those classes. You can create classes with primary constructors for simple initialization, or secondary constructors for more flexibility. Classes can have properties and methods that can be accessed by creating objects. This structured approach to defining and using classes enhances code reusability and readability, providing an essential foundation for object-oriented design.

4.2 Constructors and Initialization Blocks

In Kotlin, constructors and initialization blocks are used to initialize the properties of a class when an object is created. Kotlin provides a simple and flexible way to define constructors and initialize objects.

Types of Constructors in Kotlin

Kotlin has two types of constructors:

Primary Constructor
Secondary Constructor

1. Primary Constructor

The primary constructor is the simplest way to define a class in Kotlin. It is declared directly after the class name and is used to initialize the class properties. You can define parameters in the primary constructor and initialize class properties using these parameters.

Syntax of Primary Constructor

kotlin
Copy code
```
class ClassName(val param1: Type, var param2: Type) {
    // Properties and methods can be defined here
}
```

Example of Primary Constructor

kotlin
Copy code
```
class Car(val make: String, val model: String, var year: Int) {
    fun displayInfo() {
        println("Car: $make $model, Year: $year")
    }
}
```

In this example:

The Car class has a primary constructor with three parameters: make, model, and year.
The properties make and model are immutable (val), while year is mutable (var).

Creating an Object Using Primary Constructor

kotlin
Copy code
```
fun main() {
    val car = Car("Tesla", "Model S", 2021)
    car.displayInfo()  // Output: Car: Tesla Model S, Year: 2021
}
```

The object car is created with values for make, model, and year using the primary constructor.

2. Secondary Constructor

The secondary constructor is used when more flexibility is required during object initialization. It is declared using the constructor keyword. Secondary constructors can call the primary constructor (if present) and perform additional initialization.

Syntax of Secondary Constructor

kotlin
Copy code
```kotlin
class ClassName {
    constructor(param1: Type, param2: Type) {
        // Initialization code
    }
}
```

Example of Secondary Constructor

kotlin
Copy code
```kotlin
class Car(val make: String, val model: String) {
    var year: Int = 0
```

```kotlin
    // Secondary constructor
    constructor(make: String, model: String, year: Int) :
this(make, model) {
        this.year = year
    }

    fun displayInfo() {
        println("Car: $make $model, Year: $year")
    }
}
```

In this example:

The Car class has a secondary constructor that allows you to initialize year after the object is created, in addition to make and model.

Creating an Object Using Secondary Constructor

kotlin
Copy code
```kotlin
fun main() {
    val car1 = Car("Ford", "Mustang")
    car1.displayInfo()  // Output: Car: Ford Mustang, Year: 0

    val car2 = Car("Chevrolet", "Camaro", 2022)
```

car2.displayInfo() // Output: Car: Chevrolet Camaro, Year: 2022
}

The secondary constructor allows for flexible object creation, with or without the year parameter.

Initialization Blocks in Kotlin

An initialization block is a block of code that runs when an object is created. It is used to perform additional initialization after the constructor is called. In Kotlin, initialization blocks are defined using the init keyword.

You can use init blocks to initialize properties, perform validations, or call functions.

Syntax of Initialization Block

```kotlin
Copy code
class ClassName {
    init {
        // Initialization code
    }
}
```

Example of Initialization Block

```kotlin
class Car(val make: String, val model: String, var year: Int) {
    init {
        println("Car object is being created...")
    }

    fun displayInfo() {
        println("Car: $make $model, Year: $year")
    }
}
```

In this example:

The init block prints a message whenever a Car object is created.
Creating an Object with Initialization Block

```kotlin
fun main() {
    val car = Car("Tesla", "Model 3", 2021)
    car.displayInfo()  // Output: Car object is being created...
                //      Car: Tesla Model 3, Year: 2021
}
```

The initialization block runs as soon as the object is created, before any other method or property access.

Combining Constructors and Initialization Blocks

You can combine primary constructors, secondary constructors, and initialization blocks to create flexible and powerful class initializations. If you have both primary and secondary constructors, the init block runs after the primary constructor is called.

Example: Using Primary Constructor, Secondary Constructor, and Init Block

kotlin
Copy code
```kotlin
class Car(val make: String, val model: String) {
    var year: Int = 0

    // Secondary constructor
    constructor(make: String, model: String, year: Int) :
this(make, model) {
        this.year = year
    }

    init {
```

```kotlin
        println("Car object is being created with make: $make
and model: $model")
    }

    fun displayInfo() {
        println("Car: $make $model, Year: $year")
    }
}
```

Creating an Object with Combined Initialization

kotlin
Copy code
```kotlin
fun main() {
    val car = Car("BMW", "X5", 2021)
    car.displayInfo()  // Output: Car object is being created
with make: BMW and model: X5
                //      Car: BMW X5, Year: 2021
}
```

In this example:

The init block prints a message each time a Car object is created.
The secondary constructor is used to initialize the year property.

Conclusion

In Kotlin, constructors and initialization blocks provide flexible ways to initialize objects. The primary constructor is the simplest way to initialize properties, while secondary constructors provide additional initialization options. The init block allows for extra initialization code to run when an object is created. Using these features together allows for cleaner, more readable, and maintainable Kotlin code when working with classes and objects.

4.3 Understanding Objects and Companion Objects

In Kotlin, objects and companion objects serve specific purposes for defining behavior and managing state in a class. While both are related to creating instances and managing data, they have distinct roles.

1. Objects in Kotlin

An object in Kotlin is a singleton — a class that only has one instance. Kotlin makes it simple to define an object using the object keyword, which ensures that there is only a single instance of the object throughout the application.

What is an Object?

An object can be used in various scenarios, including:

Defining a singleton.

Holding utility functions or constants.
Implementing a behavior without requiring instantiation of a class.

Creating and Using an Object

Here's the syntax for defining and using an object:

kotlin
Copy code
```kotlin
object SingletonExample {
    var counter = 0

    fun incrementCounter() {
        counter++
    }
```

```kotlin
    fun displayCounter() {
        println("Counter value: $counter")
    }
}

fun main() {
    // Accessing object properties and methods without
creating an instance
    SingletonExample.incrementCounter()
    SingletonExample.displayCounter()  // Output: Counter
value: 1
}
```

In this example:

SingletonExample is an object, and it has a property (counter) and methods (incrementCounter and displayCounter).
The object is accessed directly, and there is no need to instantiate it.

Key Features of Objects in Kotlin:

Singleton Pattern: Kotlin objects are automatically singletons, meaning there is only one instance of the object in the entire program.

Lazy Initialization: The object is initialized lazily, meaning it will only be created when it is first accessed.

No Instantiation Required: You don't need to create an instance of the object — it is accessed directly by its name.

2. Companion Objects in Kotlin

A companion object in Kotlin is a special object that is declared inside a class. It is used to define methods and properties that are tied to the class itself rather than to instances of the class. This concept is similar to static members in Java but is more flexible.

What is a Companion Object?

A companion object is used to create class-level properties or methods that are shared by all instances of the class. It is also the place where you can define factory methods or constants.

Defining a Companion Object

You define a companion object inside a class using the companion object keyword.

Syntax of a Companion Object:

kotlin

```
Copy code
class MyClass {
    companion object {
        val constantValue = 42

        fun createInstance(): MyClass {
            return MyClass()
        }
    }
}
```

In this example:

The companion object is inside the MyClass class.
It contains a property (constantValue) and a method (createInstance()).

Using a Companion Object
You access the properties and methods of the companion object using the class name (just like static members in Java).

Example of Using a Companion Object:

.

kotlin
Copy code
```
fun main() {
    println(MyClass.constantValue)  // Output: 42
```

```kotlin
    val instance = MyClass.createInstance()   // Creating
instance using companion object's method
    println(instance) // Output: MyClass@...
}
```

In this example:

constantValue is accessed directly from the class, as it is part of the companion object.

The createInstance() method is used to create an instance of MyClass.

Accessing Companion Object Members

Companion Object as a Singleton

The companion object is also a singleton, which means it will have only one instance, even though it is associated with the class.

You can access companion object members directly using the class name without needing an instance of the class.

Example of Direct Access to Companion Object:

kotlin
Copy code

```kotlin
class ExampleClass {
    companion object {
        val message = "Hello from Companion!"
    }
}

fun main() {
    println(ExampleClass.message)  // Output: Hello from Companion!
}
```

In this example:

The message property is part of the companion object inside the ExampleClass.
You access it directly via ExampleClass.message without creating an instance of ExampleClass.

Using Named Companion Objects

In Kotlin, you can also provide a name for the companion object. By default, the companion object is referenced by the keyword Companion, but you can give it a custom name if you wish.

Example of Named Companion Object:

kotlin

```
Copy code
class MyClass {
    companion object Factory {
        fun create(): MyClass {
            return MyClass()
        }
    }
}

fun main() {
    val instance = MyClass.Factory.create()   // Accessing
companion object with a custom name
    println(instance) // Output: MyClass@...
}
```

In this example:

The companion object is given the name Factory.
You can access the create() method using MyClass.Factory.create().

Factory Methods in Companion Objects

A common use case for companion objects is creating factory methods. These are methods that return an instance of the class but encapsulate the creation logic. This approach allows you to control how instances are created and provides additional flexibility, such as returning cached instances or performing initialization tasks.

Example of Factory Method in Companion Object:

kotlin
Copy code
```kotlin
class Car private constructor(val make: String, val model: String) {
    companion object Factory {
        fun createCar(make: String, model: String): Car {
            return Car(make, model)
        }
    }
}

fun main() {
    val car = Car.Factory.createCar("Tesla", "Model 3")
    println("Car: ${car.make} ${car.model}")  // Output: Car: Tesla Model 3
}
```

In this example:

The constructor of Car is private, so instances can only be created through the companion object's createCar() method.

The Factory companion object handles the instantiation of the Car class.

Conclusion

In Kotlin:

Objects are singletons that ensure a single instance of the class. They are useful for managing global state or defining utility functions.
Companion objects provide a way to define class-level properties and methods, similar to static members in Java, but with more flexibility. They can be used for factory methods, constants, or shared state between instances.

Both objects and companion objects help streamline code and provide better organization when managing behavior that is shared across multiple instances or globally in an application. By understanding when to use each, you can write clean, efficient Kotlin code.

Chapter 5
Working with Properties and Methods

In Kotlin, properties and methods are fundamental parts of a class, defining its state and behavior. Properties store data, while methods perform actions on that data.

1. Properties in Kotlin

Properties in Kotlin are similar to variables but are associated with a class or object. They can be mutable (var) or immutable (val).

Defining Properties

kotlin
Copy code
```kotlin
class Person(val name: String, var age: Int) {
    var city: String = "Unknown"
}
```

name is an immutable property (val).
age is a mutable property (var).
city is a property initialized with a default value.

Accessing Properties

.

kotlin
Copy coded
```kotlin
fun main() {
    val person = Person("Alice", 25)
    println(person.name) // Output: Alice
    person.age = 26
    println(person.age) // Output: 26
}
```

Properties are accessed using dot notation.

Mutable properties (var) can be modified, while immutable ones (val) cannot.

2. Methods in Kotlin

Methods (or functions) define the behavior of a class. They operate on properties and perform specific tasks.

Defining Methods

kotlin
Copy code
```kotlin
class Person(val name: String, var age: Int) {
```

```kotlin
    fun introduce() {
        println("Hello, my name is $name and I am $age years
old.")
    }
}
```

Calling Methods

kotlin
Copy code
```kotlin
fun main() {
    val person = Person("Bob", 30)
    person.introduce()  // Output: Hello, my name is Bob and
I am 30 years old.
}
```

Methods are called using dot notation on an object.

3. Getters and Setters

Kotlin automatically generates getter and setter methods for properties, but you can customize them.

Custom Getters and Setters

kotlin
Copy code

```kotlin
class Person(var age: Int) {
    var isAdult: Boolean
        get() = age >= 18
        set(value) {
            age = if (value) 18 else age
        }
}
```

kotlin
Copy code
```kotlin
fun main() {
    val person = Person(16)
    println(person.isAdult) // Output: false
    person.isAdult = true // Sets age to 18
    println(person.age) // Output: 18
}
```
Custom getter computes isAdult based on age.

Custom setter ensures age is set to 18 if isAdult is set to true.

Conclusion

Kotlin provides a clean and concise way to work with properties and methods. Properties store class data, while methods define class behavior. With getters and setters, you can add logic to property access, making Kotlin's OOP approach efficient and flexible.

5.1 Kotlin Properties: var vs val

In Kotlin, properties are used to store values inside a class, object, or function. When declaring properties or variables, Kotlin provides two keywords: var and val. Understanding their differences is crucial for writing efficient and maintainable Kotlin code.

1. var (Mutable Properties)

The var keyword is used to declare mutable properties, meaning their values can be changed after initialization.

Syntax:

kotlin
Copy code
var variableName: DataType = value

Example:

```kotlin
Copy code
class Person {
    var age: Int = 25
}

fun main() {
    val person = Person()
    println(person.age) // Output: 25

    person.age = 30 // Value changed
    println(person.age) // Output: 30
}
```

Key Features of var:

Can be reassigned to a new value.
Used for dynamic or changing data.
Commonly used for counters, UI state, and configuration settings.

2. val (Immutable Properties)

The val keyword is used to declare immutable properties, meaning their values cannot be changed after initialization.

Syntax:

kotlin
Copy code
val variableName: DataType = value

Example:

kotlin
Copy code
```
class Car {
    val brand: String = "Tesla"
}

fun main() {
    val car = Car()
    println(car.brand)  // Output: Tesla

    // car.brand = "BMW"  // Error: Val cannot be reassigned
}
```

Key Features of val:

Cannot be reassigned once initialized.
Ensures data integrity and thread safety.
Commonly used for constants, configuration settings, and read-only values.

Key Differences Between var and val

Feature	var (Mutable)	val (Immutable)
Can Change Value?	Yes	No
Reassignment Allowed?	Yes	No
Memory Efficiency	Slightly higher due to changes	More optimized
Use Case	Changing values (e.g., counters, UI state)	Constants, IDs, fixed values

4. Using val with Mutable Collections

A common misconception is that val makes collections completely immutable. However, val only prevents reassignment, not modifications to the collection itself.

Example:
.kotlin
Copy code
val numbers = mutableListOf(1, 2, 3)
numbers.add(4) // Allowed
println(numbers) // Output: [1, 2, 3, 4]

numbers = mutableListOf(5, 6)   // Error: Val cannot be reassigned

The list itself is mutable, but val prevents assigning a new list to numbers.

5. When to Use var vs val?

Use val when the value should not change after assignment (default choice).
Use var only if the value needs to change dynamically.

Best Practice: Prefer val over var

Kotlin encourages immutability as a best practice. Using val whenever possible leads to safer and more predictable code.

Conclusion

Understanding var and val helps in writing clean, maintainable, and bug-free Kotlin code. While var allows for mutability, val enforces immutability, improving code safety and performance. Always prefer val unless mutability is required.

5.2 Member Functions and Overloading

In Kotlin, member functions are functions defined within a class, allowing objects of that class to perform actions or modify their properties. Function overloading enables multiple functions with the same name but different parameters, improving flexibility and readability.

1. Member Functions in Kotlin

A member function is a function declared inside a class. It has direct access to the class's properties and can manipulate them.

Defining a Member Function

kotlin
Copy code
```
class Car(val brand: String, var speed: Int) {
    fun accelerate(increase: Int) {
        speed += increase
        println("$brand is now moving at $speed km/h.")
    }
}
```

Calling a Member Function

kotlin
Copy code
```
fun main() {
    val car = Car("Tesla", 60)
    car.accelerate(20)  // Output: Tesla is now moving at 80 km/h.
}
```

The function accelerate() modifies the speed property.
It is accessed using an object of the class (car.accelerate(20)).

2. Function Overloading in Kotlin

Function overloading allows defining multiple functions with the same name but different parameter lists. The correct function is determined based on:

Number of parameters

Type of parameters

Order of parameters

Example of Function Overloading
kotlin
Copy code

```kotlin
class MathOperations {
    fun multiply(a: Int, b: Int): Int {
        return a * b
    }

    fun multiply(a: Double, b: Double): Double {
        return a * b
    }

    fun multiply(a: Int, b: Int, c: Int): Int {
        return a * b * c
    }
```

}

Calling Overloaded Functions

kotlin
Copy code
fun main() {
  val math = MathOperations()

    println(math.multiply(2, 3))   **// Output: 6 (calls**
multiply(Int, Int))
    println(math.multiply(2.5, 3.5))   **// Output: 8.75 (calls**
multiply(Double, Double))
    println(math.multiply(2, 3, 4))   **// Output: 24 (calls**
multiply(Int, Int, Int))
}

Kotlin selects the appropriate function based on argument types and count.

3. Advantages of Function Overloading

Improves Readability – Uses a consistent function name for similar operations.
Enhances Code Reusability – Avoids defining different function names for similar tasks.

Provides Flexibility – Allows handling different data types and parameter variations efficiently.

Conclusion

Member functions define a class's behavior, while function overloading provides multiple ways to handle different inputs using the same function name. Overloading improves code clarity, reusability, and flexibility, making Kotlin code more concise and efficient.

5.3 Visibility Modifiers and Scoping

In Kotlin, visibility modifiers control the accessibility of classes, properties, and functions, ensuring encapsulation and security. Scoping helps manage how variables and functions are accessed within different parts of the code.

1. Visibility Modifiers in Kotlin

Kotlin provides four visibility modifiers to define access control:

Modifier	Accessible From
public (default)	Anywhere in the project
private	Only within the same class or file
protected	Within the same class and its subclasses
internal	Within the same module

1.1 Public (Default)

If no modifier is specified, the declaration is public, meaning it is accessible from anywhere.

kotlin
Copy code
```kotlin
class Car {
    fun startEngine() {
        println("Engine started")
    }
}

fun main() {
    val car = Car()
    car.startEngine() // Accessible from anywhere
}
```

1.2 Private

A private member is only accessible within the class or file where it is declared.

kotlin
Copy code

```
class Car {
    private fun startEngine() {
        println("Engine started")
    }

    fun drive() {
        startEngine() // Allowed, since it's inside the class
        println("Car is moving")
    }
}

fun main() {
    val car = Car()
    // car.startEngine()   // Error: Cannot access private function
    car.drive() // Works fine
}
```

1.3 Protected

A protected member is like private, but it is also accessible in subclasses.

```kotlin
Copy code
open class Vehicle {
    protected fun honk() {
        println("Honking...")
    }
}

class Car : Vehicle() {
    fun useHorn() {
        honk()  // Accessible in the subclass
    }
}

fun main() {
    val car = Car()
    car.useHorn()  // Works fine
    // car.honk()  // Error: honk() is protected
}
```

1.4 Internal

An internal member is accessible within the same module (a group of related Kotlin files compiled together).

kotlin

Copy code
```
internal class InternalClass {
    internal fun showMessage() {
        println("Hello from internal class")
    }
}

fun main() {
    val obj = InternalClass()
    obj.showMessage()  // Works within the same module
}
```

If another module tries to access InternalClass, it will get an error.

2. Scoping in Kotlin

Scoping helps organize variable access and function execution within specific blocks, reducing unnecessary global variables.

2.1 Block Scope

Variables declared inside a block {} are only accessible within that block.

kotlin
Copy code
```
fun main() {
```

```kotlin
    if (true) {
        val message = "Inside block"
        println(message) // Works fine
    }
    // println(message)  // Error: message is not accessible
here
}
```

2.2 Function Scope

Variables declared inside a function are only accessible within that function.

```kotlin
kotlin
Copy code
fun greet() {
    val greeting = "Hello"
    println(greeting)
}

fun main() {
    greet() // Output: Hello
    // println(greeting)  // Error: Not accessible outside
greet()
}
```

2.3 Class Scope

Class properties can be accessed within any member function of that class.

kotlin
Copy code
```kotlin
class Person {
    var name: String = "Alice"  // Class-level scope

    fun display() {
        println("Name: $name")  // Accessible here
    }
}

fun main() {
    val person = Person()
    person.display()  // Output: Name: Alice
}
```

2.4 Object Scope (With apply, let, run)

Kotlin provides scoping functions (let, apply, run, with, also) to simplify object initialization and property access.

Example: Using apply for Object Initialization

```kotlin
kotlin
Copy code
class Car {
    var brand: String = ""
    var speed: Int = 0
}

fun main() {
    val myCar = Car().apply {
        brand = "Toyota"
        speed = 100
    }
    println("${myCar.brand} is moving at ${myCar.speed} km/h")
}
```

Conclusion

Visibility modifiers (public, private, protected, internal) control the accessibility of classes, properties, and functions.

Scoping rules define how and where variables and functions can be accessed within blocks, functions, and objects.

Scoping functions (apply, let, run, etc.) improve code readability and efficiency.

Understanding these concepts helps write cleaner, safer, and more maintainable Kotlin code.

Chapter 6
Inheritance and Interfaces

Kotlin supports inheritance and interfaces as key object-oriented programming (OOP) concepts to promote code reuse and flexibility.

1. Inheritance in Kotlin

Inheritance allows a class to derive properties and behaviors from another class. Kotlin uses the open keyword to make a class inheritable since classes are final by default.

Example: Basic Inheritance

```kotlin
Copy code
open class Animal(val name: String) {
    fun eat() {
        println("$name is eating.")
    }
}
```

```kotlin
class Dog(name: String) : Animal(name) {
    fun bark() {
        println("$name is barking.")
    }
}

fun main() {
    val myDog = Dog("Buddy")
    myDog.eat() // Inherited from Animal
    myDog.bark() // Defined in Dog
}
```

Animal is the parent (superclass).
Dog is the child (subclass), inheriting eat() from Animal.

Overriding Functions in Inheritance

A subclass can override a function from its superclass using the open and override keywords.

kotlin
Copy code
```kotlin
open class Animal {
    open fun makeSound() {
        println("Some generic animal sound")
```

```kotlin
    }
}

class Cat : Animal() {
    override fun makeSound() {
        println("Meow!")
    }
}

fun main() {
    val myCat = Cat()
    myCat.makeSound()  // Output: Meow!
}
```

2. Interfaces in Kotlin

An interface defines a contract that a class must follow but does not provide implementations for functions. A class can implement multiple interfaces.

Example: Defining and Implementing an Interface

kotlin
Copy code
```kotlin
interface Drivable {
    fun drive()
}
```

```kotlin
class Car : Drivable {
  override fun drive() {
    println("Car is driving")
  }
}

fun main() {
  val myCar = Car()
  myCar.drive()  // Output: Car is driving
}
```

Drivable defines a function without implementation.
Car implements the interface by providing the function body.
Multiple Interface Implementation
A class can implement multiple interfaces.

kotlin
Copy code
```kotlin
interface Flyable {
  fun fly()
}

class Airplane : Drivable, Flyable {
  override fun drive() {
    println("Airplane is taxiing on the runway")
  }
```

```kotlin
    override fun fly() {
        println("Airplane is flying")
    }
}

fun main() {
    val plane = Airplane()
    plane.drive()
    plane.fly()
}
```

Airplane implements both Drivable and Flyable, making it multi-functional.

Conclusion

Inheritance allows code reuse by letting a subclass inherit from a superclass.
Interfaces define a contract that multiple classes can implement.
Kotlin supports multiple interfaces but only single inheritance, promoting better design flexibility.
Understanding inheritance and interfaces helps in writing scalable and maintainable Kotlin applications.

6.1 Extending Classes in Kotlin

Kotlin supports class extension through inheritance and extension functions, allowing developers to reuse and enhance functionality without modifying existing code.

1. Inheritance: Extending a Class

By default, classes in Kotlin are final (cannot be inherited). To allow inheritance, a class must be marked with the open keyword.

Example: Basic Class Inheritance

```kotlin
Copy code
open class Animal(val name: String) {
    fun eat() {
        println("$name is eating.")
    }
}

class Dog(name: String) : Animal(name) {
    fun bark() {
        println("$name is barking.")
    }
```

```kotlin
}

fun main() {
    val dog = Dog("Buddy")
    dog.eat()  // Inherited from Animal
    dog.bark() // Defined in Dog
}
```

Key Points:

Animal is an open class, allowing Dog to inherit from it.
Dog extends Animal and gets access to its eat() function.
Dog adds its own bark() function.

2. Overriding Functions in a Subclass

A subclass can override functions of a superclass using override, but the function in the superclass must be marked with open.

Example: Overriding a Function
kotlin
Copy code
```kotlin
open class Animal {
    open fun makeSound() {
        println("Some generic animal sound")
    }
}
```

```kotlin
class Cat : Animal() {
    override fun makeSound() {
        println("Meow!")
    }
}

fun main() {
    val cat = Cat()
    cat.makeSound()  // Output: Meow!
}
```

Key Points:

makeSound() in Animal is marked open, allowing override.
Cat provides its own implementation of makeSound().

3. Using the super Keyword

A subclass can call the parent class's method using super.

kotlin
Copy code
```kotlin
open class Animal {
    open fun makeSound() {
        println("Some generic animal sound")
    }
```

```kotlin
}

class Dog : Animal() {
    override fun makeSound() {
        super.makeSound()  // Calls parent function
        println("Woof! Woof!")
    }
}

fun main() {
    val dog = Dog()
    dog.makeSound()
}
```

Key Points:

super.makeSound() calls the parent's function before adding custom behavior.

4. Extending Classes with Extension Functions

Kotlin allows adding functions to existing classes using extension functions without modifying their code.

Example: Adding an Extension Function

kotlin

Copy code

```
class Car(val brand: String)

fun Car.drive() {
    println("$brand is driving!")
}

fun main() {
    val car = Car("Tesla")
    car.drive()  // Output: Tesla is driving!
}
```

Key Points:

drive() is an extension function for the Car class.

It allows adding functionality without modifying the original class.

Conclusion

Inheritance allows extending a class using the open keyword.

Function overriding customizes behavior in subclasses.

The super keyword accesses parent class methods.

Extension functions add functionality to existing classes without modifying them.

Extending classes in Kotlin improves code reusability, maintainability, and flexibility.

6.2 Abstract Classes and Methods

In Kotlin, abstract classes and abstract methods are used to create a blueprint for other classes. They define common behavior while allowing subclasses to provide specific implementations.

1. What is an Abstract Class?

An abstract class is a class that cannot be instantiated and is meant to be inherited. It may contain abstract methods (without implementation) and regular methods (with implementation).

Declaring an Abstract Class

kotlin
Copy code
```kotlin
abstract class Animal(val name: String) {
    abstract fun makeSound()   // Abstract method (no implementation)
```

```kotlin
    fun eat() { // Concrete method (has implementation)
        println("$name is eating.")
    }
}
```

abstract keyword is used to define an abstract class.
Abstract classes can have both abstract and concrete methods.

2. Implementing an Abstract Class

A subclass must implement all abstract methods of the parent class.

Example: Implementing Abstract Methods

kotlin
Copy code
```kotlin
abstract class Animal(val name: String) {
    abstract fun makeSound()

    fun eat() {
        println("$name is eating.")
    }
}
```

```kotlin
class Dog(name: String) : Animal(name) {
    override fun makeSound() {
        println("$name barks: Woof! Woof!")
    }
}

fun main() {
    val dog = Dog("Buddy")
    dog.makeSound() // Output: Buddy barks: Woof! Woof!
    dog.eat() // Output: Buddy is eating.
}
```

Key Points:

Dog extends Animal and implements makeSound().
eat() is inherited from Animal and can be used without overriding.

3. Using Abstract Properties

Abstract classes can also have abstract properties (variables without initialization).

kotlin
Copy code
abstract class Vehicle {

```kotlin
    abstract val maxSpeed: Int

    fun showSpeed() {
        println("Max speed is $maxSpeed km/h")
    }
}

class Car : Vehicle() {
    override val maxSpeed: Int = 200
}

fun main() {
    val car = Car()
    car.showSpeed()  // Output: Max speed is 200 km/h
}
```

Abstract properties must be overridden in subclasses.
The Car class provides a specific maxSpeed value.

4. Difference Between Abstract Class and Interface

Feature	Abstract Class	Interface
Can have constructors?	Yes	No
Can have method	Yes	Only default

implementations?		methods (since Kotlin 1.2)
Supports multiple inheritance?	No (single inheritance only)	Yes (multiple interfaces can be implemented)
Can contain abstract properties?	Yes	Yes

5. When to Use Abstract Classes?

When creating a base class that shares common behavior.
When some functions need to be mandatory for subclasses.
When defining a class with state (properties) and behavior.

Conclusion

Abstract classes define a template for other classes.
Abstract methods and properties must be overridden in subclasses.
Unlike interfaces, abstract classes can have constructors and fields.

Using abstract classes ensures code reusability and structure in Kotlin applications.

6.3 Interfaces: Multiple Inheritance in Kotlin

Kotlin supports multiple inheritance using interfaces. Unlike classes, an interface can be implemented by multiple classes, allowing code reuse and flexibility without the limitations of single inheritance.

1. What is an Interface in Kotlin?
An interface in Kotlin is similar to an abstract class but:

Cannot store state (no instance variables).
Cannot have constructors.
Supports multiple implementations in a single class.

Defining an Interface

kotlin
Copy code
```
interface Drivable {
    fun drive()
```

}

Uses the interface keyword.

Contains abstract methods (without implementation) by default.

2. Implementing an Interface

A class implements an interface using : and must provide implementations for all abstract methods.

```kotlin
Copy code
class Car : Drivable {
    override fun drive() {
        println("Car is driving")
    }
}

fun main() {
    val car = Car()
    car.drive()  // Output: Car is driving
}
```

Car implements Drivable and provides the drive() method.

3. Multiple Interface Implementation

A class can implement multiple interfaces, enabling multiple inheritance.

Example: Implementing Multiple Interfaces

kotlin

Copy code

```kotlin
interface Drivable {
    fun drive()
}

interface Flyable {
    fun fly()
}

class Airplane : Drivable, Flyable {
    override fun drive() {
        println("Airplane is taxiing on the runway")
    }

    override fun fly() {
        println("Airplane is flying")
    }
}

fun main() {
    val plane = Airplane()
    plane.drive()
```

```kotlin
    plane.fly()
}
```

Key Points:

Airplane implements both Drivable and Flyable.
The class must override all abstract methods.

4. Default Method Implementation in Interfaces

Kotlin interfaces can have default implementations using default
methods.

```kotlin
Copy code
interface Logger {
    fun log(message: String) {
        println("Logging: $message")
    }
}

class FileLogger : Logger

fun main() {
    val logger = FileLogger()
    logger.log("File saved!")  // Output: Logging: File saved!
}
```

FileLogger inherits log() without overriding it.

5. Resolving Method Conflicts in Multiple Inheritance

If multiple interfaces provide the same method, the class must override it.

Example: Handling Conflicts

kotlin

Copy code

```kotlin
interface A {
    fun show() {
        println("Interface A")
    }
}

interface B {
    fun show() {
        println("Interface B")
    }
}

class C : A, B {
    override fun show() {
        super<A>.show()  // Choose method from A
        super<B>.show()  // Choose method from B
    }
```

```
}

fun main() {
    val obj = C()
    obj.show()
}
```

Key Points:

C inherits conflicting show() methods.
Explicitly calls super<A>.show() and super<B>.show().

6. Abstract Class vs. Interface

Feature	Abstract Class	Interface
State (properties)	Yes	No (only val properties)
Constructors	Yes	No
Multiple Inheritance	No	Yes.

Default Implementations	Yes	Yes (since Kotlin 1.2)

7. When to Use Interfaces?

When multiple inheritance is needed.
When defining common behavior for unrelated classes.
When defining shared contracts for different implementations.

Conclusion

Interfaces enable multiple inheritance in Kotlin.
A class can implement multiple interfaces.
Default methods reduce redundancy.
Method conflicts require explicit resolution using super<>.
Using interfaces helps build scalable and modular Kotlin applications.

Chapter 7
Advanced Object-Oriented Concepts

.Beyond basic OOP principles like encapsulation, inheritance, and polymorphism, Kotlin offers advanced OOP features that enhance code flexibility, reusability, and maintainability.

1. Abstract Classes and Interfaces

Abstract classes provide a base for subclasses but cannot be instantiated.
Interfaces allow multiple inheritance and can have default method implementations.

Example: Combining Abstract Classes and Interfaces

kotlin
Copy code

```kotlin
abstract class Animal(val name: String) {
    abstract fun makeSound()
}

interface Movable {
    fun move() {
        println("Moving...")
    }
}

class Dog(name: String) : Animal(name), Movable {
    override fun makeSound() {
        println("$name barks")
    }
}

fun main() {
    val dog = Dog("Buddy")
    dog.makeSound()
    dog.move()
}
```

Dog inherits from Animal and implements Movable.

2. Data Classes and Object Declarations

Data classes provide built-in functionalities like toString(), equals(), and copy().

Object declarations create single instances (singletons).

Example: Data Class and Object Singleton

kotlin

Copy code

```
data class User(val name: String, val age: Int)

object Database {
    fun connect() = println("Connected to Database")
}

fun main() {
    val user = User("Alice", 25)
    println(user)

    Database.connect()
}
```

User is a data class.

Database is an object declaration (singleton).

3. Companion Objects and Factory Patterns

Companion objects allow static-like methods inside a class.

Factory patterns create objects in a controlled way.

Example: Companion Object as a Factory
kotlin
Copy code

```kotlin
class Car(val brand: String) {
  companion object {
    fun createTesla() = Car("Tesla")
  }
}

fun main() {
  val tesla = Car.createTesla()
  println("Car brand: ${tesla.brand}")
}
```

The companion object acts as a factory to create Car instances.

4. Delegation: Code Reusability Without Inheritance

Instead of extending a class, Kotlin allows delegation for code reuse.

Example: Class Delegation
kotlin
Copy code

```kotlin
interface Logger {
```

```kotlin
    fun log(message: String)
}

class ConsoleLogger : Logger {
    override fun log(message: String) = println("Log:
$message")
}

class Service(logger: Logger) : Logger by logger

fun main() {
    val service = Service(ConsoleLogger())
    service.log("Service started")
}
```

Service delegates logging functionality to ConsoleLogger.

5. Sealed Classes for Restricted Inheritance

Sealed classes limit which classes can inherit from them, useful for representing states.

Example: Sealed Class for State Handling

kotlin
Copy code
```kotlin
sealed class Result {
```

```kotlin
    object Success : Result()
    data class Error(val message: String) : Result()
}

fun handleResult(result: Result) {
    when (result) {
        is Result.Success -> println("Operation successful")
        is Result.Error -> println("Error: ${result.message}")
    }
}
```

Result allows only predefined subclasses (Success, Error).

Conclusion

Abstract classes & interfaces enhance polymorphism.

Data classes & object declarations simplify object management.

Companion objects & factory patterns improve object creation.

Delegation replaces unnecessary inheritance.

Sealed classes make state management safer.

Mastering these concepts helps build scalable, maintainable, and efficient Kotlin applications.

7.1 Data Classes: Simplified Data Management

Kotlin data classes provide a simple way to handle data storage with minimal boilerplate code. They automatically generate useful functions like toString(), equals(), hashCode(), and copy(), making data management easier.

1. Declaring a Data Class
A data class is defined using the data keyword before class.

Example: Basic Data Class
kotlin
Copy code
```kotlin
data class User(val name: String, val age: Int)

fun main() {
    val user = User("Alice", 25)
    println(user)  // Output: User(name=Alice, age=25)
}
```

Key Features:

Automatically generates toString(), equals(), and hashCode().
Requires at least one property in the constructor.

2. Built-in Functions of Data Classes

Data classes come with several useful functions:

a) copy() Function

Creates a duplicate object with modified properties.

kotlin

Copy code

val user1 = User("Alice", 25)

val user2 = user1.copy(age = 30)

println(user2) // Output: User(name=Alice, age=30)

copy() helps create variations without modifying the original object.

b) equals() and hashCode() Functions

Data classes automatically compare objects by their content, not memory reference.

kotlin

Copy code

val user1 = User("Alice", 25)

val user2 = User("Alice", 25)

println(user1 == user2) // Output: true

Without data, classes compare memory references instead of values.

3. Destructuring Declarations

Data classes allow destructuring, making it easy to extract values.

kotlin

Copy code

```kotlin
val (name, age) = User("Alice", 25)
println(name) // Output: Alice
println(age)  // Output: 25
```

This feature is useful when working with lists or function returns.

4. Using Data Classes in Collections

Data classes are ideal for lists and sets because they have equals() and hashCode().

kotlin

Copy code

```kotlin
val users = listOf(User("Alice", 25), User("Bob", 30))
println(users.contains(User("Alice", 25))) // Output: true
```

Allows efficient lookups and comparisons in collections.

5. Data Classes with toString() for Debugging

Data classes automatically generate readable output, making debugging easier.

kotlin
Copy code
val user = User("Alice", 25)
println(user) // Output: User(name=Alice, age=25)

No need to manually override toString().

6. Limitations of Data Classes

Cannot be abstract, open, sealed, or inner.
Primary constructor must have at least one property.
Inheritance is not allowed, but they can implement interfaces.

7. When to Use Data Classes?

When storing simple data structures (e.g., user profiles, API responses).
When working with collections where equality matters.
When creating immutable objects that need easy copying.

Conclusion

Kotlin data classes simplify data management by reducing boilerplate code. They provide automatic comparison, copying, destructuring, and readability, making them perfect for storing and handling structured data efficiently.

7.2 Sealed Classes and Enum Classes

Kotlin provides sealed classes and enum classes to represent restricted sets of values in a structured and type-safe manner. Both are useful for defining state-based logic and ensuring exhaustive handling in when expressions.

1. Sealed Classes: Restricted Inheritance

A sealed class allows a fixed set of subclasses, preventing inheritance outside the declared scope. This makes them ideal for representing different states in a structured way.

Declaring a Sealed Class

kotlin
Copy code
sealed class Result {

```kotlin
    object Success : Result()
    data class Error(val message: String) : Result()
}

fun handleResult(result: Result) {
    when (result) {
        is Result.Success -> println("Operation successful")
        is Result.Error -> println("Error: ${result.message}")
    }
}

fun main() {
    val success = Result.Success
    val failure = Result.Error("Network failure")

    handleResult(success)  // Output: Operation successful
    handleResult(failure)  // Output: Error: Network failure
}
```

Key Features:

sealed class restricts inheritance to the same file.
Ensures exhaustive when checks without needing an else branch.
Supports objects, data classes, and regular classes as subclasses.

2. Enum Classes: Fixed Set of Constants

An enum class is used for defining a predefined set of constant values, often when the values are known at compile time.

Declaring an Enum Class

kotlin
Copy code
```
enum class Direction {
    NORTH, SOUTH, EAST, WEST
}

fun getDirectionMessage(direction: Direction) {
    when (direction) {
        Direction.NORTH -> println("You are heading north")
        Direction.SOUTH -> println("You are heading south")
        Direction.EAST -> println("You are heading east")
        Direction.WEST -> println("You are heading west")
    }
}

fun main() {
    getDirectionMessage(Direction.EAST)  // Output: You are heading east
}
```

Key Features:

Defines a fixed set of constants.

Used with when expressions for exhaustive checks.

Each value is a singleton.

3. Enum Classes with Properties and Methods

Enum constants can have custom properties and methods.

kotlin
Copy code
```kotlin
enum class Planet(val mass: Double, val radius: Double) {
    EARTH(5.97, 6371.0),
    MARS(0.64, 3389.5),
    JUPITER(1898.0, 69911.0);

    fun gravity(): Double = (mass / (radius * radius))
}

fun main() {
    println("Earth's gravity: ${Planet.EARTH.gravity()}")
}
```

Each enum constant has associated properties.

Enum classes can contain methods.

4. Sealed Class vs. Enum Class

Feature	Sealed Class	Enum Class
Usage	Represents complex state hierarchies	Represents predefined constant values
Can have data classes?	Yes	No
Can have different properties per subclass?	Yes	No (all must have the same properties)
Supports object inheritance?	Yes	No
Used in when expressions?	Yes (ensures exhaustive checks)	Yes (ensures exhaustive checks)

5. When to Use Sealed Classes vs. Enum Classes?

Use Case	Use Sealed Class	Use Enum Class
Different states with unique properties	■	✗
Representing constant values (e.g., colors, directions)	✗	■
Handling API responses (Success, Error)	■	✗
Fixed list of values at compile time	✗	■

Conclusion

Sealed classes are great for handling state-based logic, API responses, and error handling.

Enum classes are best for fixed sets of constants, such as days of the week or directions.

Both enforce exhaustive when checks, improving code safety and readability.

Using sealed and enum classes properly helps in writing cleaner, safer, and more maintainable Kotlin code.

7.3 Nested and Inner Classes

Kotlin supports nested and inner classes to help organize code and define class hierarchies. These allow a class to be declared inside another class, improving encapsulation and logical grouping of related components.

1. Nested Classes (Static by Default)

A nested class is a class declared inside another class. In Kotlin, nested classes do not have access to the outer class's members because they are static by default.

Example: Defining a Nested Class

```kotlin
Copy code
class Outer {
  class Nested {
    fun greet() = "Hello from Nested class"
  }
}

fun main() {
    val nested = Outer.Nested()   // No need for Outer instance
    println(nested.greet())   // Output: Hello from Nested class
}
```

Key Features:

Declared inside another class.

Cannot access outer class members.

Instantiated without an outer class instance.

2. Inner Classes (Access Outer Class Members)

An inner class is a nested class that can access the outer class's properties and methods. It is marked with the inner keyword.

Example: Inner Class Accessing Outer Class Properties

kotlin
Copy code

```kotlin
class Outer(val outerData: String) {
    inner class Inner {
        fun greet() = "Hello from Inner class, accessing: $outerData"
    }
}

fun main() {
    val outer = Outer("Outer Data")
    val inner = outer.Inner() // Requires an Outer instance
    println(inner.greet()) // Output: Hello from Inner class, accessing: Outer Data
}
```

Key Features:

Marked with the inner keyword.

Has access to outer class members.

Requires an instance of the outer class to create an inner class instance.

3. Differences Between Nested and Inner Classes

Feature	Nested Class	Inner Class
Access to outer class members	✘ No	◼ Yes
Requires an instance of outer class	✘ No	◼ Yes
Marked with inner keyword	✘ No	◼ Yes
Use case	Grouping related logic	Interacting with outer class

4. When to Use Nested vs. Inner Classes?

Use Case	Use Nested Class	Use Inner Class

Grouping logically related classes	■	✗
Independent functionality inside another class	■	✗
Needs access to outer class members	✗	■
Reducing class clutter in large applications	■	■

Conclusion

Nested classes are like static classes, useful when the inner class does not need access to the outer class.

Inner classes are used when the inner class needs to access outer class members.

Choosing between them depends on whether outer class access is required.

Using nested and inner classes correctly improves code organization and maintainability in Kotlin.

Chapter 8
Design Patterns in Kotlin

Design patterns are proven solutions to common software development problems. In Kotlin, these patterns improve code structure, maintainability, and scalability.

1. Creational Patterns (Object Creation)

a) Singleton Pattern (Ensures a single instance of a class)
Kotlin provides a built-in way to create singletons using the object keyword.

kotlin
Copy code
```kotlin
object Database {
    fun connect() = println("Connected to Database")
}

fun main() {
    Database.connect() // Output: Connected to Database
}
```

b) Factory Pattern (Creates objects without exposing instantiation logic)

kotlin

Copy code

```kotlin
class Car(val brand: String) {
    companion object {
        fun createTesla() = Car("Tesla")
    }
}

fun main() {
    val car = Car.createTesla()
    println(car.brand)  // Output: Tesla
}
```

2. Structural Patterns (Organizing Code)

a) Adapter Pattern (Bridges incompatible interfaces)
Useful for integrating third-party libraries or legacy code.

kotlin

Copy code

```kotlin
interface OldSystem {
    fun legacyMethod(): String
}

class NewSystem {
```

```kotlin
    fun newMethod() = "Using new system"
}

class Adapter(private val newSystem: NewSystem) :
OldSystem {
    override fun legacyMethod() = newSystem.newMethod()
}

fun main() {
    val adapter = Adapter(NewSystem())
    println(adapter.legacyMethod())   // Output: Using new
system
}
```

b) Delegate Pattern (Reuses behavior without inheritance)

kotlin
Copy code
```kotlin
interface Logger {
    fun log(message: String)
}

class ConsoleLogger : Logger {
    override fun log(message: String) = println("Log:
$message")
}
```

```kotlin
class Service(logger: Logger) : Logger by logger

fun main() {
    val service = Service(ConsoleLogger())
    service.log("Service started")   // Output: Log: Service started
}
```

3. Behavioral Patterns (Managing Object Interactions)

a) Observer Pattern (Notifies subscribers of changes)
kotlin
Copy code

```kotlin
class EventManager {
    private val listeners = mutableListOf<(String) -> Unit>()

    fun subscribe(listener: (String) -> Unit) {
        listeners.add(listener)
    }

    fun notify(event: String) {
        listeners.forEach { it(event) }
    }
}

fun main() {
    val eventManager = EventManager()
```

```kotlin
    eventManager.subscribe { println("Listener 1: $it") }
    eventManager.subscribe { println("Listener 2: $it") }

    eventManager.notify("Event occurred")
}
```

b) Strategy Pattern (Selects behavior at runtime)

```kotlin
Copy code
interface PaymentStrategy {
    fun pay(amount: Double)
}

class CreditCardPayment : PaymentStrategy {
    override fun pay(amount: Double) = println("Paid
$amount using Credit Card")
}

class PayPalPayment : PaymentStrategy {
    override fun pay(amount: Double) = println("Paid
$amount using PayPal")
}

fun main() {
```

```kotlin
    val paymentMethod: PaymentStrategy =
CreditCardPayment()
    paymentMethod.pay(100.0)  // Output: Paid 100.0 using
Credit Card
}
```

Conclusion

Creational patterns simplify object creation.
Structural patterns help organize and reuse code efficiently.
Behavioral patterns improve communication between objects.
Using design patterns in Kotlin leads to cleaner, more scalable, and maintainable applications.

8.1 Singleton Pattern

The Singleton Pattern ensures that a class has only one instance throughout the application and provides a global access point to it. In Kotlin, the object declaration makes implementing a singleton simple and concise.

1 Implementing Singleton in Kotlin

In Java, a singleton requires private constructors, static methods, or synchronized blocks. In Kotlin, the object keyword automatically ensures a single instance is created.

Example: Basic Singleton
kotlin
Copy code

```kotlin
object Database {
    fun connect() = println("Connected to Database")
}

fun main() {
    Database.connect() // Output: Connected to Database
}
```

Key Features:

Automatically thread-safe.
Cannot have constructors (as it's instantiated once).
Global access point without needing static methods.

2. Singleton with Properties and Methods

A singleton can store state and have additional functionality.

kotlin

```
Copy code
object Logger {
    private val logs = mutableListOf<String>()

    fun log(message: String) {
        logs.add(message)
        println("Log: $message")
    }

    fun showLogs() = logs.forEach { println(it) }
}

fun main() {
    Logger.log("App started")
    Logger.log("User logged in")
    Logger.showLogs()
}
```

The logs list stores messages persistently in the singleton.

3. Singleton with Lazy Initialization

If you need lazy initialization, use lazy with a companion object.

kotlin
Copy code
```
class Database private constructor() {
```

```kotlin
    init {
        println("Database Initialized")
    }

    companion object {
        val instance: Database by lazy { Database() }
    }
}

fun main() {
    val db1 = Database.instance
    val db2 = Database.instance
    println(db1 === db2)  // Output: true (Same instance)
}
```

The lazy initialization ensures the instance is created only when first accessed.

4. Thread Safety in Singleton

The object declaration in Kotlin is thread-safe by default, unlike Java's synchronized singleton approach.

kotlin
Copy code
```kotlin
object Configuration {
    init {
```

```kotlin
    println("Configuration Initialized")
  }
}

fun main() {
  val config1 = Configuration
  val config2 = Configuration
    println(config1 === config2)  // Output: true (Same instance)
}
```

The instance is created only once, even in multi-threaded environments.

5. When to Use the Singleton Pattern?

Use Case	Use Singleton?
Managing database connections	■ Yes
Centralized logging.	■ Yes
Caching and configuration settings	■ Yes
Storing temporary session data	■ Yes
Managing UI state (not recommended)	✘ Avoid

6. Conclusion

The object keyword makes singleton implementation simple and thread-safe.

Companion objects allow lazy initialization when needed.

Best for logging, configuration, and shared resources but should be used carefully to avoid global state issues.

Using the Singleton Pattern correctly ensures efficiency and consistency in Kotlin applications.

8.2 Factory Pattern

The Factory Pattern is a creational design pattern used to create objects without exposing instantiation logic. Instead of calling constructors directly, a factory method handles object creation, making the code more flexible and maintainable.

1. Why Use the Factory Pattern?

Encapsulates object creation logic to avoid direct new instantiation.

Supports polymorphism, allowing different object types to be created dynamically.

Improves maintainability by centralizing object creation.

Useful for complex object creation where different conditions determine which class instance is needed.

2. Basic Factory Pattern in Kotlin

A simple factory method creates instances based on a condition.

Example: Car Factory
kotlin
Copy code
```kotlin
interface Car {
    fun drive()
}

class Sedan : Car {
    override fun drive() = println("Driving a Sedan")
}

class SUV : Car {
    override fun drive() = println("Driving an SUV")
}

class CarFactory {
```

```kotlin
    fun createCar(type: String): Car {
        return when (type) {
            "Sedan" -> Sedan()
            "SUV" -> SUV()
            else -> throw IllegalArgumentException("Unknown car type")
        }
    }
}

fun main() {
    val factory = CarFactory()
    val car1 = factory.createCar("Sedan")
    car1.drive() // Output: Driving a Sedan

    val car2 = factory.createCar("SUV")
    car2.drive() // Output: Driving an SUV
}
```

Key Features:

CarFactory centralizes object creation.

when statement determines the correct class to instantiate.

Avoids direct instantiation, making the code more flexible.

3. Factory with Companion Object (Static-Like Factory Method)

Using a companion object allows factory methods to be accessed without creating an instance of the factory class.

```kotlin
Copy code
interface Animal {
    fun makeSound()
}

class Dog : Animal {
    override fun makeSound() = println("Woof!")
}

class Cat : Animal {
    override fun makeSound() = println("Meow!")
}

class AnimalFactory {
    companion object {
        fun createAnimal(type: String): Animal {
            return when (type) {
                "Dog" -> Dog()
                "Cat" -> Cat()
                            else -> throw
IllegalArgumentException("Unknown animal type")
```

```
            }
        }
    }
}

fun main() {
    val dog = AnimalFactory.createAnimal("Dog")
    dog.makeSound()  // Output: Woof!

    val cat = AnimalFactory.createAnimal("Cat")
    cat.makeSound()  // Output: Meow!
}
```

Advantages:

No need to instantiate AnimalFactory (companion object behaves like a static method).
Easy to call: AnimalFactory.createAnimal("Dog").

4. Factory with Enum for Cleaner Code

Using enums improves readability and eliminates string comparisons.

kotlin

189

```
Copy code
enum class CarType { SEDAN, SUV }

class CarFactory {
   companion object {
     fun createCar(type: CarType): Car {
       return when (type) {
         CarType.SEDAN -> Sedan()
         CarType.SUV -> SUV()
       }
     }
   }
}

fun main() {
   val sedan = CarFactory.createCar(CarType.SEDAN)
   sedan.drive()  // Output: Driving a Sedan
}
```

Enums reduce errors caused by misspelled strings.
Makes the code cleaner and safer.

5. When to Use the Factory Pattern?

Use Case	Use Factory Pattern?
Object creation logic is complex	▇ Yes

Need to encapsulate object creation	■ Yes
Need to return different subclasses dynamically	■ Yes
Creating a single instance (Singleton needed)	✖ No

6. Conclusion

The Factory Pattern centralizes object creation, making the code cleaner and more maintainable.
Using a companion object simplifies factory method access.
Enums improve safety by eliminating hardcoded strings.
This pattern is ideal for cases where object instantiation varies based on conditions or configurations.

8.3 Observer Pattern

The Observer Pattern is a behavioral design pattern that allows one object (subject) to notify multiple other objects (observers) when its state changes. It is commonly used in event-driven systems, UI frameworks, and real-time applications.

1. Why Use the Observer Pattern?

Decouples subjects and observers, making the code more flexible.
Allows multiple observers to react to state changes dynamically.
Useful for real-time updates, such as UI changes, event handling, and notifications.

2. Implementing Observer Pattern in Kotlin

Example: Basic Observer Pattern (Custom Implementation)
In this example, we create a Subject (Publisher) that notifies
Observers (Subscribers) when its state changes.

```kotlin
Copy code
// Observer Interface
interface Observer {
    fun update(message: String)
}

// Subject Class
class EventManager {
    private val observers = mutableListOf<Observer>()

    fun subscribe(observer: Observer) {
        observers.add(observer)
    }

    fun unsubscribe(observer: Observer) {
        observers.remove(observer)
    }

    fun notifyObservers(message: String) {
```

```kotlin
        observers.forEach { it.update(message) }
    }
}

// Concrete Observers
class User(val name: String) : Observer {
    override fun update(message: String) {
        println("$name received update: $message")
    }
}

fun main() {
    val eventManager = EventManager()

    val user1 = User("Alice")
    val user2 = User("Bob")

    eventManager.subscribe(user1)
    eventManager.subscribe(user2)

    eventManager.notifyObservers("New Event Available!")

    eventManager.unsubscribe(user1)
            eventManager.notifyObservers("Another    Event
Happened!")
}
```
Output:

sql
Copy code
Alice received update: New Event Available!
Bob received update: New Event Available!
Bob received update: Another Event Happened!

Key Features:

The EventManager (Subject) maintains a list of subscribers.
Observers (User instances) implement an Observer interface.
When an event occurs, all subscribed users are notified automatically.

3. Observer Pattern Using Kotlin's Built-in Observable

Kotlin provides Observable and Observer classes from java.util that simplify the implementation.

kotlin
Copy code

```kotlin
import java.util.Observable
import java.util.Observer

// Observable (Subject)
class NewsPublisher : Observable() {
```

```kotlin
    fun publishNews(news: String) {
        setChanged()
        notifyObservers(news)
    }
}

// Observer (Subscriber)
class NewsReader(val name: String) : Observer {
    override fun update(o: Observable?, arg: Any?) {
        println("$name received news: $arg")
    }
}

fun main() {
    val newsPublisher = NewsPublisher()

    val reader1 = NewsReader("Alice")
    val reader2 = NewsReader("Bob")

    newsPublisher.addObserver(reader1)
    newsPublisher.addObserver(reader2)

    newsPublisher.publishNews("Breaking News: Kotlin 2.0 Released!")
}
```

Output:

yaml
Copy code
Alice received news: Breaking News: Kotlin 2.0 Released!
Bob received news: Breaking News: Kotlin 2.0 Released!

Advantages of Using Observable:

Reduces boilerplate code.
Built-in support for observer management (addObserver() and notifyObservers()).

4. When to Use the Observer Pattern?

Use Case.	Use Observer Pattern?
UI event handling (button clicks, data binding)	■ Yes
Real-time notifications (news updates, chat messages)	Yes ■
Decoupling components (avoiding tight dependencies)	Yes ■
One-to-one communication (e.g., direct method calls)	No ✖

5. Conclusion

The Observer Pattern is ideal for event-driven programming.

It helps in decoupling subjects and observers, making applications more modular.

Kotlin's custom implementation allows more flexibility, while Observable simplifies usage for Java interoperability.

This pattern is widely used in UI frameworks, event systems, and real-time applications.

8.4 Builder Pattern

The Builder Pattern is a creational design pattern that simplifies object construction, especially for objects with many optional parameters. It provides a step-by-step approach to building complex objects, making the code more readable and maintainable.

1. Why Use the Builder Pattern?

Handles complex object creation with multiple parameters.

Improves readability by replacing long constructor calls with a fluent API.

Supports immutability by allowing controlled object construction.

Reduces constructor overloads when dealing with multiple optional parameters.

2. Implementing Builder Pattern in Kotlin

Example: Traditional Builder Pattern

kotlin

Copy code

```kotlin
class Car private constructor(
    val brand: String,
    val model: String,
    val year: Int,
    val color: String?,
    val sunroof: Boolean
) {
    class Builder {
        private var brand: String = ""
        private var model: String = ""
        private var year: Int = 0
```

```kotlin
        private var color: String? = null
        private var sunroof: Boolean = false

        fun brand(brand: String) = apply { this.brand = brand
}
        fun model(model: String) = apply { this.model = model
}
        fun year(year: Int) = apply { this.year = year }
        fun color(color: String?) = apply { this.color = color }
        fun sunroof(sunroof: Boolean) = apply { this.sunroof =
sunroof }

        fun build(): Car {
            return Car(brand, model, year, color, sunroof)
        }
    }
}

fun main() {
    val car = Car.Builder()
        .brand("Tesla")
        .model("Model S")
        .year(2023)
        .color("Red")
        .sunroof(true)
        .build()
```

```
    println("${car.brand} ${car.model} (${car.year}), Color:
${car.color}, Sunroof: ${car.sunroof}")
}
```

Output:

yaml

Copy code

Tesla Model S (2023), Color: Red, Sunroof: true

Key Features:

Private constructor ensures objects can only be created using the builder.

Fluent API (apply) improves readability.

Avoids large constructors by setting only required properties.

3. Kotlin-Specific Alternative: Using Data Class with copy()
Kotlin's data class and copy() function can serve as a lightweight alternative to the Builder Pattern.

kotlin

Copy code

```
data class Car(
    val brand: String,
    val model: String,
    val year: Int,
```

```kotlin
    val color: String? = null,
    val sunroof: Boolean = false
)

fun main() {
    val defaultCar = Car(brand = "Tesla", model = "Model S",
year = 2023)
        val customizedCar = defaultCar.copy(color = "Red",
sunroof = true)

    println(customizedCar)
}
```

Advantages of Using copy():

Less boilerplate (no need for a separate builder class).
Immutability is maintained.
Easier to modify objects without affecting the original.

4. When to Use the Builder Pattern?

Use Case	Use Builder Pattern?	
Object has many optional parameters	■	Yes
Avoiding large constructors with many arguments	■	Yes
Creating immutable objects step by step	■	Yes

Simple object creation with few properties ✘ No (Use constructor)

5. Conclusion

The Builder Pattern is ideal for constructing complex objects step by step.

In Kotlin, data classes and copy() can be a simpler alternative for modifying immutable objects.
The pattern improves readability, flexibility, and maintainability in object creation.
Use the Builder Pattern when dealing with complex configurations, optional parameters, or fluent APIs.

Chapter 9
Error Handling and Exception Management

Error handling is essential in any application to prevent crashes, ensure robustness, and provide meaningful feedback to users. Kotlin provides a structured approach to handling exceptions using try-catch blocks, custom exceptions, and functional programming techniques.

1. Exception Handling in Kotlin

Kotlin uses standard Java-style exception handling with try, catch, finally, and throw.

Example: Basic Try-Catch Block

```kotlin
Copy code
fun divide(a: Int, b: Int): Int {
    return try {
        a / b // May throw ArithmeticException
    } catch (e: ArithmeticException) {
        println("Error: Division by zero is not allowed!")
        0 // Default return value
    }
}
```

```kotlin
fun main() {
    println(divide(10, 2))  // Output: 5
    println(divide(10, 0))  // Output: Error: Division by zero
is not allowed! 0
}
```

try block attempts to execute the code.

catch block handles any thrown exceptions.

The program continues running instead of crashing.

2. Throwing Custom Exceptions

You can define and throw custom exceptions for better error representation.

kotlin
Copy code

```kotlin
class InvalidAgeException(message: String) : Exception(message)

fun validateAge(age: Int) {
    if (age < 18) throw InvalidAgeException("Age must be 18 or above")
    println("Age is valid")
```

```kotlin
}

fun main() {
    try {
        validateAge(16)
    } catch (e: InvalidAgeException) {
        println("Exception: ${e.message}")
    }
}
```

Custom exceptions provide clearer error messages.
throw is used to manually raise an exception.

3. Finally Block

The finally block always executes, useful for resource cleanup.

kotlin
Copy code
```kotlin
fun readFile() {
    try {
        println("Reading file...")
        throw Exception("File not found")
    } catch (e: Exception) {
        println("Error: ${e.message}")
    } finally {
```

```kotlin
        println("Closing file")
    }
}

fun main() {
    readFile()
}
```
Output:
mathematica
Copy code
Reading file...
Error: File not found
Closing file

finally ensures resources like files, databases, or network connections are properly closed.

4. Using runCatching() for Functional Error Handling

Instead of try-catch, Kotlin provides runCatching, which returns a Result object.

kotlin
Copy code
```kotlin
fun riskyOperation(): Int = throw Exception("Something went wrong")
```

```
fun main() {
    val result = runCatching { riskyOperation() }
    println(result.getOrElse { "Default Value" })  // Output:
Default Value
}
```

runCatching avoids explicit try-catch blocks, improving readability.
.getOrElse { } provides a fallback value if an exception occurs.

5. When to Use Different Error Handling Techniques?

Scenario Use Case

Recoverable errors (e.g., file not found)	Try-Catch
Defining custom business logic errors	Custom Exceptions
Ensuring resource cleanup	Finally Block
Functional programming style	runCatching()

6. Conclusion

Try-catch blocks are the standard way to handle exceptions.
Custom exceptions improve error clarity.
finally ensures resource cleanup.

Functional error handling (runCatching) makes code cleaner. Proper error handling ensures reliability and stability in Kotlin applications!

9.1 Using try-catch Blocks

Kotlin provides try-catch blocks to handle exceptions and prevent runtime crashes. This mechanism allows developers to gracefully manage errors, ensuring smooth application execution.

1. Syntax of try-catch

The try block contains code that might throw an exception, and the catch block handles the error.

Basic Example
kotlin
Copy code
```kotlin
fun divide(a: Int, b: Int): Int {
    return try {
        a / b  // May throw ArithmeticException
    } catch (e: ArithmeticException) {
        println("Error: Division by zero is not allowed!")
        0  // Default return value
```

```kotlin
    }
}

fun main() {
    println(divide(10, 2)) // Output: 5
    println(divide(10, 0)) // Output: Error: Division by zero
is not allowed! 0
}
```

The try block executes risky code.

The catch block handles exceptions gracefully instead of crashing the program.

The function returns a fallback value when an exception occurs.

2. Multiple Catch Blocks

You can handle different exceptions separately using multiple catch blocks.

kotlin
Copy code
```kotlin
fun parseNumber(input: String): Int {
    return try {
        input.toInt()
    } catch (e: NumberFormatException) {
        println("Error: Invalid number format")
        -1
```

```kotlin
    } catch (e: Exception) {
        println("Unexpected error: ${e.message}")
        -1
    }
}

fun main() {
    println(parseNumber("123"))   // Output: 123
    println(parseNumber("abc"))   // Output: Error: Invalid
number format -1
}
```

Specific exceptions (NumberFormatException) are handled first.
A generic catch block (Exception) catches all other errors.

3. Using finally for Cleanup

The finally block always executes, whether an exception occurs or
not. It is useful for resource cleanup.

kotlin
Copy code
```kotlin
fun readFile() {
    try {
        println("Opening file...")
        throw Exception("File not found") // Simulating an
error
```

```kotlin
    } catch (e: Exception) {
        println("Error: ${e.message}")
    } finally {
        println("Closing file")
    }
}

fun main() {
    readFile()
}
```
Output:
mathematica
Copy code
Opening file...
Error: File not found
Closing file

The finally block ensures the file is closed even if an exception occurs.

4. Assigning try-catch Result to a Variable

In Kotlin, try can return a value, making it useful for handling default values in case of errors.

kotlin

Copy code

```
fun safeDivision(a: Int, b: Int): Int {
    val result = try {
        a / b
    } catch (e: ArithmeticException) {
        0  // Default value if an error occurs
    }
    return result
}

fun main() {
    println(safeDivision(10, 2))  // Output: 5
    println(safeDivision(10, 0))  // Output: 0
}
```

The result of try is assigned to result.

If an exception occurs, the catch block returns a fallback value.

5. When to Use try-catch Blocks?

ScenarioUse try-catch?

Handling runtime errors (e.g., division by zero)　　■ Yes

Parsing user input (e.g., converting strings to numbers)　　■
Yes

Reading from files or databases　　■ Yes

Preventing crashes due to unexpected conditions Yes

Validating input (prefer if-statements instead) ✖ No

6. Conclusion

try-catch blocks prevent crashes by handling runtime exceptions.

Multiple catch blocks can handle different types of errors.

finally ensures resource cleanup even when an exception occurs.

Returning a fallback value from try-catch improves code robustness.

Using try-catch effectively ensures a smooth user experience and stable application performance in Kotlin.

9.2 Custom Exceptions in Kotlin

Kotlin allows developers to define custom exceptions to handle application-specific errors in a structured way. This improves error clarity, makes debugging easier, and helps enforce business rules.

1. Why Use Custom Exceptions?

Provides more meaningful error messages.
Helps categorize errors specific to your application.
Improves code readability and maintainability.
Allows handling specific errors differently in catch blocks.

2. Creating a Custom Exception

In Kotlin, custom exceptions are created by extending the Exception or RuntimeException class.

Example: Custom Exception for Invalid Age
kotlin
Copy code

```kotlin
class InvalidAgeException(message: String) : Exception(message)

fun validateAge(age: Int) {
    if (age < 18) throw InvalidAgeException("Age must be 18 or above")
    println("Age is valid")
}

fun main() {
    try {
```

```
    validateAge(16) // This will throw an exception
  } catch (e: InvalidAgeException) {
    println("Exception: ${e.message}")
  }
}
```

Output:

makefile

Copy code

Exception: Age must be 18 or above

The InvalidAgeException extends Exception.
It is thrown when the age is below 18.
The catch block handles the error gracefully.

3. Extending RuntimeException vs Exception

Exception → Checked exception (must be handled explicitly).
RuntimeException → Unchecked exception (can be ignored but may crash at runtime).

Example: Using RuntimeException

kotlin

Copy code

class DatabaseConnectionException(message: String) : RuntimeException(message)

```kotlin
fun connectToDatabase() {
    throw DatabaseConnectionException("Unable to connect
to database")
}

fun main() {
    try {
        connectToDatabase()
    } catch (e: DatabaseConnectionException) {
        println("Database Error: ${e.message}")
    }
}
```

Use RuntimeException for unexpected failures (e.g., network issues).
Use Exception for business logic errors (e.g., invalid input).

4. Custom Exception with Additional Properties

You can add properties to exceptions for more detailed error information.

kotlin
Copy code
class PaymentFailedException(val errorCode: Int, message: String) : Exception(message)

```
fun processPayment(amount: Double) {
    if (amount <= 0) throw PaymentFailedException(400,
"Invalid payment amount: $amount")
}

fun main() {
  try {
    processPayment(-50.0)
  } catch (e: PaymentFailedException) {
    println("Error ${e.errorCode}: ${e.message}")
  }
}
```

Output:

javascript

Copy code

Error 400: Invalid payment amount: -50.0

The exception includes an errorCode for better debugging.

5. When to Use Custom Exceptions?

ScenarioUse Custom.   Exception?

Invalid input (e.g., negative age)   ■ Yes
Business rule violations (e.g., insufficient balance)   ■ Yes
System failures (e.g., database errors)   ■ Yes
Minor validation checks (use if-else instead)   ✗ No

6. Conclusion

Custom exceptions improve clarity and maintainability.

Use Exception for business logic and RuntimeException for system errors.

Add custom properties to store extra error details.

Custom exceptions make error handling more meaningful and structured.

By using custom exceptions effectively, you can write cleaner, more robust Kotlin applications!

9.3 Best Practices for Handling Errors

Effective error handling ensures that applications are robust, maintainable, and user-friendly. Kotlin provides multiple ways to handle errors, including try-catch blocks, custom exceptions, and functional error handling. Here are some best practices to manage errors efficiently.

1. Use Specific Exceptions

Avoid catching generic Exception unless absolutely necessary. Instead, catch specific exceptions to handle different error types appropriately.

Bad Practice (Catching Generic Exception)

kotlin

Copy code

```kotlin
try {
    val number = "abc".toInt()
} catch (e: Exception) {  // Too generic
    println("An error occurred!")
}
```

Good Practice (Catching Specific Exception)

kotlin

Copy code

```kotlin
try {
    val number = "abc".toInt()
} catch (e: NumberFormatException) {
    println("Invalid number format!")
}
```

Why?

Helps pinpoint the exact cause of failure.
Prevents swallowing unexpected exceptions.

2. Use Custom Exceptions for Business Logic Errors

For application-specific errors, define custom exceptions instead of using generic ones.

kotlin
Copy code

```kotlin
class InsufficientBalanceException(message: String) : Exception(message)

fun withdraw(amount: Double, balance: Double) {
    if (amount > balance) throw InsufficientBalanceException("Insufficient balance!")
}

fun main() {
    try {
        withdraw(100.0, 50.0)
    } catch (e: InsufficientBalanceException) {
        println(e.message)
    }
}
```

Why?

Improves error clarity,

Makes debugging easier.

. Always Clean Up Resources (finally Block)

When working with files, databases, or network connections, ensure they are properly closed using finally or use Kotlin's use function.

Using finally

kotlin

Copy code

```kotlin
fun readFile() {
    val file = java.io.File("data.txt")
    val reader = file.bufferedReader()

    try {
        println(reader.readLine()) // Read file
    } catch (e: Exception) {
        println("Error reading file: ${e.message}")
    } finally {
        reader.close() // Ensures file is closed
    }
}
```

Using use Function (Recommended)

kotlin

Copy code

```kotlin
fun readFile() {
    java.io.File("data.txt").bufferedReader().use { reader ->
        println(reader.readLine()) // File is automatically closed
    }
}
```

Why?

Prevents memory leaks and resource locks.
Ensures resources are always cleaned up, even if an error occurs.

4. Avoid Silent Failures

Never catch exceptions without handling or logging them properly.

Bad Practice (Swallowing Exception)

kotlin
Copy code
```kotlin
try {
    val number = "abc".toInt()
} catch (e: NumberFormatException) {
    // No action taken (silent failure)
}
```

Good Practice (Logging the Error)

```kotlin
Copy code
try {
    val number = "abc".toInt()
} catch (e: NumberFormatException) {
    println("Error: ${e.message}")  // Logs error message
}
```

Why?

Helps diagnose issues quickly.
Prevents silent failures that lead to unpredictable behavior.

5. Use Functional Error Handling (runCatching)

Instead of traditional try-catch, Kotlin provides runCatching for cleaner functional error handling.

```kotlin
Copy code
fun riskyOperation(): Int = throw Exception("Something went wrong")

fun main() {
    val result = runCatching { riskyOperation() }
        .getOrElse { println("Handled error: ${it.message}"); 0 }
```

```
    println(result)   // Output: Handled error: Something
went wrong 0
}
```

Why?

Avoids unnecessary try-catch clutter.
Improves readability in functional-style code.

6. Handle Expected Errors with Null Safety and Optionals

Use null safety (? and ?:) to handle expected failures instead of
throwing exceptions.

Example: Handling Null Values with Elvis Operator (?:)

kotlin
Copy code
```kotlin
fun getUserName(user: String?): String {
    return user ?: "Guest"  // Default value if user is null
}

fun main() {
    println(getUserName(null)) // Output: Guest
}
```

Why?

Reduces unnecessary exceptions.

Improves code readability and safety.

7. Use Logging Instead of Printing Errors

Instead of println(), use a logging framework like SLF4J or Logback for better error tracking.

kotlin
Copy code
```kotlin
import org.slf4j.LoggerFactory

val logger = LoggerFactory.getLogger("MyApp")

fun main() {
    try {
        val result = 10 / 0
    } catch (e: ArithmeticException) {
        logger.error("Math error: ${e.message}")
    }
}
```

Why?

Logs can be stored, searched, and monitored.

Printing to console (println) is not suitable for production.

8. Don't Overuse Exceptions for Control Flow

Exceptions should be used only for exceptional cases, not regular logic.

Bad Practice (Using Exception for Control Flow)

kotlin
Copy code

```kotlin
fun getUser(users: Map<String, String>, id: String): String {
    return try {
        users[id] ?: throw NoSuchElementException("User not found")
    } catch (e: NoSuchElementException) {
        "Guest"  // Default user
    }
}
```

Good Practice (Using Safe Lookup Instead)

kotlin
Copy code

```kotlin
fun getUser(users: Map<String, String>, id: String): String {
    return users[id] ?: "Guest"
```

}

Why?

Improves performance by avoiding unnecessary exceptions.
Kotlin provides safe alternatives like null checks and default values.

9. Provide Meaningful Error Messages

Error messages should be clear and actionable for debugging.

Bad Practice (Vague Error Message)

kotlin
Copy code
throw Exception("Something went wrong")

Good Practice (Detailed Error Message)
kotlin
Copy code
throw Exception("Failed to process order: Order ID is missing")

Why?

Helps developers understand the issue faster.

Makes debugging easier.

10. Test Error Handling Scenarios

Always test how your code behaves when exceptions occur.

Example: Unit Test for Exception Handling (Using JUnit)

```kotlin
Copy code
import org.junit.jupiter.api.assertThrows
import kotlin.test.Test

class ExceptionTest {
    @Test
    fun testInvalidAgeException() {
        assertThrows<InvalidAgeException> { validateAge(16)
}
    }
}
```

Why?

Ensures proper error handling under different conditions.
Prevents unexpected crashes in production.

Conclusion

■ Catch specific exceptions instead of using generic Exception.

■ Use custom exceptions for business logic errors.

■ Always clean up resources using finally or use.

■ Log errors instead of printing them.

■ Use functional error handling (runCatching) for cleaner code.

■ Handle expected failures with null safety, not exceptions.

■ Never use exceptions for regular logic flow.

■ Write clear error messages and test exception scenarios.

By following these best practices, you can write reliable, maintainable, and efficient Kotlin applications!

Chapter 10

Writing Clean and Efficient Kotlin Code

Writing clean and efficient Kotlin code enhances readability, maintainability, and performance. Here are key principles to follow:

1. Use Idiomatic Kotlin

Kotlin offers expressive syntax that simplifies code. Prefer Kotlin-specific features over Java-style coding.

█ Good (Idiomatic Kotlin)

```kotlin
Copy code
val names = listOf("Alice", "Bob", "Charlie")
val filteredNames = names.filter { it.startsWith("A") }
```

✗ Bad (Verbose Java-like Style)
```kotlin
Copy code
val names = listOf("Alice", "Bob", "Charlie")
val filteredNames = ArrayList<String>()
for (name in names) {
    if (name.startsWith("A")) {
        filteredNames.add(name)
```

```
  }
}
```

Why?

Uses higher-order functions (filter) for concise and readable code.
Avoids unnecessary loops and mutable lists.

2. Prefer Immutable Variables (val over var)

Immutable variables make the code safer and easier to debug.

■ Good (Immutable)

kotlin
Copy code
val age = 30

✗ Bad (Mutable When Not Needed)
kotlin
Copy code
var age = 30
Why?

Prevents unintended modifications.
Improves thread safety in concurrent programming.

3. Use Data Classes for Simple Data Holders
Data classes reduce boilerplate code for models.

■ Good (Data Class)

kotlin
Copy code
data class User(val name: String, val age: Int)

✖ Bad (Regular Class with Boilerplate)
kotlin
Copy code
```kotlin
class User(val name: String, val age: Int) {
    override fun toString() = "User(name=$name, age=$age)"
}
```

Why?

Automatically provides toString(), equals(), and hashCode().
Reduces redundant code.

4. Use Extension Functions for Readability

Extension functions help add functionality to existing classes
without modifying them.

■ Good (Extension Function)

kotlin
Copy code
```kotlin
fun String.isEmailValid() = contains("@") && contains(".")
```

✖ Bad (Utility Function)
kotlin
Copy code
```kotlin
fun isEmailValid(email: String) = email.contains("@") && email.contains(".")
```

Why?

Improves code readability and maintainability.
Makes code more intuitive by calling email.isEmailValid().

5. Use Smart Casts Instead of Explicit Casting

Kotlin automatically casts variables when necessary.

■ Good (Smart Casts)
kotlin
Copy code
```kotlin
fun printLength(value: Any) {
    if (value is String) {
        println(value.length) // No need for explicit cast
    }
```

}

✕ Bad (Manual Casting)

kotlin

Copy code

```kotlin
fun printLength(value: Any) {
  if (value is String) {
    println((value as String).length) // Unnecessary explicit cast
  }
}
```

Why?

Avoids redundant type casting.
Improves readability and safety.

6. Use Null Safety (?., ?:, !!)
Kotlin's null safety features prevent NullPointerException (NPE).

■ Good (Safe Calls and Elvis Operator)

kotlin

Copy code

```kotlin
val length = name?.length ?: 0  // Returns length or default value 0
```

✕ Bad (Forcing Non-Null)

kotlin

Copy code
val length = name!!.length // Risky: May cause crash if null
Why?

Prevents app crashes due to null references.

7
. Use Sealed Classes Instead of Enums for Hierarchical Data
Sealed classes allow defining restricted hierarchies.

■ Good (Sealed Class)

kotlin
Copy code
```
sealed class Result
data class Success(val data: String) : Result()
data class Error(val message: String) : Result()
```

✖ Bad (Using Enum)
kotlin
Copy code
```
enum class Result { SUCCESS, ERROR }
```

Why?

Sealed classes can hold data, enums cannot.
Provides better flexibility for handling different outcomes.

8. Avoid Unnecessary Object Creation

Creating unnecessary objects increases memory usage.

■ Good (Singleton Object)

```kotlin
Copy code
object Logger {
    fun log(message: String) = println(message)
}
```

✖ Bad (Multiple Object Creation)

```kotlin
Copy code
class Logger {
    fun log(message: String) = println(message)
}
```

Why?

Using object ensures only one instance exists.
Improves performance and memory efficiency.

9. Favor Higher-Order Functions and Lambdas

Kotlin supports functional programming with higher-order functions.

■ Good (Lambda Expression)

kotlin
Copy code
val numbers = listOf(1, 2, 3, 4)
val squares = numbers.map { it * it }

✘ Bad (Traditional Loop)

kotlin
Copy code
val numbers = listOf(1, 2, 3, 4)
val squares = ArrayList<Int>()
for (number in numbers) {
    squares.add(number * number)
}

Why?

More concise and easier to read.

10. Write Readable Code with Proper Naming Conventions
Use descriptive and consistent names for variables and functions.

■ Good

kotlin

Copy code

```kotlin
fun calculateTotalPrice(price: Double, quantity: Int): Double
```

✕ Bad

kotlin

Copy code

```kotlin
fun calc(p: Double, q: Int): Double
```

Why?

Improves readability and understandability.

Conclusion

■ Write idiomatic Kotlin code using higher-order functions and extension functions.

■ Use val instead of var for immutability.

■ Leverage data classes to reduce boilerplate code.

■ Utilize null safety features to prevent runtime crashes.

■ Write concise and expressive code using lambdas and functional programming.

By following these practices, you can write clean, efficient, and maintainable Kotlin applications!

10.1 Using Extension Functions for Cleaner Code

Kotlin's extension functions allow you to add functionality to existing classes without modifying their source code. This feature makes your code more concise, expressive, and easier to maintain. Extension functions are particularly useful for extending the behavior of libraries or classes that you cannot modify directly, such as built-in Kotlin types or third-party libraries.

1. What are Extension Functions?

An extension function is a function that can be called on an object, but it's not a part of the object's class. These functions allow you to "extend" the behavior of existing types. In Kotlin, an extension function is defined by prefixing the function name with the type being extended, followed by a dot (.).

Syntax:
kotlin
Copy code
```kotlin
fun ClassName.functionName(parameters) {
    // Function body
}
```

2. Example of Extension Function

Here's a simple example of an extension function that adds functionality to the String class.

```kotlin
Copy code
fun String.isPalindrome(): Boolean {
    return this == this.reversed()
}

fun main() {
    val word = "madam"
    println(word.isPalindrome()) // Output: true
}
```

In this example, the isPalindrome() function is added to the String class, and you can now call it on any String object like a built-in function.

Why Use?

Enhances readability and clarity of your code.
Encapsulates logic in a function without changing the class definition.

3. Using Extension Functions on Collections

Extension functions are especially useful when working with collections like lists, maps, etc. You can easily add custom behavior to the Kotlin collections.

Example: Adding an Extension Function to List
kotlin
Copy code
```kotlin
fun List<Int>.sumEvenNumbers(): Int {
    return this.filter { it % 2 == 0 }.sum()
}

fun main() {
    val numbers = listOf(1, 2, 3, 4, 5, 6)
    println(numbers.sumEvenNumbers()) // Output: 12
}
```

In this case, sumEvenNumbers() is an extension function that filters the even numbers from a list and calculates their sum.

Why Use?

Makes your collection manipulation more readable and expressive.
Allows you to create custom functionality without altering the original classes.

4. Extension Functions for Null Safety

You can also use extension functions to safely operate on nullable types. This makes your code cleaner and avoids null pointer exceptions.

Example: Safe Extension Function for Nullable Types

kotlin
Copy code
```kotlin
fun String?.isNotEmptyOrNull(): Boolean {
    return this?.isNotEmpty() ?: false
}

fun main() {
    val text: String? = "Hello, Kotlin!"
    println(text.isNotEmptyOrNull()) // Output: true
}
```
Here, isNotEmptyOrNull() is an extension function that ensures null safety when checking if the string is not empty.

Why Use?

Helps avoid null pointer exceptions.
Keeps null safety logic separate and clean.

5. Adding Extension Functions to Custom Classes

Extension functions can be added to your custom classes as well, making it easy to extend their behavior without altering their code.

Example: Extension Function on Custom Class

```kotlin
Copy code
class Person(val name: String, val age: Int)

fun Person.isAdult() = this.age >= 18

fun main() {
    val person = Person("Alice", 25)
    println(person.isAdult()) // Output: true
}
```

Here, the isAdult() function is added to the Person class as an extension, allowing you to check whether a person is an adult without modifying the original Person class.

Why Use?

Extends behavior of custom classes without inheritance or modification.
Promotes cleaner, more reusable code.

6. Limitations of Extension Functions

While extension functions are powerful, there are some limitations to keep in mind:

Extension functions do not modify the class itself: They are just syntactic sugar that provides a more readable way to call a function. They are not truly part of the class.

Example: If you define an extension function isAdult() for Person, you can call it on a Person object, but it doesn't alter the Person class definition.

Overridden methods in subclasses: Extension functions are resolved statically, meaning they are resolved at compile-time, not at runtime. This may cause unexpected behavior when the extension function is called on an object that belongs to a subclass.

No access to private members: Extension functions cannot access private or protected members of the class they extend.

7. Best Practices for Extension Functions
Here are some best practices for using extension functions in Kotlin:

1. Use Extension Functions for Readability
Use them when they make the code more readable and concise. Avoid creating extensions just for the sake of it.

2. Avoid Overusing Extensions

While extension functions are convenient, using them excessively may make your code less maintainable and harder to follow.

3. Keep Extensions in Separate Files

Organize your extension functions in dedicated files to maintain clarity, especially when they are extensive.

4. Name Extensions Meaningfully

Choose meaningful and descriptive names for extension functions so that their purpose is immediately clear.

8. Conclusion

Extension functions in Kotlin provide a clean and efficient way to extend the functionality of existing classes without modifying their source code. They promote readable, concise, and expressive code. Use extension functions to enhance the flexibility of your code, keep it clean, and avoid clutter. However, remember to use them judiciously, as overusing them can lead to confusion or potential issues with code maintenance.

By leveraging extension functions, you can make your Kotlin code more modular and maintainable, and enhance the overall development experience!

10.2 Delegation and Lazy Initialization

Kotlin provides powerful features like delegation and lazy initialization, which simplify code and improve performance. These concepts help in reducing boilerplate code, managing resources efficiently, and creating more maintainable and modular software. Let's explore both features in detail.

1. Delegation in Kotlin

Delegation is a design pattern where an object hands over some of its responsibilities to another object. In Kotlin, delegation is used to delegate tasks or responsibilities to other classes. This concept allows you to reuse functionality and compose behavior rather than relying on inheritance.

Types of Delegation in Kotlin:

a. Class Delegation (Automatic Delegation with by keyword)

In Kotlin, you can use the by keyword to delegate interface methods to another object. The object that handles the method calls is called the delegate.

Example of Class Delegation:
kotlin
Copy code

```kotlin
interface Printer {
   fun printDocument()
}

class SimplePrinter : Printer {
   override fun printDocument() {
     println("Printing document...")
   }
}

class AdvancedPrinter(printer: Printer) : Printer by printer
```

```
fun main() {
    val simplePrinter = SimplePrinter()
    val advancedPrinter = AdvancedPrinter(simplePrinter)
        advancedPrinter.printDocument()   // Output: Printing
document...
}
```

In this example:

The AdvancedPrinter class delegates its printDocument method to an instance of SimplePrinter.
The keyword by tells Kotlin to automatically implement the interface methods by delegating them to the given object (simplePrinter).

Advantages of Class Delegation:

Composition over inheritance: Avoids the rigidity of inheritance and promotes code reuse.
Simplifies code: Automatically implements interface methods via delegation.

b. Property Delegation

Kotlin allows you to delegate the getter and setter behavior of properties to another object. This is commonly used for cases like lazy initialization, observable properties, and storing properties in a map.

Example of Property Delegation:

kotlin
Copy code

```kotlin
import kotlin.reflect.KProperty

class Example {
    var name: String by Delegate()
}

class Delegate {
    private var field: String = "Initial value"

    operator fun getValue(thisRef: Any?, property: KProperty<*>): String {
        return field
    }

    operator fun setValue(thisRef: Any?, property: KProperty<*>, value: String) {
        field = value
    }
}
```

```
fun main() {
    val example = Example()
    println(example.name) // Output: Initial value
    example.name = "New value"
    println(example.name) // Output: New value
}
```

In this example:

The name property in Example class is delegated to Delegate.
The getValue and setValue methods are used to define custom getter and setter logic.

Use Cases of Property Delegation:

Observable properties: Automatically notify when a property changes.
Lazy initialization: Initialize the property when it is first accessed.
Storing properties in a map: For more complex storage needs.

2. Lazy Initialization in Kotlin

Lazy initialization is a technique where an object or value is not initialized until it is actually needed. This is particularly useful when dealing with expensive objects or resources that should not be created until the first time they are used.

Using lazy in Kotlin:

Kotlin provides a lazy delegate for lazy initialization, which allows you to delay the creation of a value until it's actually required. It ensures that the value is created only once and is thread-safe by default.

Example of Lazy Initialization:

```kotlin
Copy code
val myValue: String by lazy {
    println("Initializing myValue...")
    "Hello, Kotlin!"
}

fun main() {
    println("Before accessing myValue")
    println(myValue)   // Output: Initializing myValue... Hello, Kotlin!
    println(myValue)   // Output: Hello, Kotlin! (No initialization this time)
}
```

In this example:

The myValue is lazily initialized: the block inside lazy {} is executed only when myValue is accessed for the first time.
The message "Initializing myValue..." is printed only once during the first access.

Advantages of Lazy Initialization:

Efficiency: Expensive objects or calculations are deferred until required.
Thread safety: The default lazy implementation is thread-safe, ensuring the value is computed only once in a multi-threaded environment.

Lazy Initialization with Custom Threading:

You can customize the thread behavior with lazy(LazyThreadSafetyMode) if you want to avoid the default thread safety mechanism for performance reasons.

kotlin
Copy code
```kotlin
val myValue: String by lazy(LazyThreadSafetyMode.NONE) {
    "Hello, Kotlin!"
}
```

3. Combining Delegation and Lazy Initialization

Kotlin allows you to combine delegation and lazy initialization for more powerful and flexible code. For example, you could have a property that is delegated to an object while being lazily initialized.

Example: Using Delegation with Lazy Initialization:

```kotlin
Copy code
class MyClass {
    val config: String by lazy {
        println("Loading configuration...")
        "Configuration Loaded"
    }

    val name: String by Delegate()
}

class Delegate {
    private var field: String = "Default Name"

    operator fun getValue(thisRef: Any?, property: KProperty<*>):
    String {
        return field
    }
```

```kotlin
    operator fun setValue(thisRef: Any?, property: KProperty<*>,
value: String) {
        field = value
    }
}

fun main() {
    val myClass = MyClass()

    // Lazy initialization of 'config'
        println(myClass.config)  // Output: Loading configuration...
Configuration Loaded
        println(myClass.config)  // Output: Configuration Loaded
(No loading this time)

    // Delegate usage for 'name'
    println(myClass.name) // Output: Default Name
    myClass.name = "John"
    println(myClass.name) // Output: John
}
```

In this example:

The config property is lazily initialized when accessed.
The name property is delegated to an instance of Delegate.

4. Benefits of Delegation and Lazy Initialization

1. Reduces Boilerplate Code:
Both features reduce the need for boilerplate code. Delegation eliminates the need for complex inheritance, and lazy initialization prevents the premature creation of resources.

2. Enhances Flexibility:

Delegation allows flexible composition of behaviors, making code easier to extend and maintain.
Lazy initialization ensures that expensive operations are only performed when necessary, improving performance.

3. Improves Code Readability:

Both techniques promote clear and concise code. Delegation makes it easy to extend functionality, while lazy initialization ensures that initialization logic is contained and easy to understand.

5. Conclusion

Kotlin's delegation and lazy initialization are powerful tools for writing clean, efficient, and maintainable code. Delegation enables flexible composition and code reuse, while lazy initialization ensures that resources are only consumed when necessary. Both features can dramatically simplify your codebase and improve performance, making them essential techniques for every Kotlin developer to master.

By applying these concepts appropriately, you can build modular, scalable, and efficient applications with Kotlin.

10.3 Best Practices for Writing Maintainable Code

Writing maintainable code is a crucial skill for software developers, especially when working on large or long-term projects. Code that is easy to understand, modify, and extend helps teams collaborate more effectively, reduces bugs, and ensures that future developers can build upon existing work with minimal friction. In Kotlin, as with any other programming language, there are several best practices that can help make your code more maintainable.

1. Write Clean and Readable Code

a. Follow Naming Conventions

Use descriptive, clear names for classes, functions, and variables. Avoid vague names like temp or data, and instead use names that clearly indicate the purpose, such as userList or getUserData().

CamelCase for variables, functions, and properties, and PascalCase for class names. Example: calculateTotalAmount(), UserProfile.

b. Keep Code Simple

Avoid unnecessary complexity. Keep functions and classes focused on one responsibility and keep them small. If a function is getting too long, it might be doing too much.

Stick to the KISS principle (Keep It Simple, Stupid) and make your code as simple and intuitive as possible.

c. Use Comments and Documentation

Use comments to explain complex or non-obvious logic in your code. However, avoid redundant comments like // increments the counter. Instead, focus on why something is done rather than how.

In Kotlin, use KDoc for documenting functions, classes, and properties. This provides useful documentation for future developers and makes your code easier to understand.

Example of KDoc:

kotlin

Copy code

```
/**
 * Calculates the total price after tax.
 *
 * @param price The original price of the item.
 * @param taxRate The applicable tax rate.
 * @return The price including tax.
 */
fun calculatePriceWithTax(price: Double, taxRate: Double): Double {
    return price * (1 + taxRate)
}
```

2. Follow SOLID Principles

The SOLID principles are a set of five object-oriented design principles that, when followed, make your code more maintainable, flexible, and scalable.

S - Single Responsibility Principle (SRP): A class should have one reason to change, meaning it should have only one responsibility.
O - Open/Closed Principle (OCP): Software entities (classes, modules, functions) should be open for extension, but closed for modification.

L - Liskov Substitution Principle (LSP): Objects of a superclass should be replaceable with objects of a subclass without affecting the functionality of the program.

I - Interface Segregation Principle (ISP): Clients should not be forced to depend on interfaces they do not use.

D - Dependency Inversion Principle (DIP): High-level modules should not depend on low-level modules; both should depend on abstractions.

3. Modularize Your Code

a. Break Code into Smaller Functions

Small, reusable functions are easier to understand and test. Functions should ideally do one thing and do it well.

Avoid large monolithic classes. Break them down into smaller, logically grouped classes.

b. Use Packages and Modules

Organize related classes and functions into packages or modules to improve code readability and structure. This helps other developers understand the context and find the necessary code more easily.

Avoid placing too many classes in one file; separate them based on functionality.

4. Leverage Kotlin Features

Kotlin has many features that can help write more concise and readable code, making it easier to maintain.

a. Use Null Safety

Take advantage of Kotlin's null safety features to avoid NullPointerException. Use nullable types (?), safe calls (?.), and the Elvis operator (?:) to manage null values efficiently.

Example:

```kotlin
Copy code
val result = user?.name ?: "Unknown"
```

b. Use Data Classes

Kotlin's data classes are perfect for classes that mainly hold data. They automatically provide useful functions like toString(), equals(), hashCode(), and copy(), reducing the need for boilerplate code.

```kotlin
Copy code
data class User(val name: String, val age: Int)
```

c. Take Advantage of Extension Functions

Extension functions allow you to add new behavior to existing classes without modifying them. This makes your code more modular and easier to extend.

kotlin
Copy code
```kotlin
fun String.isPalindrome(): Boolean {
    return this == this.reversed()
}
```

5. Write Testable Code

Testing is key to maintaining high-quality code, and writing code that is easy to test is vital.

a. Write Unit Tests

Write unit tests for your functions and methods to ensure they work as expected. This will also make it easier to catch regressions when you make changes.
Use libraries like JUnit or KotlinTest for writing and running tests.

b. Keep Code Testable

Design your code with testability in mind. Avoid hard-to-test components, such as tightly coupled classes or those that have many dependencies.
Use dependency injection to make your classes more testable by passing dependencies rather than creating them within the class.

Example of dependency injection:

kotlin
Copy code

```kotlin
class UserService(private val userRepository: UserRepository) {
    fun getUser(id: Int): User = userRepository.getUserById(id)
}
```

6. Use Immutable Data Structures

Immutable data structures help avoid unintended side effects and make your code easier to reason about.

a. Use val for Immutable Properties

Use immutable properties (val) as much as possible. This makes the state of your objects predictable and reduces the chances of bugs.

kotlin
Copy code

```kotlin
val user = User("John", 25)
```

b. Prefer Immutable Collections

Prefer immutable collections (like List, Set, Map) over mutable ones when you don't need to change the collection.

kotlin
Copy code

```kotlin
val numbers: List<Int> = listOf(1, 2, 3)
```

7. Handle Errors Gracefully

a. Use Exceptions Wisely

Use exceptions to handle unexpected situations, but avoid overusing them for normal control flow. Make sure your exception handling is meaningful and provides clear error messages.

Example:

kotlin
Copy code

```kotlin
try {
    // Code that may throw an exception
} catch (e: Exception) {
    println("An error occurred: ${e.message}")
}
```

b. Provide Clear Error Messages

When exceptions occur, make sure to log clear, detailed error messages that help developers understand the problem.

8. Refactor Regularly

As your codebase evolves, it's important to refactor your code to keep it clean, efficient, and maintainable. Regularly review your code to find areas for improvement.

Remove duplication: If you find similar code blocks, consider extracting them into functions or classes to reduce duplication.
Improve readability: Refactor long functions or classes into smaller, more manageable pieces.

9. Prioritize Performance and Scalability

Write code that is optimized for performance, but avoid premature optimization. Focus on making the code clear and maintainable first, and optimize when necessary.
Scalability is important in large applications. Make sure that your design can handle increased load or additional functionality without a complete redesign.

Conclusion

Writing maintainable code is about balancing clarity, simplicity, and flexibility. By following best practices like adhering to SOLID principles, modularizing your code, writing tests, and using Kotlin's features like null safety and extension functions, you can create code that is clean, scalable, and easy to maintain.

Remember, maintainable code is an ongoing effort, so always be proactive in refactoring and improving your codebase, and encourage your team to follow these practices for long-term success.

Chapter 11
Testing and Debugging Kotlin Applications

.

Testing and debugging are crucial for ensuring the reliability, stability, and maintainability of Kotlin applications. Effective testing helps catch bugs early, while debugging tools help developers identify and fix issues efficiently. Kotlin provides robust support for testing frameworks and debugging tools to streamline the development process.

1. Testing in Kotlin

a. Unit Testing with JUnit

Kotlin supports JUnit (JUnit 4 & 5) for unit testing.
Unit tests focus on testing individual functions or components in isolation.
Use assertions (assertEquals, assertTrue, etc.) to validate expected behavior.

Example using JUnit:

kotlin
Copy code

```kotlin
import org.junit.Test
import kotlin.test.assertEquals

class MathUtilsTest {

  @Test
  fun testAddition() {
    val result = 2 + 3
    assertEquals(5, result)
  }
}
```

b. Mocking Dependencies with MockK

Use MockK for creating mock objects in Kotlin.
Helps in testing classes that have dependencies without requiring actual implementations.

Example using MockK:

kotlin
Copy code
```kotlin
import io.mockk.*
import org.junit.Test
import kotlin.test.assertEquals

class UserServiceTest {
```

```kotlin
    private val userRepository = mockk<UserRepository>()
    private val userService = UserService(userRepository)

    @Test
    fun testGetUser() {
        every { userRepository.getUserById(1) } returns User(1,
"John Doe")

        val user = userService.getUser(1)

        assertEquals("John Doe", user.name)
        verify { userRepository.getUserById(1) }
    }
}
```

c. UI Testing with Espresso

For Android applications, Espresso is used for testing UI interactions.
Simulates user actions like button clicks and text inputs.

2. Debugging in Kotlin

a. Using IntelliJ IDEA Debugger
Kotlin integrates seamlessly with IntelliJ IDEA and Android Studio for debugging.

Features include:

Breakpoints: Pause execution at specific lines.
Step Over / Step Into: Navigate through code execution.
Watches and Variables: Inspect variable values during runtime.

b. Logging with Kotlin's Log and println

For quick debugging, use println() to print values in the console.
In Android, use Log:
kotlin
Copy code
import android.util.Log

Log.d("DEBUG_TAG", "This is a debug message")

c. Exception Handling for Debugging

Use try-catch blocks to catch and log exceptions.
kotlin
Copy code
```kotlin
try {
    val result = 10 / 0
} catch (e: ArithmeticException) {
    println("Error: ${e.message}")
}
```

d. Analyzing Stack Traces

When an error occurs, check the stack trace to find the root cause. It shows the sequence of function calls leading to the error.

3. Best Practices for Testing and Debugging

Write tests before fixing bugs to verify issues and prevent regressions.
Automate testing using CI/CD pipelines for consistent validation.
Use structured logging to capture useful debug information.
Break problems down and test/debug smaller units before full integration.

By following these best practices, developers can build stable, reliable Kotlin applications with fewer errors and faster issue resolution.

11.1 Unit Testing with Kotlin

Unit testing is an essential part of software development that ensures individual components of an application work as expected. In Kotlin, unit testing is primarily done using JUnit and enhanced with libraries like MockK for mocking dependencies. Well-written unit tests improve code reliability, catch bugs early, and make refactoring safer.

1. Setting Up Unit Testing in Kotlin

a. Adding Dependencies
To enable unit testing in a Kotlin project, add the necessary dependencies to your Gradle build file:

kotlin
Copy code

```
dependencies {
    testImplementation 'org.junit.jupiter:junit-jupiter:5.7.1'  // JUnit 5
    testImplementation 'io.mockk:mockk:1.12.0' // MockK for mocking
    testImplementation 'org.jetbrains.kotlin:kotlin-test' // Kotlin test utilities
}
```

2. Writing Unit Tests with JUnit

JUnit is the most commonly used testing framework for Kotlin. It provides various annotations and assertions to verify expected outcomes.

a. Basic Test Case Example

A simple test function to check basic arithmetic operations:

```kotlin
import org.junit.jupiter.api.Test
import kotlin.test.assertEquals

class MathUtilsTest {

    @Test
    fun testAddition() {
        val result = 5 + 3
        assertEquals(8, result, "Addition should return the correct sum")
    }
}
```

b. Using @BeforeEach and @AfterEach

JUnit provides lifecycle annotations to set up and tear down test environments.

```kotlin
Copy code
```

```kotlin
import org.junit.jupiter.api.*

class SampleTest {

    @BeforeEach
    fun setup() {
        println("Before each test")
    }

    @AfterEach
    fun tearDown() {
        println("After each test")
    }

    @Test
    fun sampleTest() {
        assertEquals(2 * 2, 4)
    }
}
```

3. Mocking Dependencies with MockK

When testing components that rely on external dependencies, MockK allows us to create mock objects and define expected behaviors.

a. Mocking a Repository

Consider a UserService that depends on UserRepository to fetch user data.

```kotlin
Copy code
import io.mockk.*
import org.junit.jupiter.api.Test
import kotlin.test.assertEquals

class UserServiceTest {
    private val userRepository = mockk<UserRepository>()
    private val userService = UserService(userRepository)

    @Test
    fun testGetUser() {
        every { userRepository.getUserById(1) } returns User(1, "John Doe")

        val user = userService.getUser(1)

        assertEquals("John Doe", user.name)
        verify { userRepository.getUserById(1) }  // Verify method call
    }
}
```

b. Mocking Behavior and Verifying Interactions

MockK allows verifying method calls and simulating exceptions.

```kotlin
Copy code
@Test
fun testExceptionHandling() {
        every { userRepository.getUserById(any()) } throws
RuntimeException("Database error")

  try {
    userService.getUser(1)
  } catch (e: RuntimeException) {
    assertEquals("Database error", e.message)
  }
}
```

4. Parameterized Tests

JUnit 5 allows running tests with multiple input values using Parameterized Tests.

```kotlin
Copy code
import org.junit.jupiter.params.ParameterizedTest
import org.junit.jupiter.params.provider.CsvSource
```

```kotlin
import kotlin.test.assertEquals

class MathUtilsTest {

    @ParameterizedTest
    @CsvSource("2,3,5", "4,5,9", "6,7,13")
    fun testAddition(a: Int, b: Int, expected: Int) {
        assertEquals(expected, a + b)
    }
}
```

5. Best Practices for Unit Testing in Kotlin

Write small, focused tests for individual functions or classes.
Use meaningful test names to describe expected behavior.
Follow the AAA pattern: Arrange, Act, Assert.
Mock external dependencies to isolate test logic.
Run tests automatically using CI/CD pipelines.
Cover edge cases to ensure robustness.
By following these practices, developers can write effective and maintainable unit tests in Kotlin, improving software reliability and maintainability.

11.2 Debugging Tools and Techniques

Debugging is a critical part of software development, helping developers identify and fix issues efficiently. Kotlin offers powerful debugging tools and techniques, especially when using IntelliJ IDEA or Android Studio. Effective debugging reduces development time, improves code quality, and ensures better application stability.

1. Debugging with IntelliJ IDEA and Android Studio

a. Setting Breakpoints

Breakpoints allow developers to pause execution at specific lines to inspect variable values and execution flow.

Set a Breakpoint: Click on the left margin of a line number in IntelliJ IDEA/Android Studio.
Run Debugger: Click the debug button (bug icon) or press Shift + F9.

Step Through Code:

Step Over (F8): Move to the next line without entering functions.
Step Into (F7): Enter a function to debug inside it.

Step Out (Shift + F8): Exit the current function.

b. Evaluating Expressions

During debugging, use the Evaluate Expression (Alt + F8) feature to inspect and modify variable values dynamically.

2. Using Logs for Debugging

Logging is a simple but effective debugging technique, especially when breakpoints aren't practical (e.g., debugging API calls or background threads).

a. Logging in Kotlin

For simple applications:

```kotlin
Copy code
println("Debug message: Variable x = $x")
```
For Android applications:

```kotlin
Copy code
import android.util.Log
```

```
Log.d("DEBUG_TAG", "User data: $user")
```

Log.e("ERROR_TAG", "Something went wrong!", exception)

b. Structured Logging

Use structured logging frameworks like SLF4J with Logback for better log management in Kotlin backend applications.

Example using SLF4J:

```kotlin
Copy code
import org.slf4j.LoggerFactory

val logger = LoggerFactory.getLogger("MyApp")
logger.info("Application started")
logger.error("An error occurred", exception)
```

3. Exception Handling for Debugging

Using try-catch blocks helps prevent crashes and provides useful error messages.

```kotlin
Copy code
try {
    val result = 10 / 0
} catch (e: ArithmeticException) {
```

```kotlin
    println("Error: ${e.message}")
}
```

a. Using Custom Exception Messages

```kotlin
Copy code
class          InvalidInputException(message:          String)          :
Exception(message)

fun validateInput(input: Int) {
    if (input < 0) throw InvalidInputException("Input cannot be
negative")
}
```

4. Analyzing Stack Traces

A stack trace helps trace the sequence of function calls that led to
an error.

Example:

```php
Copy code
Exception in thread "main" java.lang.ArithmeticException: / by
zero
    at MainKt main(Main.kt:5)
```

Locate the error: Check the file name and line number (Main.kt:5).

Check the function call chain to understand where the issue originated.

5. Remote Debugging

For debugging applications running on remote servers or Android devices:

Enable Remote Debugging in IntelliJ IDEA.
Use adb logcat for debugging Android logs.
Attach a Debugger to JVM-based applications using a debug port.

6. Best Practices for Effective Debugging

Reproduce the issue before debugging.
Use breakpoints strategically instead of println().
Log meaningful messages with relevant data.
Isolate the problem by testing smaller components separately.

Write unit tests to catch and prevent regressions.
By using these debugging tools and techniques, developers can efficiently troubleshoot and resolve issues in Kotlin applications, ensuring a smoother development process.

11.3 Using Mocking Frameworks

Mocking frameworks are essential for unit testing, allowing developers to isolate components and test them independently. In Kotlin, MockK is the most popular mocking library, offering powerful features like stubbing, spying, and verification. Mocking frameworks help in writing cleaner, faster, and more maintainable tests.

1. Why Use Mocking Frameworks?
Mocking frameworks help:

✔ Isolate dependencies – Test a class without requiring real implementations of its dependencies.
✔ Simulate behaviors – Define expected behavior for dependencies.
✔ Verify interactions – Check if methods were called with the correct arguments.
✔ Improve test speed – Avoid slow operations like database or API calls.

2. Setting Up MockK in a Kotlin Project

a. Adding Dependencies

To use MockK, add the following dependency in your Gradle (Kotlin DSL) file:

kotlin
Copy code
```
dependencies {
    testImplementation("io.mockk:mockk:1.12.0") // MockK
for mocking
    testImplementation("org.jetbrains.kotlin:kotlin-test") //
Kotlin test utilities

testImplementation("org.junit.jupiter:junit-jupiter:5.7.1")
// JUnit 5
}
```

3. Mocking with MockK

a. Creating Mocks and Stubbing Methods
Mocks replace real objects with test doubles that return predefined values.

Example: Mocking a UserRepository inside a UserService test:

kotlin

```kotlin
Copy code
import io.mockk.*
import org.junit.jupiter.api.Test
import kotlin.test.assertEquals

// Sample data class
data class User(val id: Int, val name: String)

// Interface to be mocked
interface UserRepository {
    fun getUserById(id: Int): User?
}

// Service class that depends on UserRepository
class UserService(private val repository: UserRepository) {
    fun getUser(id: Int): String {
        val user = repository.getUserById(id) ?: return "User
not found"
        return user.name
    }
}

class UserServiceTest {
    private val userRepository = mockk<UserRepository>()
// Create a mock instance
    private val userService = UserService(userRepository)
```

```kotlin
@Test
fun `test getUser returns correct user name`() {
    // Stubbing: Define mock behavior
    every { userRepository.getUserById(1) } returns User(1, "John Doe")

    // Act: Call method being tested
    val result = userService.getUser(1)

    // Assert: Verify expected output
    assertEquals("John Doe", result)

    // Verify interaction with mock
    verify { userRepository.getUserById(1) }
  }
}
```

4. Verifying Method Calls

MockK allows verifying if a function was called and how many times.

Example:

kotlin
Copy code
@Test

```kotlin
fun `test method call verification`() {
    every { userRepository.getUserById(any()) } returns
User(2, "Alice")

    userService.getUser(2)

    verify(exactly = 1) { userRepository.getUserById(2) } //
Ensures method was called once
}
```

5. Mocking Exceptions

You can simulate exceptions using throws.

```kotlin
kotlin
Copy code
@Test
fun `test exception handling`() {
    every { userRepository.getUserById(any()) } throws
RuntimeException("Database error")

    try {
        userService.getUser(1)
    } catch (e: RuntimeException) {
        assertEquals("Database error", e.message)
    }
}
```

6. Using Spies for Partial Mocking

Spies allow testing real object behavior while still controlling specific methods.

kotlin
Copy code

```kotlin
@Test
fun `test spying on a real object`() {
    val realRepo = UserRepositoryImpl() // Assume a real implementation exists
    val spyRepo = spyk(realRepo)

    every { spyRepo.getUserById(1) } returns User(1, "Mocked User") // Overriding one method

    val result = spyRepo.getUserById(1)
    assertEquals("Mocked User", result?.name)
}
```

7. Mocking Singleton Objects

MockK allows mocking Kotlin object singletons using mockkObject().

kotlin

Copy code

```
object Logger {
    fun log(message: String) = println(message)
}

@Test
fun `test mocking a singleton object`() {
    mockkObject(Logger)
    every { Logger.log(any()) } just Runs

    Logger.log("Test message")

    verify { Logger.log("Test message") }
}
```

8. Best Practices for Using Mocking Frameworks

Mock only what is necessary – Avoid excessive mocking; prefer real objects when feasible.

Use verify sparingly – Over-verifying method calls can make tests fragile.

Prefer constructor injection – Makes it easier to replace dependencies with mocks.

Combine unit tests with integration tests – Mocking is useful, but real-world integration tests are essential.

Use spies wisely – Partial mocking should be avoided when possible, as it can make tests less predictable.

By leveraging MockK and following best practices, Kotlin developers can write clean, reliable, and efficient unit tests, improving software quality and maintainability.

Chapter 12
Integrating Functional Programming with OOP in Kotlin

Kotlin is a hybrid language that seamlessly combines Object-Oriented Programming (OOP) and Functional Programming (FP) paradigms. By integrating FP principles into OOP-based designs, developers can write more concise, maintainable, and scalable code.

1. Key Functional Programming Features in Kotlin

a. First-Class and Higher-Order Functions

Functions in Kotlin can be assigned to variables, passed as arguments, and returned from other functions.

Example of a higher-order function:

kotlin
Copy code
```kotlin
fun operate(a: Int, b: Int, operation: (Int, Int) -> Int): Int {
    return operation(a, b)
}

val sum = operate(5, 3) { x, y -> x + y }
```

println(sum) // Output: 8

b. Lambda Expressions

Lambdas allow writing concise functions without explicit method declarations.

kotlin
Copy code
```kotlin
val square: (Int) -> Int = { it * it }
println(square(4)) // Output: 16
```

c. Immutability and Data Transformation

Functional programming promotes immutability and avoids changing state.

kotlin
Copy code
```kotlin
val numbers = listOf(1, 2, 3, 4, 5)
val squaredNumbers = numbers.map { it * it }
println(squaredNumbers) // Output: [1, 4, 9, 16, 25]
```

2. Applying Functional Programming in OOP-Based Kotlin Applications

a. Using Functional Interfaces

Kotlin allows defining interfaces with a single abstract method (SAM), making them compatible with lambda expressions.

kotlin
Copy code
```kotlin
fun interface Transformer {
    fun transform(value: Int): Int
}

val doubleValue = Transformer { it * 2 }
println(doubleValue.transform(5)) // Output: 10
```

b. Functional Composition with Extension Functions

Kotlin's extension functions enhance OOP by adding behavior without modifying the original class.

kotlin
Copy code
```kotlin
fun String.reverseAndUppercase(): String = this.reversed().uppercase()

println("hello".reverseAndUppercase()) // Output: "OLLEH"
```

c. Combining FP and OOP with Sealed Classes

Sealed classes help structure functional-style handling of different cases.

kotlin
Copy code

```kotlin
sealed class Result {
    data class Success(val data: String) : Result()
    object Error : Result()
}

fun handleResult(result: Result): String {
    return when (result) {
        is Result.Success -> "Success: ${result.data}"
        Result.Error -> "An error occurred"
    }
}

println(handleResult(Result.Success("Data    loaded"))) // Output: Success: Data loaded
```

3. Benefits of Combining FP with OOP

✔ Improved code readability with concise lambda expressions and higher-order functions.
✔ Better maintainability by reducing side effects and using immutable data structures.

✔ More reusable components through extension functions and functional interfaces.

✔ Enhanced safety with sealed classes and functional error handling.

By leveraging functional programming techniques within an OOP structure, Kotlin developers can write more expressive and efficient code while maintaining the benefits of both paradigms.

12.1 Kotlin's Functional Features

Kotlin is a modern programming language that seamlessly blends Object-Oriented Programming (OOP) with Functional Programming (FP). It provides a variety of functional features that enable developers to write concise, expressive, and immutable code while maintaining high performance and readability.

1. First-Class and Higher-Order Functions

a. First-Class Functions
Functions in Kotlin are treated as first-class citizens, meaning they can be:

Assigned to variables

Passed as arguments

Returned from other functions

Example:

kotlin

Copy code

```kotlin
val greet: (String) -> String = { name -> "Hello, $name!" }
println(greet("Alice")) // Output: Hello, Alice!
```

b. Higher-Order Functions

A function that takes another function as a parameter or returns a function is called a higher-order function.

Example:

kotlin

Copy code

```kotlin
fun operate(a: Int, b: Int, operation: (Int, Int) -> Int): Int {
    return operation(a, b)
}

val sum = operate(5, 3) { x, y -> x + y }
println(sum) // Output: 8
```

2. Lambda Expressions and Anonymous Functions

Lambda expressions allow defining short, inline functions without explicitly declaring them.

Example:

kotlin
Copy code
```
val square: (Int) -> Int = { it * it }
println(square(4)) // Output: 16
```

Anonymous functions provide a more explicit syntax:

kotlin
Copy code
```
val multiply = fun(a: Int, b: Int): Int { return a * b }
println(multiply(3, 4)) // Output: 12
```

3. Immutability and Data Transformation

Kotlin encourages immutability by favoring val over var and provides functional collection transformations like map, filter, and reduce.

Example:

kotlin
Copy code

```kotlin
val numbers = listOf(1, 2, 3, 4, 5)
val squaredNumbers = numbers.map { it * it }
println(squaredNumbers) // Output: [1, 4, 9, 16, 25]
```

Filtering values:

kotlin
Copy code
```kotlin
val evenNumbers = numbers.filter { it % 2 == 0 }
println(evenNumbers) // Output: [2, 4]
```

4. Extension Functions

Extension functions allow adding new functionality to existing classes without modifying them.

Example:

kotlin
Copy code
```kotlin
fun String.reverseAndUppercase(): String =
this.reversed().uppercase()

println("hello".reverseAndUppercase()) // Output:
"OLLEH"
```

5. Function Composition

Kotlin supports function composition using lambda chaining.

Example:

kotlin
Copy code
val double: (Int) -> Int = { it * 2 }
val increment: (Int) -> Int = { it + 1 }

val doubleThenIncrement = double.andThen(increment)

println(doubleThenIncrement(4)) // Output: 9

6. Sealed Classes for Functional Data Handling

Sealed classes are a functional way to represent restricted class hierarchies, often used in functional error handling.

Example:

kotlin
Copy code
sealed class Result {
    data class Success(val data: String) : Result()
    object Error : Result()
}

```kotlin
fun handleResult(result: Result): String {
    return when (result) {
        is Result.Success -> "Success: ${result.data}"
        Result.Error -> "An error occurred"
    }
}
```

```kotlin
println(handleResult(Result.Success("Data    loaded")))   //
Output: Success: Data loaded
```

7. Lazy Evaluation

Kotlin supports lazy evaluation, meaning computations are deferred until needed.

Example:

kotlin
Copy code
```kotlin
val lazyValue: String by lazy {
    println("Computed only when accessed")
    "Hello, Kotlin!"
}
```

```kotlin
println("Before accessing lazyValue")
println(lazyValue) // Computation happens here
```

println(lazyValue) // No computation this time

8. Functional Error Handling with Result API

Kotlin provides the Result type for handling errors in a functional style.

Example:

kotlin
Copy code
```kotlin
fun divide(a: Int, b: Int): Result<Int> {
                    return    if    (b    ==    0)
Result.failure(ArithmeticException("Cannot    divide    by
zero"))
    else Result.success(a / b)
}

val result = divide(10, 2)
result.onSuccess { println("Result: $it") }
    .onFailure { println("Error: ${it.message}") }
```

9. Coroutines: Asynchronous Functional Programming

Kotlin's coroutines make asynchronous programming easy by eliminating callback hell.

Example:

```kotlin
Copy code
import kotlinx.coroutines.*

fun main() = runBlocking {
    launch {
        delay(1000)
        println("Hello from coroutine!")
    }
    println("Before coroutine")
}
```

Conclusion

Kotlin's functional programming features make code more expressive, concise, and safer. By leveraging higher-order functions, lambdas, immutability, extension functions, and coroutines, developers can write highly efficient and maintainable applications while integrating seamlessly with object-oriented concepts.

12.2 Combining OOP and Functional Programming

Kotlin is a hybrid language that seamlessly integrates Object-Oriented Programming (OOP) and Functional Programming (FP). By combining these paradigms, developers can write cleaner, more efficient, and scalable code while benefiting from the best of both worlds.

1. Why Combine OOP and FP?

✔ Encapsulation & Reusability (OOP) – Classes, objects, and inheritance help in structuring large applications.
✔ Immutability & Conciseness (FP) – Functional programming reduces side effects and simplifies data transformations.
✔ Better Readability & Maintainability – Combining FP concepts in OOP-based code leads to more expressive logic.
✔ Improved Performance & Safety – FP techniques like pure functions and immutability reduce bugs and enhance concurrency.

2. Key Ways to Combine OOP and FP in Kotlin

a. Using Functional Interfaces in OOP
Kotlin allows defining interfaces with a single abstract method (SAM interfaces), making them compatible with lambdas.

Example:

```kotlin
Copy code
fun interface Transformer {
    fun transform(value: Int): Int
}

val doubleValue = Transformer { it * 2 }
println(doubleValue.transform(5)) // Output: 10
```

This blends OOP (interface-based design) with FP (lambda expressions).

b. Functional Extensions for OOP Classes

Extension functions allow adding behavior to existing classes without modifying them.

Example:

```kotlin
Copy code
class Person(val name: String)

fun Person.greet() = "Hello, my name is $name"

val person = Person("Alice")
println(person.greet()) // Output: Hello, my name is Alice
```

This combines OOP (class-based design) with FP (higher-order functions).

c. Immutable Data Classes with Functional Operations

Kotlin's data classes support immutability while leveraging functional transformation methods.

Example:

kotlin
Copy code
```
data class User(val name: String, val age: Int)

val users = listOf(User("Alice", 25), User("Bob", 30))

val adultUsers = users.filter { it.age >= 18 }.map {
it.copy(name = it.name.uppercase()) }
println(adultUsers) // Output: [User(name=ALICE,
age=25), User(name=BOB, age=30)]
```

Here, we apply FP concepts (immutability, map, and filter) within an OOP structure.

d. Higher-Order Functions Inside Classes

OOP classes can define higher-order functions that take lambdas as parameters.

Example:

kotlin
Copy code

```
class Calculator {
    fun operate(a: Int, b: Int, operation: (Int, Int) -> Int): Int {
        return operation(a, b)
    }
}

val calc = Calculator()
println(calc.operate(10, 5) { x, y -> x - y }) // Output: 5
```

This allows for OOP-based encapsulation while enabling FP-style flexible behavior.

e. Sealed Classes for Functional Data Handling

Sealed classes provide an OOP-based structure for handling multiple states in a functional style.

Example:

```kotlin
Copy code
sealed class Result {
    data class Success(val data: String) : Result()
    object Error : Result()
}

fun handleResult(result: Result): String {
    return when (result) {
        is Result.Success -> "Success: ${result.data}"
        Result.Error -> "An error occurred"
    }
}

println(handleResult(Result.Success("Data    loaded")))    // Output: Success: Data loaded
```

This merges OOP-based inheritance with FP-style pattern matching.

f. Functional Composition with Objects

Kotlin objects can use function composition to chain multiple operations.

Example:

```kotlin
Copy code
object MathUtils {
    fun double(x: Int) = x * 2
    fun square(x: Int) = x * x
}

val result = MathUtils.square(MathUtils.double(3))
println(result) // Output: 36
```

This blends OOP (object-based design) with FP (pure functions and composition).

g. Coroutines for Asynchronous Functional Programming in OOP

Kotlin's coroutines simplify async programming while maintaining OOP structure.

Example:

```kotlin
Copy code
import kotlinx.coroutines.*

class AsyncProcessor {
    suspend fun fetchData(): String {
```

```kotlin
        delay(1000) // Simulating network call
        return "Data Loaded"
    }
}


fun main() = runBlocking {
    val processor = AsyncProcessor()
    launch {
        println(processor.fetchData())
    }
}
```

This maintains OOP-based class structure while using FP-style coroutine-based concurrency.

3. Best Practices for Mixing OOP and FP in Kotlin

✔ Use FP for data transformations – Prefer map, filter, reduce over loops.

✔ Leverage immutability – Use val and data classes to avoid unintended state changes.

✔ Encapsulate behavior in OOP classes – Organize logic inside classes and objects, while using FP for processing.

✔ Use extension functions – Add functionality without modifying the original class.

✔ Adopt higher-order functions – Pass functions as parameters for flexible behavior.

✔ Utilize sealed classes – Handle multiple states in a structured, functional way.

✔ Combine coroutines with OOP – Structure async tasks within objects and classes for better maintainability.

Conclusion

By blending OOP's encapsulation and structure with FP's immutability and expressiveness, Kotlin enables cleaner, more efficient, and scalable applications. Whether designing object-oriented systems or data-driven functional pipelines, Kotlin offers the flexibility to use both paradigms seamlessly.

12.3 Real-World Use Cases

Kotlin's hybrid nature allows developers to leverage both Object-Oriented Programming (OOP) and Functional Programming (FP) to build scalable, maintainable, and efficient applications. Below are some real-world use cases where combining these paradigms enhances software development.

1. Android App Development

Why Kotlin?

✔ Officially supported by Google for Android development.
✔ Combines OOP for UI components and FP for data processing.
✔ Reduces boilerplate with extension functions and higher-order functions.

Example: Using OOP for UI and FP for Data Handling

```kotlin
Copy code
class UserViewModel {
    fun fetchUsers(): List<String> {
        return listOf("Alice", "Bob", "Charlie").map { it.uppercase() }
    }
}
```

Here, OOP (class-based ViewModel) handles state management, while FP (map function) processes data efficiently.

2. Backend Development with Kotlin and Spring Boot

Why Kotlin?

✔ Strong OOP support for service-oriented architecture (SOA)

✔ Functional programming simplifies API response transformations.

✔ Coroutines enable asynchronous, non-blocking operations.

Example: Handling API Responses

kotlin
Copy code
```
@RestController
class UserController(val userService: UserService) {
  @GetMapping("/users")
  fun getUsers(): List<String> = userService.getUsers().map
{ it.name.uppercase() }
}
```

This integrates OOP (Spring Boot's controller-service architecture) with FP (map function for transformation).

3. Data Processing and ETL Pipelines

Why Kotlin?

✔ FP simplifies data transformation and filtering.

✔ Sealed classes help with structured error handling.

✔ Extension functions allow cleaner syntax for processing data.

Example: Processing and Filtering Data

kotlin

Copy code

data class Transaction(val id: Int, val amount: Double)

val transactions = listOf(Transaction(1, 100.0), Transaction(2, -50.0), Transaction(3, 200.0))

val validTransactions = transactions.filter { it.amount > 0 }.map { it.copy(amount = it.amount * 1.1) }
println(validTransactions) // Output: [Transaction(id=1, amount=110.0), Transaction(id=3, amount=220.0)]

This OOP-based data modeling benefits from FP's declarative filtering and transformation.

4. Machine Learning and Data Science

Why Kotlin?

✔ Functional programming simplifies mathematical transformations.
✔ Immutability prevents accidental data modifications.
✔ Coroutines allow parallel data processing.

Example: Functional Approach to Data Transformation

kotlin

Copy code

```kotlin
val numbers = listOf(1, 2, 3, 4, 5)
val squaredNumbers = numbers.map { it * it }
println(squaredNumbers) // Output: [1, 4, 9, 16, 25]
```

This showcases how FP principles (map, immutability) make data transformations straightforward.

5. Financial Applications (FinTech)

Why Kotlin?

✔ OOP for transaction management and account structures.
✔ FP for real-time calculations and risk analysis.
✔ Coroutines for asynchronous market data processing.

Example: Functional Interest Calculation

kotlin

Copy code

```kotlin
fun calculateInterest(principal: Double, rate: Double, years: Int): Double =
    principal * (1 + rate).pow(years)
```

println(calculateInterest(1000.0, 0.05, 5)) // Output: 1276.28

This uses FP (pure function, immutability) within an OOP-based financial model.

6. Game Development

Why Kotlin?

✔ OOP for game objects and UI interactions.

✔ FP for game physics and transformations.

✔ Coroutines for smooth animations and concurrency.

Example: Applying Functional Composition to Game Mechanics

```kotlin
Copy code
data class Player(val name: String, val score: Int)

fun Player.increaseScore(points: Int): Player = this.copy(score = this.score + points)

val player = Player("Alice", 10).increaseScore(5)
println(player) // Output: Player(name=Alice, score=15)
```

This blends OOP (data classes) with FP (immutability and transformation functions).

7. IoT and Edge Computing

Why Kotlin?

✔ OOP for device abstraction and communication models.

✔ FP for sensor data aggregation and filtering.

✔ Coroutines for non-blocking device communication.

Example: Processing IoT Sensor Data

kotlin
Copy code

```kotlin
data class SensorReading(val id: Int, val temperature: Double)

val readings = listOf(SensorReading(1, 22.5), SensorReading(2, 30.0), SensorReading(3, 25.0))
val highReadings = readings.filter { it.temperature > 25 }

println(highReadings)   //   Output:   [SensorReading(id=2, temperature=30.0)]
```

This efficiently combines OOP-based data representation with FP's transformation functions.

8. Blockchain and Cryptography Applications
Why Kotlin?

✔ OOP for block and transaction structures.

✔ FP for data immutability and hashing functions.

✔ Coroutines for asynchronous transaction validation.

Example: Functional Hashing in Blockchain
kotlin
Copy code
import java.security.MessageDigest

```kotlin
fun hash(data: String): String {
    return MessageDigest.getInstance("SHA-256")
        .digest(data.toByteArray())
        .joinToString("") { "%02x".format(it) }
}

println(hash("Block123")) // Output: (a unique SHA-256 hash)
```

This showcases FP-style pure functions within an OOP-based blockchain model.

Conclusion

By integrating OOP's structure and encapsulation with FP's immutability, transformation, and concurrency, Kotlin enables the development of high-performance, scalable applications across various domains. Whether building Android apps, financial systems, machine learning models, or real-time IoT solutions,

Kotlin's hybrid paradigm ensures clean, efficient, and maintainable code.

.

Chapter 13
Case Studies and Real-World Applications

Kotlin's versatility has made it a popular choice across various industries, from mobile and web development to finance and data science. Below are some real-world applications and case studies showcasing how Kotlin's blend of Object-Oriented Programming (OOP) and Functional Programming (FP) enhances development.

1. Android App Development – Google's Adoption of Kotlin

Case Study: Google's Migration from Java to Kotlin
Google officially adopted Kotlin as the preferred language for Android development, citing:
✔ Less Boilerplate – Improved code readability and maintainability.
✔ Safer Code – Reduced NullPointerExceptions with Kotlin's null safety.
✔ Functional Features – Use of higher-order functions and coroutines for better performance.

Example: Google Play Console

The Google Play Console team migrated its Android app to Kotlin, leading to 30% fewer crashes and faster feature delivery.

2. Backend Development – Pinterest's Kotlin Migration

Case Study: Pinterest Adopting Kotlin for Backend Services
Pinterest transitioned its backend microservices to Kotlin, achieving:
✔ Better Maintainability – Cleaner, more expressive code.
✔ Improved Performance – Faster execution with coroutines.
✔ Seamless Java Interoperability – Smooth migration from Java-based services.

Result: The switch led to a 20% improvement in API performance and more maintainable code.

3. Financial Technology (FinTech) – Square's Use of Kotlin

Case Study: Square's Payment Processing System
Square, a leading FinTech company, uses Kotlin for its mobile and server-side payment solutions, benefiting from:
✔ Reliability – Using Kotlin's type safety and functional programming to prevent transaction errors.
✔ Concurrency – Leveraging coroutines for real-time payment processing.
✔ Cross-Platform Development – Sharing business logic between Android and iOS via Kotlin Multiplatform.

Impact: Square's Kotlin-based system processes millions of transactions daily with improved stability.

4. AI and Machine Learning – Data Science with Kotlin

Case Study: JetBrains' Kotlin for Data Science Initiative
JetBrains developed Kotlin for Data Science to compete with Python, highlighting:

✔ Functional Programming for Data Processing – Using map, filter, reduce for transformations.
✔ Immutability for Data Safety – Reducing unintended mutations in large datasets.
✔ Kotlin Jupyter Integration – Enabling interactive data analysis.

Example: Kotlin is used in real-time fraud detection models in banking applications.

5. Blockchain and Cryptography – Kotlin in Distributed Ledgers

Case Study: Corda Blockchain (R3's Kotlin-Based DLT Platform)
Corda, a blockchain platform for financial transactions, is entirely built on Kotlin due to:
✔ Concise and Readable Code – Compared to Java-based blockchain solutions.

✔ Better Security – Sealed classes for immutability and state handling.

✔ Functional Hashing and Encryption – Using pure functions for cryptographic operations.

Impact: Corda is used by banks, insurers, and stock exchanges worldwide for secure transactions.

6. Cloud Computing – Kotlin in Microservices

Case Study: Netflix's Microservices with Kotlin and Spring Boot
Netflix has integrated Kotlin into its Spring Boot-based microservices, gaining:

✔ Non-Blocking Asynchronous Execution – Using Kotlin coroutines.

✔ Better Maintainability – Cleaner APIs with functional constructs.

✔ Scalability – Handling millions of concurrent requests efficiently.

Example: Kotlin is used in real-time video recommendation engines at Netflix.

Conclusion

From Android development (Google, Pinterest) to backend microservices (Netflix, Square) and blockchain solutions (Corda),

Kotlin has proven to be a powerful, flexible, and scalable language. Its combination of OOP and FP makes it an ideal choice for modern software development, improving performance, maintainability, and security.

13.1 Building a Scalable Kotlin Project

Building a scalable Kotlin project requires a combination of good architecture, solid coding practices, and efficient tools that ensure your codebase can grow without compromising performance or maintainability. Kotlin's features, including its support for Object-Oriented Programming (OOP), Functional Programming (FP), and Coroutines, provide developers with the tools needed to build robust, scalable applications. Below is a step-by-step guide to building a scalable Kotlin project.

1. Define Project Architecture

A clear architecture is crucial for scaling a project, as it helps organize code logically and promotes separation of concerns. Some common architectural patterns in Kotlin are:

a. Microservices Architecture

For larger systems, breaking down the project into independent microservices allows for better scalability. Each service can be developed, deployed, and scaled independently, ensuring the overall system remains flexible.

b. Modular Architecture

In modular architecture, the project is divided into smaller, independent modules, each responsible for a specific domain or feature. This separation makes it easier to maintain and scale the project over time. In Kotlin, this could involve creating separate modules for API handling, database interactions, UI, etc.

c. Layered Architecture

A Layered Architecture separates the application into different layers, such as the presentation, business logic, and data access layers. This pattern allows for easy changes and scaling of individual parts of the system.

2. Leverage Kotlin Features for Scalability

a. Coroutines for Asynchronous Programming

Kotlin's built-in support for coroutines allows for writing non-blocking, asynchronous code, making it ideal for scalable applications. Coroutines allow efficient handling of multiple operations, such as network requests, I/O operations, and background tasks, without blocking the main thread.

Example:

```kotlin
Copy code
suspend fun fetchData(): String {
    return withContext(Dispatchers.IO) {
        // Simulate network or I/O operation
        delay(1000)
        "Data fetched"
    }
}
```

Using coroutines, tasks can run concurrently, improving performance and scalability, especially when dealing with high concurrency.

b. Kotlin Multiplatform for Cross-Platform Scalability

Kotlin's support for Kotlin Multiplatform allows you to share code across different platforms (Android, iOS, Web, Backend), which promotes code reuse and reduces duplication. This approach is ideal when building large, multi-platform projects.

3. Database Design for Scalability

A well-designed database is fundamental to building scalable systems. You need to select the right type of database and schema that can handle a growing amount of data efficiently.

a. Relational Databases

For structured data with relationships, you can use relational databases like PostgreSQL or MySQL. Kotlin has great support for working with databases through libraries like Exposed (a Kotlin SQL framework) or JPA (Hibernate).

b. NoSQL Databases

For highly dynamic or unstructured data, NoSQL databases like MongoDB or Cassandra can handle horizontal scaling and are often used in scalable systems that need to store vast amounts of data.

c. Caching

For high-performance applications, caching is crucial. Use caching solutions such as Redis to reduce database load and speed up data access for frequently requested data.

4. Implementing Clean Code Practices

a. Modularity and Code Reusability

In large projects, maintaining clean, reusable code is essential. Kotlin supports extension functions and higher-order functions, which help reduce duplication and increase the reusability of code.

b. Testing for Scalability

Testing plays a critical role in ensuring the scalability of your project. Use unit tests, integration tests, and load tests to ensure that your application can handle growth. Libraries like JUnit for testing, and MockK for mocking dependencies in Kotlin, will help ensure robust testing practices.

5. Optimize Performance for Scalability

As your project grows, optimizing performance becomes crucial to maintain scalability.

a. Profiling and Performance Monitoring

Use profiling tools like YourKit or JProfiler to identify performance bottlenecks, such as slow database queries or inefficient algorithms. Kotlin's native support for JVM allows you to use these tools effectively.

b. Concurrency and Thread Management

For scalable applications, managing concurrency is essential. Kotlin's coroutines offer a more efficient, lightweight alternative to traditional threads, and help in writing highly concurrent code. Use Dispatchers (such as Dispatchers.IO, Dispatchers.Main) to control where tasks run (on the main thread, background, etc.).

6. Use Dependency Injection (DI)

In a scalable Kotlin project, dependency injection is essential for decoupling components and making the system easier to test and maintain. Kotlin works well with DI frameworks such as Koin and Dagger.

Example with Koin:
kotlin
Copy code
val appModule = module {
   single { MyDatabase() }
   single { MyRepository(get()) }

}

startKoin { modules(appModule) }

Dependency injection simplifies managing object creation and dependencies, making it easier to scale the project as new features are added.

7. Version Control and Continuous Integration

a. Git for Version Control

Use Git for version control to manage changes in your project as it scales. Proper branching strategies (such as GitFlow) ensure smooth collaboration among team members.

b. Continuous Integration (CI) and Continuous Deployment (CD)

Implement CI/CD pipelines using tools like Jenkins, GitLab CI, or GitHub Actions. Automate testing, builds, and deployments to ensure rapid, reliable delivery of new features without compromising on stability.

8. Documentation and Collaboration

a. Code Documentation

As the project grows, code documentation becomes essential. Kotlin's support for KDoc (Kotlin's documentation tool) helps document the codebase effectively. Proper documentation ensures that team members can understand and maintain the code as the project scales.

b. Collaboration Tools

Use collaboration tools like Jira, Confluence, or Trello to manage tasks, sprints, and project timelines. Effective collaboration and task management are crucial when building large-scale applications.

9. Cloud Deployment and Scaling

As your project scales, moving to the cloud is essential for handling increased load and ensuring scalability.

a. Cloud Platforms

Use cloud platforms like AWS, Google Cloud, or Azure for deploying your Kotlin application. These platforms provide services such as load balancing, auto-scaling, and serverless computing to handle growing traffic and workloads efficiently.

b. Containerization with Docker

Containerize your Kotlin project with Docker to create portable and isolated environments. Kubernetes can then be used for orchestration, ensuring that your application can scale horizontally by adding more containers as needed.

Conclusion

Building a scalable Kotlin project involves using the language's powerful features like coroutines, modularization, and Kotlin Multiplatform, along with implementing best practices for architecture, performance optimization, and testing. By combining Object-Oriented Programming (OOP) with Functional Programming (FP) principles, you can create a project that is both maintainable and capable of handling growth. As your project scales, focus on optimizing performance, leveraging cloud services, and maintaining a solid CI/CD pipeline to ensure smooth operations as the system evolves.

13.2 Refactoring Legacy Code with Kotlin OOP

Refactoring legacy code is an essential part of maintaining and improving an application's long-term health, performance, and scalability. Over time, legacy codebases can become harder to maintain, leading to issues such as reduced developer productivity, higher error rates, and slower release cycles. Refactoring legacy code with Kotlin's Object-Oriented Programming (OOP) features allows teams to modernize their codebases, improve readability, and make systems easier to extend, test, and scale.

In this article, we'll explore how Kotlin's features can be used effectively to refactor legacy code with an emphasis on OOP principles such as Encapsulation, Inheritance, Abstraction, and Polymorphism.

1. Understanding Legacy Code Challenges

Legacy code refers to older codebases that are often outdated, hard to read, or poorly structured. Some common challenges include:

Tightly coupled code: Components are highly dependent on one another, making them difficult to modify or extend.

Lack of modularity: The code lacks clear separation of concerns, resulting in scattered logic and complex interdependencies.

No or poor testing: Legacy systems might not have sufficient tests, making refactoring risky and difficult to validate.

Difficult to scale: As new features are added, the system becomes increasingly difficult to extend without breaking existing functionality.

Refactoring involves making changes to the code without changing its behavior, improving readability, maintainability, and scalability.

2. Applying Object-Oriented Principles to Legacy Code

a. Encapsulation: Hiding Complexity

In many legacy codebases, data and functions are often mixed together in ways that make it difficult to understand or modify. Encapsulation helps by hiding the internal details and exposing only the necessary parts of an object to other components.

In Kotlin, encapsulation can be implemented with:

Private properties and methods to limit access to internal state. Public getter and setter methods to control how data is accessed and modified.

Example:
kotlin
Copy code
```kotlin
class Employee(private var salary: Double) {
```

```kotlin
fun getSalary(): Double {
    return salary
}

fun increaseSalary(increase: Double) {
    if (increase > 0) {
        salary += increase
    }
}
}
```

By encapsulating the salary property and exposing controlled access through methods, we prevent other parts of the code from directly manipulating it.

b. Inheritance: Reusing Code and Creating Hierarchies

Legacy code often involves repetitive logic that could benefit from inheritance, which allows for code reuse. By creating a class hierarchy, you can move common functionality to a base class, enabling specialized behavior in derived classes.

Kotlin makes inheritance easy with its open and override keywords, allowing you to create class hierarchies with ease.

Example:

```kotlin
Copy code
open class Animal(val name: String) {
  open fun makeSound() {
    println("Some generic animal sound")
  }
}

class Dog(name: String) : Animal(name) {
  override fun makeSound() {
    println("Bark")
  }
}

class Cat(name: String) : Animal(name) {
  override fun makeSound() {
    println("Meow")
  }
}
```

Here, the Animal class provides common behavior, while Dog and Cat specialize it with their own implementations.

c. Abstraction: Simplifying Complex Systems

Legacy code often has complex, tightly coupled components that need to be simplified. Abstraction is used to hide unnecessary details and only expose relevant functionality. Kotlin supports abstraction with abstract classes and interfaces.

Using abstraction helps isolate the logic and make the system easier to extend and maintain.

Example with Abstract Class:
kotlin
Copy code

```kotlin
abstract class PaymentProcessor {
    abstract fun processPayment(amount: Double)
}

class PayPalProcessor : PaymentProcessor() {
    override fun processPayment(amount: Double) {
        println("Processing PayPal payment of $$amount")
    }
}

class StripeProcessor : PaymentProcessor() {
    override fun processPayment(amount: Double) {
        println("Processing Stripe payment of $$amount")
    }
}
```

The PaymentProcessor class defines a common interface, while different classes (PayPalProcessor, StripeProcessor) implement their specific behaviors.

d. Polymorphism: Making Code Flexible

Polymorphism allows different classes to be treated as instances of a common superclass, making the code more flexible and extensible. This allows different objects to be used interchangeably, enabling you to handle new types without changing existing code.

Kotlin makes polymorphism easy through overriding methods in subclasses and using interfaces to define flexible contract behavior.

Example:
kotlin
Copy code

```kotlin
fun printPaymentDetails(paymentProcessor: PaymentProcessor, amount: Double) {
    paymentProcessor.processPayment(amount)
}

val paypal = PayPalProcessor()
val stripe = StripeProcessor()
```

printPaymentDetails(paypal, 100.0) // **Outputs: Processing PayPal payment of $100.0**
printPaymentDetails(stripe, 150.0) // **Outputs: Processing Stripe payment of $150.0**

This allows you to replace payment processor types without altering the logic of how payments are processed, demonstrating polymorphic behavior.

3. Refactoring Steps for Legacy Code with Kotlin

Step 1: Understand the Current Codebase
Before refactoring, it's essential to understand the current state of the legacy codebase. Focus on identifying areas that are tightly coupled, hard to test, or lacking abstraction.

Step 2: Write Tests (If None Exist)

Legacy systems often lack sufficient test coverage. Begin by writing unit tests for the existing code, ensuring that its behavior is well-documented and verifiable.

Step 3: Isolate and Modularize Code

Using Kotlin's features like extension functions, sealed classes, and data classes, break down large, monolithic classes into smaller, manageable modules.

For example, you might break a large function that handles multiple tasks into several smaller, more focused functions.

Step 4: Use Kotlin Features for Simplification

Refactor the legacy code by utilizing Kotlin's advanced features:

Data classes for simplifying model objects.
Extension functions to add new behavior without modifying the original code.
Sealed classes to represent restricted class hierarchies.

Step 5: Eliminate Code Duplication

Remove code duplication by applying inheritance and composition. Where possible, move shared logic to base classes or utility functions, making the codebase more maintainable and extensible.

Step 6: Refactor to Immutable Data
Use Kotlin's immutable variables (val) to reduce the potential for unexpected changes in state, making the code easier to reason about and safer.

4. Benefits of Refactoring with Kotlin OOP

Increased Readability: Kotlin's concise syntax, type system, and OOP features make code more readable and easier to maintain.

Reduced Technical Debt: By modernizing the legacy code with better design patterns, you reduce technical debt and prepare the system for future growth.

Improved Testability: Encapsulation, abstraction, and modularity improve testability, making it easier to write unit tests and achieve greater test coverage.

Better Performance: Kotlin's support for coroutines and modern programming practices can lead to performance improvements as you refactor the system.

5. Conclusion

Refactoring legacy code with Kotlin's OOP principles allows for a more organized, maintainable, and scalable codebase. By leveraging Encapsulation, Inheritance, Abstraction, and Polymorphism, you can improve code clarity, reduce duplication, and prepare the system for future growth. Kotlin's features such as coroutines, data classes, and extension functions offer additional power to streamline and modernize the legacy code, making it a perfect choice for refactoring efforts.

13.3 Practical Applications in Mobile and Web Development

.

Kotlin has become a popular programming language for mobile and web development due to its modern features, concise syntax, and full interoperability with Java. Kotlin's versatility allows it to be used in both mobile applications (primarily for Android) and web applications (both backend and frontend), making it a powerful tool for full-stack development.

In this article, we will explore the practical applications of Kotlin in mobile and web development, highlighting how it can be utilized to build efficient, scalable, and maintainable applications.

1. Kotlin in Mobile Development

a. Android Development

Kotlin has officially been recognized as the preferred language for Android development by Google. It is fully interoperable with Java, which makes it easy to integrate into existing Java-based Android projects. Kotlin offers significant improvements over Java in terms of conciseness, readability, and safety, making Android development faster and less error-prone.

Key Benefits of Kotlin for Android:

Concise Syntax: Kotlin's expressive syntax reduces the need for boilerplate code (e.g., null checks, getters/setters, and data classes).

Null Safety: Kotlin's type system helps avoid NullPointerException by distinguishing nullable and non-nullable types at compile time.

Coroutines for Asynchronous Programming: Kotlin provides built-in support for coroutines, enabling easy management of background tasks, such as network requests, without blocking the UI thread.

Extension Functions: Kotlin allows you to extend existing classes with new functionality without modifying their code, making Android development more flexible and reusable.

Example - Simple Android Activity in Kotlin:

```kotlin
Copy code
class MainActivity : AppCompatActivity() {

    override fun onCreate(savedInstanceState: Bundle?) {
        super.onCreate(savedInstanceState)
        setContentView(R.layout.activity_main)

        val button: Button = findViewById(R.id.myButton)
        button.setOnClickListener {
                Toast.makeText(this, "Button Clicked!",
Toast.LENGTH_SHORT).show()
```

```
        }
      }
    }
```

In the above example, the Kotlin syntax is concise and eliminates the need for boilerplate code (such as type declarations).

b. Android Libraries and Frameworks with Kotlin

Many popular Android libraries, such as Retrofit, Glide, and Room, offer Kotlin-friendly APIs that allow for more efficient and readable code. Kotlin's compatibility with Java ensures that developers can continue using existing libraries while benefiting from Kotlin's modern features.

Retrofit + Kotlin: Retrofit simplifies network operations in Android, and with Kotlin's support for coroutines, network calls become even more streamlined.
Room + Kotlin: Room is a persistence library for Android that simplifies database interactions. Kotlin's data classes and coroutines are perfect for managing data efficiently with Room.

2. Kotlin in Web Development

a. Backend Development with Kotlin
Kotlin is also an excellent choice for backend development. It runs on the JVM, meaning that Kotlin can leverage existing Java-based

frameworks and libraries. Several popular web frameworks support Kotlin, including Ktor, Spring Boot, and Vert.x.

Key Benefits of Kotlin for Backend Development:

Null Safety: Kotlin's type system prevents null pointer exceptions, which are common in backend systems.

Coroutines: Kotlin's native support for coroutines simplifies the handling of asynchronous operations, such as database queries, file I/O, and HTTP requests, while keeping the code non-blocking and efficient.

Expressive Syntax: Kotlin's concise and expressive syntax makes backend code easier to write and maintain, reducing boilerplate and improving readability.

Example - Simple Ktor Server in Kotlin:

```kotlin
Copy code
import io.ktor.application.*
import io.ktor.features.ContentNegotiation
import io.ktor.http.HttpStatusCode
import io.ktor.request.receive
import io.ktor.response.respond
import io.ktor.routing.Routing
```

```kotlin
import io.ktor.routing.get
import io.ktor.routing.post
import io.ktor.server.engine.embeddedServer
import io.ktor.server.netty.Netty
import io.ktor.serialization.json
import io.ktor.application.install
import io.ktor.features.StatusPages

fun Application.module() {
  install(ContentNegotiation) {
    json()
  }

  routing {
    get("/hello") {
      call.respond(HttpStatusCode.OK, "Hello, World!")
    }
  }
}

fun main() {
    embeddedServer(Netty, port = 8080, module =
Application::module).start(wait = true)
}
```

This example shows how easily Kotlin can be used to create a
simple REST API using Ktor, a lightweight framework for

building web applications. The use of coroutines and Kotlin's built-in features make the code minimal and efficient.

b. Full-Stack Development with Kotlin

In full-stack development, Kotlin is not limited to just the backend; it can also be used on the frontend with Kotlin/JS, a technology that compiles Kotlin code to JavaScript. Kotlin/JS allows developers to write frontend web applications with Kotlin while taking advantage of modern features such as type-safe nullability, extension functions, and lambda expressions.

Kotlin + JavaScript + React:

Kotlin/JS can be integrated with popular frontend frameworks like React. Using the Kotlin React bindings, developers can build reactive web applications with Kotlin and reuse existing JavaScript libraries.

Kotlin React: Write React components in Kotlin, making use of Kotlin's type safety and concise syntax while interacting with the JavaScript ecosystem.

3. Kotlin Multiplatform: Cross-Platform Mobile and Web Development

One of the most exciting features of Kotlin is Kotlin Multiplatform, which allows developers to write shared code that works across multiple platforms, including Android, iOS, Web, and backend systems. This enables true cross-platform development, reducing duplication of code and improving maintainability.

Key Benefits of Kotlin Multiplatform:

Shared Business Logic: Code shared between mobile (Android and iOS), backend, and web platforms can be written once and used across platforms, reducing development time and errors.

Platform-Specific Code: While Kotlin Multiplatform enables code sharing, it also allows platform-specific code for UI or features that require custom implementation.

Faster Time to Market: With shared code across platforms, teams can develop applications for multiple platforms simultaneously, accelerating the release cycle.

Example - Shared Code in Kotlin Multiplatform:

```kotlin
Copy code
// Shared code (commonMain)
expect fun getPlatformName(): String

// Android specific implementation
```

```
actual fun getPlatformName(): String {
  return "Android"
}


// iOS-specific implementation
actual fun getPlatformName(): String {
  return "iOS"
}
```

The expect/actual mechanism allows developers to define a common API and implement platform-specific code as needed, reducing duplication and improving consistency across platforms.

4. Kotlin for WebAssembly

Kotlin also supports WebAssembly (Wasm), a binary instruction format designed for fast execution on the web. WebAssembly allows Kotlin code to run in web browsers with near-native performance, enabling the development of web applications that require high performance, such as games, simulations, or intensive data processing tasks.

Benefits of Kotlin for WebAssembly:

Performance: WebAssembly offers performance close to native code, which can be ideal for performance-sensitive web applications.

Cross-Browser Compatibility: WebAssembly works in all major web browsers, ensuring compatibility across platforms

5. Conclusion

Kotlin is a powerful and versatile programming language for both mobile and web development. In mobile development, Kotlin shines as the preferred language for Android, offering concise, null-safe code, and robust libraries like Retrofit and Room. For backend and web development, Kotlin excels with frameworks like Ktor and Spring Boot, offering asynchronous programming through coroutines and a concise syntax.

Moreover, Kotlin's Multiplatform capabilities make it a strong contender for building cross-platform applications, sharing business logic across Android, iOS, web, and backend systems. By using Kotlin for both mobile and web development, teams can streamline their development process, reduce duplication, and maintain a consistent codebase across platforms.

Whether you are building a mobile app, a web server, or a full-stack system, Kotlin provides the tools to build efficient, scalable, and maintainable applications.

National Institute of Standards and Technology Interagency or Internal Report 7298r2
222 pages (May 2013)

National Institute of Standards and Technology
Attn: Computer Security Division, Information Technology Laboratory
100 Bureau Drive (Mail Stop 8930) Gaithersburg, MD 20899-8930
Email: secglossary@nist.gov

Reports on Computer Systems Technology

The Information Technology Laboratory (ITL) at the National Institute of Standards and Technology (NIST) promotes the U.S. economy and public welfare by providing technical leadership for the Nation's measurement and standards infrastructure. ITL develops tests, test methods, reference data, proof of concept implementations, and technical analyses to advance the development and productive use of information technology. ITL's responsibilities include the development of management, administrative, technical, and physical standards and guidelines for the cost-effective security and privacy of other than national security-related information in Federal information systems.

Abstract

The National Institute of Standards and Technology (NIST) has received numerous requests to provide a summary glossary for our publications and other relevant sources, and to make the glossary available to practitioners. As a result of these requests, this glossary of common security terms has been extracted from NIST Federal Information Processing Standards (FIPS), the Special Publication (SP) 800 series, NIST Interagency Reports (NISTIRs), and from the Committee for National Security Systems Instruction 4009 (CNSSI-4009). This glossary includes most of the terms in the NIST publications. It also contains nearly all of the terms and definitions from CNSSI-4009. This glossary provides a central resource of terms and definitions most commonly used in NIST information security publications and in CNSS information assurance publications. For a given term, we do not include all definitions in NIST documents – especially not from the older NIST publications. Since draft documents are not stable, we do not refer to terms/definitions in them.

Each entry in the glossary points to one or more source NIST publications, and/or CNSSI-4009, and/or supplemental sources where appropriate. The NIST publications referenced are the most recent versions of those publications (as of the date of this document).

Keywords

Cyber Security; Definitions; Glossary; Information Assurance; Information Security; Terms

Introduction

We have received numerous requests to provide a summary glossary for our publications and other relevant sources, and to make the glossary available to practitioners. As a result of these requests, this glossary of common security terms has been extracted from NIST Federal Information Processing Standards (FIPS), the Special Publication (SP) 800 series, NIST Interagency Reports (NISTIRs), and from the Committee for National Security Systems Instruction 4009 (CNSSI-4009). The glossary includes most of the terms in the NIST publications. It also contains nearly all of the terms and definitions from CNSSI-4009. The glossary provides a central resource of terms and definitions most commonly used in NIST information security publications and in CNSS information assurance publications. For a given term, we do not include all definitions in NIST documents – especially not from the older NIST publications. Since draft documents are not stable, we do not refer to terms/definitions in them.

Each entry in the glossary points to one or more source NIST publications, and/or CNSSI-4009, and/or supplemental sources where appropriate. A list of the supplemental (non-NIST) sources may be found on pages 221-222. As we are continuously refreshing our publication suite, terms included in the glossary come from our more recent publications. The NIST publications referenced are the most recent versions of those publications (as of the date of this document).

It is our intention to keep the glossary current by providing updates online. New definitions will be added to the glossary as required, and updated versions will be posted on the Computer Security Resource Center (CSRC) Web site at http://csrc.nist.gov/.

The Editor, Richard Kissel, would like to express special thanks to Ms. Tanya Brewer for her outstanding work in the design of the original cover page and in the overall design and organization of the document. Thanks also to all who provided comments during the public review period of this document. The Editor also expresses special thanks to the CNSS Glossary Working Group for encouraging the inclusion of CNSSI-4009 terms and definitions into this glossary.

Comments and suggestions on this publication should be sent to secglossary@nist.gov.

Access –	Ability to make use of any information system (IS) resource. SOURCE: SP 800-32 Ability and means to communicate with or otherwise interact with a system, to use system resources to handle information, to gain knowledge of the information the system contains, or to control system components and functions. SOURCE: CNSSI-4009
Access Authority –	An entity responsible for monitoring and granting access privileges for other authorized entities. SOURCE: CNSSI-4009
Access Control –	The process of granting or denying specific requests to: 1) obtain and use information and related information processing services; and 2) enter specific physical facilities (e.g., federal buildings, military establishments, border crossing entrances). SOURCE: FIPS 201; CNSSI-4009
Access Control List (ACL) –	1. A list of permissions associated with an object. The list specifies who or what is allowed to access the object and what operations are allowed to be performed on the object. 2. A mechanism that implements access control for a system resource by enumerating the system entities that are permitted to access the resource and stating, either implicitly or explicitly, the access modes granted to each entity. SOURCE: CNSSI-4009
Access Control Lists (ACLs) –	A register of: 1. users (including groups, machines, processes) who have been given permission to use a particular system resource, and 2. the types of access they have been permitted. SOURCE: SP 800-12
Access Control Mechanism –	Security safeguards (i.e., hardware and software features, physical controls, operating procedures, management procedures, and various combinations of these) designed to detect and deny unauthorized access and permit authorized access to an information system. SOURCE: CNSSI-4009
Access Level –	A category within a given security classification limiting entry or system connectivity to only authorized persons. SOURCE: CNSSI-4009

Access List – | Roster of individuals authorized admittance to a controlled area.
SOURCE: CNSSI-4009

Access Point – | A device that logically connects wireless client devices operating in infrastructure to one another and provides access to a distribution system, if connected, which is typically an organization's enterprise wired network.
SOURCE: SP 800-48; SP 800-121

Access Profile – | Association of a user with a list of protected objects the user may access.
SOURCE: CNSSI-4009

Access Type – | Privilege to perform action on an object. Read, write, execute, append, modify, delete, and create are examples of access types. See Write.
SOURCE: CNSSI-4009

Account Management, User – | Involves
1) the process of requesting, establishing, issuing, and closing user accounts;
2) tracking users and their respective access authorizations; and
3) managing these functions.
SOURCE: SP 800-12

Accountability – | The security goal that generates the requirement for actions of an entity to be traced uniquely to that entity. This supports non-repudiation, deterrence, fault isolation, intrusion detection and prevention, and after-action recovery and legal action.
SOURCE: SP 800-27

Principle that an individual is entrusted to safeguard and control equipment, keying material, and information and is answerable to proper authority for the loss or misuse of that equipment or information.
SOURCE: CNSSI-4009

Accounting Legend Code (ALC) – | Numeric code used to indicate the minimum accounting controls required for items of accountable communications security (COMSEC) material within the COMSEC Material Control System.
SOURCE: CNSSI-4009

Accounting Number – | Number assigned to an item of COMSEC material to facilitate its control.
SOURCE: CNSSI-4009

Accreditation –   See Authorization.

Accreditation Authority –   See Authorizing Official.

Accreditation Boundary –   See Authorization Boundary.

Accreditation Package –   Product comprised of a System Security Plan (SSP) and a report
                                documenting the basis for the accreditation decision.

                                SOURCE: CNSSI-4009

Accrediting Authority –   Synonymous with Designated Accrediting Authority (DAA). See
                                also Authorizing Official.

                                SOURCE: CNSSI-4009

Activation Data –   Private data, other than keys, that are required to access
                                cryptographic modules.

                                SOURCE: SP 800-32

Active Attack –   An attack that alters a system or data.

                                SOURCE: CNSSI-4009

                                An attack on the authentication protocol where the Attacker
                                transmits data to the Claimant, Credential Service Provider,
                                Verifier, or Relying Party. Examples of active attacks include
                                man-in-the-middle, impersonation, and session hijacking.

                                SOURCE: SP 800-63

Active Content –   Electronic documents that can carry out or trigger actions
                                automatically on a computer platform without the intervention of a
                                user.

                                SOURCE: SP 800-28

                                Software in various forms that is able to automatically carry out or
                                trigger actions on a computer platform without the intervention of a
                                user.

                                SOURCE: CNSSI-4009

Active Security Testing –   Security testing that involves direct interaction with a target, such as
                                sending packets to a target.

                                SOURCE: SP 800-115

Activities –   An assessment object that includes specific protection-related
                                pursuits or actions supporting an information system that involve
                                people (e.g., conducting system backup operations, monitoring
                                network traffic).

                                SOURCE: SP 800-53A

Ad Hoc Network –	A wireless network that dynamically connects wireless client devices to each other without the use of an infrastructure device, such as an access point or a base station.
	SOURCE: SP 800-121
Add-on Security –	Incorporation of new hardware, software, or firmware safeguards in an operational information system.
	SOURCE: CNSSI-4009
Adequate Security –	Security commensurate with the risk and the magnitude of harm resulting from the loss, misuse, or unauthorized access to or modification of information.
	SOURCE: SP 800-53; FIPS 200; OMB Circular A-130, App. III
	Security commensurate with the risk and magnitude of harm resulting from the loss, misuse, or unauthorized access to or modification of information.
	Note: This includes assuring that information systems operate effectively and provide appropriate confidentiality, integrity, and availability, through the use of cost-effective management, personnel, operational, and technical controls.
	SOURCE: CNSSI-4009; SP 800-37
Administrative Account –	A user account with full privileges on a computer.
	SOURCE: SP 800-69
Administrative Safeguards –	Administrative actions, policies, and procedures to manage the selection, development, implementation, and maintenance of security measures to protect electronic health information and to manage the conduct of the covered entity's workforce in relation to protecting that information.
	SOURCE: SP 800-66
Advanced Encryption Standard – (AES)	The Advanced Encryption Standard specifies a U.S. government-approved cryptographic algorithm that can be used to protect electronic data. The AES algorithm is a symmetric block cipher that can encrypt (encipher) and decrypt (decipher) information. This standard specifies the Rijndael algorithm, a symmetric block cipher that can process data blocks of 128 bits, using cipher keys with lengths of 128, 192, and 256 bits.
	SOURCE: FIPS 197

A U.S. government-approved cryptographic algorithm that can be used to protect electronic data. The AES algorithm is a symmetric block cipher that can encrypt (encipher) and decrypt (decipher) information.

SOURCE: CNSSI-4009

Advanced Key Processor (AKP) –

A cryptographic device that performs all cryptographic functions for a management client node and contains the interfaces to 1) exchange information with a client platform, 2) interact with fill devices, and 3) connect a client platform securely to the primary services node (PRSN).

SOURCE: CNSSI-4009

Advanced Persistent Threats(APT) –

An adversary that possesses sophisticated levels of expertise and significant resources which allow it to create opportunities to achieve its objectives by using multiple attack vectors (e.g., cyber, physical, and deception). These objectives typically include establishing and extending footholds within the information technology infrastructure of the targeted organizations for purposes of exfiltrating information, undermining or impeding critical aspects of a mission, program, or organization; or positioning itself to carry out these objectives in the future. The advanced persistent threat: (i) pursues its objectives repeatedly over an extended period of time; (ii) adapts to defenders' efforts to resist it; and (iii) is determined to maintain the level of interaction needed to execute its objectives.

SOURCE: SP 800-39

Adversary –

Individual, group, organization, or government that conducts or has the intent to conduct detrimental activities.

SOURCE: SP 800-30

Advisory –

Notification of significant new trends or developments regarding the threat to the information systems of an organization. This notification may include analytical insights into trends, intentions, technologies, or tactics of an adversary targeting information systems.

SOURCE: CNSSI-4009

Agency –

Any executive department, military department, government corporation, government-controlled corporation, or other establishment in the executive branch of the government (including the Executive Office of the President), or any independent regulatory agency, but does not include: 1) the Government Accountability Office; 2) the Federal Election Commission; 3) the governments of the District of Columbia and of the territories and possessions of the United States, and their various subdivisions; or 4) government-owned contractor-operated facilities, including laboratories engaged in national defense research and production activities.

SOURCE: FIPS 200; 44 U.S.C., Sec. 3502

ALSO See Executive Agency.

Agency Certification Authority –
(CA)

A CA that acts on behalf of an agency and is under the operational control of an agency.

SOURCE: SP 800-32

Agent –

A program acting on behalf of a person or organization.

SOURCE: SP 800-95

Alert –

Notification that a specific attack has been directed at an organization's information systems.

SOURCE: CNSSI-4009

Allocation –

The process an organization employs to determine whether security controls are defined as system-specific, hybrid, or common.

The process an organization employs to assign security controls to specific information system components responsible for providing a particular security capability (e.g., router, server, remote sensor).

SOURCE: SP 800-37

Alternate COMSEC Custodian –

Individual designated by proper authority to perform the duties of the COMSEC custodian during the temporary absence of the COMSEC custodian.

SOURCE: CNSSI-4009

Alternate Work Site –

Governmentwide, national program allowing federal employees to work at home or at geographically convenient satellite offices for part of the work week (e.g., telecommuting).

SOURCE: CNSSI-4009

Analysis –

The examination of acquired data for its significance and probative value to the case.

SOURCE: SP 800-72

Anomaly-Based Detection –	The process of comparing definitions of what activity is considered normal against observed events to identify significant deviations. SOURCE: SP 800-94
Anti-jam –	Countermeasures ensuring that transmitted information can be received despite deliberate jamming attempts. SOURCE: CNSSI-4009
Anti-spoof –	Countermeasures taken to prevent the unauthorized use of legitimate Identification & Authentication (I&A) data, however it was obtained, to mimic a subject different from the attacker. SOURCE: CNSSI-4009
Antispyware Software –	A program that specializes in detecting both malware and non-malware forms of spyware. SOURCE: SP 800-69
Antivirus Software –	A program that monitors a computer or network to identify all major types of malware and prevent or contain malware incidents. SOURCE: SP 800-83
Applicant –	The subscriber is sometimes called an "applicant" after applying to a certification authority for a certificate, but before the certificate issuance procedure is completed. SOURCE: SP 800-32
Application –	A software program hosted by an information system. SOURCE: SP 800-37 Software program that performs a specific function directly for a user and can be executed without access to system control, monitoring, or administrative privileges. SOURCE: CNSSI-4009
Approval to Operate (ATO) –	The official management decision issued by a DAA or PAA to authorize operation of an information system and to explicitly accept the residual risk to agency operations (including mission, functions, image, or reputation), agency assets, or individuals. SOURCE: CNSSI-4009

Approved –	Federal Information Processing Standard (FIPS)-approved or National Institute of Standards and Technology (NIST)-recommended. An algorithm or technique that is either 1) specified in a FIPS or NIST Recommendation, or 2) adopted in a FIPS or NIST Recommendation.
	SOURCE: FIPS 201
	FIPS-approved and/or NIST-recommended.
	SOURCE: FIPS 140-2
	FIPS-approved and/or NIST-recommended. An algorithm or technique that is either 1) specified in a FIPS or NIST Recommendation, 2) adopted in a FIPS or NIST Recommendation, or 3) specified in a list of NIST-approved security functions.
	SOURCE: FIPS 186
Approved Mode of Operation –	A mode of the cryptographic module that employs only Approved security functions (not to be confused with a specific mode of an Approved security function, e.g., Data Encryption Standard Cipher-Block Chaining (DES CBC) mode).
	SOURCE: FIPS 140-2
Approved Security Function –	A security function (e.g., cryptographic algorithm, cryptographic key management technique, or authentication technique) that is either a) specified in an Approved Standard; b) adopted in an Approved Standard and specified either in an appendix of the Approved Standard or in a document referenced by the Approved Standard; or c) specified in the list of Approved security functions.
	SOURCE: FIPS 140-2
Assessment –	See Security Control Assessment.
Assessment Findings –	Assessment results produced by the application of an assessment procedure to a security control or control enhancement to achieve an assessment objective; the execution of a determination statement within an assessment procedure by an assessor that results in either a *satisfied* or *other than satisfied* condition.
	SOURCE: SP 800-53A
Assessment Method –	One of three types of actions (i.e., examine, interview, test) taken by assessors in obtaining evidence during an assessment.
	SOURCE: SP 800-53A

Assessment Object –	The item (i.e., specifications, mechanisms, activities, individuals) upon which an assessment method is applied during an assessment.
	SOURCE: SP 800-53A
Assessment Objective –	A set of determination statements that expresses the desired outcome for the assessment of a security control or control enhancement.
	SOURCE: SP 800-53A
Assessment Procedure –	A set of assessment objectives and an associated set of assessment methods and assessment objects.
	SOURCE: SP 800-53A
Assessor –	See Security Control Assessor.
Asset –	A major application, general support system, high impact program, physical plant, mission critical system, personnel, equipment, or a logically related group of systems.
	SOURCE: CNSSI-4009
Asset Identification –	Security Content Automation Protocol (SCAP) constructs to uniquely identify assets (components) based on known identifiers and/or known information about the assets.
	SOURCE: SP 800-128
Asset Reporting Format (ARF) –	SCAP data model for expressing the transport format of information about assets (components) and the relationships between assets and reports.
	SOURCE: SP 800-128
Assurance –	Grounds for confidence that the other four security goals (integrity, availability, confidentiality, and accountability) have been adequately met by a specific implementation. "Adequately met" includes (1) functionality that performs correctly, (2) sufficient protection against unintentional errors (by users or software), and (3) sufficient resistance to intentional penetration or by-pass.
	SOURCE: SP 800-27
	The grounds for confidence that the set of intended security controls in an information system are effective in their application.
	SOURCE: SP 800-37; SP 800-53A
	Measure of confidence that the security features, practices, procedures, and architecture of an information system accurately mediates and enforces the security policy.
	SOURCE: CNSSI-4009; SP 800-39

In the context of OMB M-04-04 and this document, assurance is defined as 1) the degree of confidence in the vetting process used to establish the identity of an individual to whom the credential was issued, and 2) the degree of confidence that the individual who uses the credential is the individual to whom the credential was issued.

SOURCE: SP 800-63

Assurance Case –

A structured set of arguments and a body of evidence showing that an information system satisfies specific claims with respect to a given quality attribute.

SOURCE: SP 800-53A; SP 800-39

Assured Information Sharing –

The ability to confidently share information with those who need it, when and where they need it, as determined by operational need and an acceptable level of security risk.

SOURCE: CNSSI-4009

Assured Software –

Computer application that has been designed, developed, analyzed, and tested using processes, tools, and techniques that establish a level of confidence in it.

SOURCE: CNSSI-4009

Asymmetric Cryptography –

See Public Key Cryptography.

SOURCE: CNSSI-4009

Asymmetric Keys –

Two related keys, a public key and a private key that are used to perform complementary operations, such as encryption and decryption or signature generation and signature verification.

SOURCE: FIPS 201

Attack –

An attempt to gain unauthorized access to system services, resources, or information, or an attempt to compromise system integrity.

SOURCE: SP 800-32

Any kind of malicious activity that attempts to collect, disrupt, deny, degrade, or destroy information system resources or the information itself.

SOURCE: CNSSI-4009

Attack Sensing and Warning (AS&W) –

Detection, correlation, identification, and characterization of intentional unauthorized activity with notification to decision makers so that an appropriate response can be developed.

SOURCE: CNSSI-4009

Attack Signature –	A specific sequence of events indicative of an unauthorized access attempt.
	SOURCE: SP 800-12
	A characteristic byte pattern used in malicious code or an indicator, or set of indicators, that allows the identification of malicious network activities.
	SOURCE: CNSSI-4009
Attribute Authority –	An entity, recognized by the Federal Public Key Infrastructure (PKI) Policy Authority or comparable agency body as having the authority to verify the association of attributes to an identity.
	SOURCE: SP 800-32
Attribute-Based Access Control –	Access control based on attributes associated with and about subjects, objects, targets, initiators, resources, or the environment. An access control rule set defines the combination of attributes under which an access may take place.
	SOURCE: SP 800-53; CNSSI-4009
Attribute-Based Authorization –	A structured process that determines when a user is authorized to access information, systems, or services based on attributes of the user and of the information, system, or service.
	SOURCE: CNSSI-4009
Audit –	Independent review and examination of records and activities to assess the adequacy of system controls, to ensure compliance with established policies and operational procedures, and to recommend necessary changes in controls, policies, or procedures.
	SOURCE: SP 800-32
	Independent review and examination of records and activities to assess the adequacy of system controls, to ensure compliance with established policies and operational procedures.
	SOURCE: CNSSI-4009
Audit Data –	Chronological record of system activities to enable the reconstruction and examination of the sequence of events and changes in an event.
	SOURCE: SP 800-32
Audit Log –	A chronological record of system activities. Includes records of system accesses and operations performed in a given period.
	SOURCE: CNSSI-4009

Audit Reduction Tools –	Preprocessors designed to reduce the volume of audit records to facilitate manual review. Before a security review, these tools can remove many audit records known to have little security significance. These tools generally remove records generated by specified classes of events, such as records generated by nightly backups. SOURCE: SP 800-12; CNSSI-4009
Audit Review –	The assessment of an information system to evaluate the adequacy of implemented security controls, assure that they are functioning properly, identify vulnerabilities, and assist in implementation of new security controls where required. This assessment is conducted annually or whenever significant change has occurred and may lead to recertification of the information system. SOURCE: CNSSI-4009
Audit Trail –	A record showing who has accessed an Information Technology (IT) system and what operations the user has performed during a given period. SOURCE: SP 800-47 A chronological record that reconstructs and examines the sequence of activities surrounding or leading to a specific operation, procedure, or event in a security relevant transaction from inception to final result. SOURCE: CNSSI-4009
Authenticate –	To confirm the identity of an entity when that identity is presented. SOURCE: SP 800-32 To verify the identity of a user, user device, or other entity. SOURCE: CNSSI-4009
Authentication –	Verifying the identity of a user, process, or device, often as a prerequisite to allowing access to resources in an information system. SOURCE: SP 800-53; SP 800-53A; SP 800-27; FIPS 200; SP 800-30 The process of establishing confidence of authenticity. SOURCE: FIPS 201 Encompasses identity verification, message origin authentication, and message content authentication. SOURCE: FIPS 190

A process that establishes the origin of information or determines an entity's identity.

SOURCE: SP 800-21

The process of verifying the identity or other attributes claimed by or assumed of an entity (user, process, or device), or to verify the source and integrity of data.

SOURCE: CNSSI-4009

The process of establishing confidence in the identity of users or information systems.

SOURCE: SP 800-63

Authentication Code –

A cryptographic checksum based on an Approved security function (also known as a Message Authentication Code [MAC]).

SOURCE: FIPS 140-2

Authentication Mechanism –

Hardware-or software-based mechanisms that force users to prove their identity before accessing data on a device.

SOURCE: SP 800-72; SP 800-124

Hardware or software-based mechanisms that forces users, devices, or processes to prove their identity before accessing data on an information system.

SOURCE: CNSSI-4009

Authentication Mode –

A block cipher mode of operation that can provide assurance of the authenticity and, therefore, the integrity of data.

SOURCE: SP 800-38B

Authentication Period –

The maximum acceptable period between any initial authentication process and subsequent reauthentication processes during a single terminal session or during the period data is being accessed.

SOURCE: CNSSI-4009

Authentication Protocol –

A defined sequence of messages between a Claimant and a Verifier that demonstrates that the Claimant has possession and control of a valid token to establish his/her identity, and optionally, demonstrates to the Claimant that he or she is communicating with the intended Verifier.

SOURCE: SP 800-63

A well-specified message exchange process between a claimant and a verifier that enables the verifier to confirm the claimant's identity.

SOURCE: CNSSI-4009

Authentication Tag –	A pair of bit strings associated to data to provide assurance of its authenticity. SOURCE: SP 800-38B
Authentication Token –	Authentication information conveyed during an authentication exchange. SOURCE: FIPS 196
Authenticator –	The means used to confirm the identity of a user, process, or device (e.g., user password or token). SOURCE: SP 800-53; CNSSI-4009
Authenticity –	The property of being genuine and being able to be verified and trusted; confidence in the validity of a transmission, a message, or message originator. See Authentication. SOURCE: SP 800-53; SP 800-53A; CNSSI-4009; SP 800-39
Authority –	Person(s) or established bodies with rights and responsibilities to exert control in an administrative sphere. SOURCE: CNSSI-4009
Authorization –	Access privileges granted to a user, program, or process or the act of granting those privileges. SOURCE: CNSSI-4009
Authorization (to operate) –	The official management decision given by a senior organizational official to authorize operation of an information system and to explicitly accept the risk to organizational operations (including mission, functions, image, or reputation), organizational assets, individuals, other organizations, and the Nation based on the implementation of an agreed-upon set of security controls. SOURCE: SP 800-53; SP 800-53A; CNSSI-4009; SP 800-37
Authorization Boundary –	All components of an information system to be authorized for operation by an authorizing official and excludes separately authorized systems, to which the information system is connected. SOURCE: CNSSI-4009; SP 800-53; SP 800-53A; SP 800-37
Authorize Processing –	See Authorization (to operate).
Authorized Vendor –	Manufacturer of information assurance equipment authorized to produce quantities in excess of contractual requirements for direct sale to eligible buyers. Eligible buyers are typically U.S. government organizations or U.S. government contractors. SOURCE: CNSSI-4009

Authorized Vendor Program(AVP) –	Program in which a vendor, producing an information systems security (INFOSEC) product under contract to NSA, is authorized to produce that product in numbers exceeding the contracted requirements for direct marketing and sale to eligible buyers. Eligible buyers are typically U.S. government organizations or U.S. government contractors. Products approved for marketing and sale through the AVP are placed on the Endorsed Cryptographic Products List (ECPL). SOURCE: CNSSI-4009
Authorizing Official –	Official with the authority to formally assume responsibility for operating an information system at an acceptable level of risk to agency operations (including mission, functions, image, or reputation), agency assets, or individuals. Synonymous with Accreditation Authority. SOURCE: FIPS 200 Senior federal official or executive with the authority to formally assume responsibility for operating an information system at an acceptable level of risk to organizational operations (including mission, functions, image, or reputation), organizational assets, individuals, other organizations, and the Nation. SOURCE: CNSSI-4009 A senior (federal) official or executive with the authority to formally assume responsibility for operating an information system at an acceptable level of risk to organizational operations (including mission, functions, image, or reputation), organizational assets, individuals, other organizations, and the Nation. SOURCE: SP 800-53; SP 800-53A; SP 800-37
Authorizing Official Designated Representative –	An organizational official acting on behalf of an authorizing official in carrying out and coordinating the required activities associated with security authorization. SOURCE: CNSSI-4009; SP 800-37; SP 800-53A
Automated Key Transport –	The transport of cryptographic keys, usually in encrypted form, using electronic means such as a computer network (e.g., key transport/agreement protocols). SOURCE: FIPS 140-2
Automated Password Generator –	An algorithm which creates random passwords that have no association with a particular user. SOURCE: FIPS 181

Automated Security Monitoring –	Use of automated procedures to ensure security controls are not circumvented or the use of these tools to track actions taken by subjects suspected of misusing the information system. SOURCE: CNSSI-4009
Automatic Remote Rekeying –	Procedure to rekey a distant crypto-equipment electronically without specific actions by the receiving terminal operator. See Manual Remote Rekeying. SOURCE: CNSSI-4009
Autonomous System (AS) –	One or more routers under a single administration operating the same routing policy. SOURCE: SP 800-54
Availability –	Ensuring timely and reliable access to and use of information. SOURCE: SP 800-53; SP 800-53A; SP 800-27; SP 800-60; SP 800-37; FIPS 200; FIPS 199; 44 U.S.C., Sec. 3542 The property of being accessible and useable upon demand by an authorized entity. SOURCE: CNSSI-4009
Awareness (Information Security) –	Activities which seek to focus an individual's attention on an (information security) issue or set of issues. SOURCE: SP 800-50
Back Door –	Typically unauthorized hidden software or hardware mechanism used to circumvent security controls. SOURCE: CNSSI-4009
Backdoor –	An undocumented way of gaining access to a computer system. A backdoor is a potential security risk. SOURCE: SP 800-82
Backtracking Resistance –	Backtracking resistance is provided relative to time T if there is assurance that an adversary who has knowledge of the internal state of the Deterministic Random Bit Generator (DRBG) at some time subsequent to time T would be unable to distinguish between observations of ideal random bitstrings and (previously unseen) bitstrings that were output by the DRBG prior to time T. The complementary assurance is called Prediction Resistance. SOURCE: SP 800-90A

Backup –

A copy of files and programs made to facilitate recovery, if necessary.

SOURCE: SP 800-34; CNSSI-4009

Banner –

Display on an information system that sets parameters for system or data use.

SOURCE: CNSSI-4009

Banner Grabbing –

The process of capturing banner information—such as application type and version—that is transmitted by a remote port when a connection is initiated.

SOURCE: SP 800-115

Baseline –

Hardware, software, databases, and relevant documentation for an information system at a given point in time.

SOURCE: CNSSI-4009

Baseline Configuration –

A set of specifications for a system, or Configuration Item (CI) within a system, that has been formally reviewed and agreed on at a given point in time, and which can be changed only through change control procedures. The baseline configuration is used as a basis for future builds, releases, and/or changes.

SOURCE: SP 800-128

Baseline Security –

The minimum security controls required for safeguarding an IT system based on its identified needs for confidentiality, integrity, and/or availability protection.

SOURCE: SP 800-16

Baselining –

Monitoring resources to determine typical utilization patterns so that significant deviations can be detected.

SOURCE: SP 800-61

Basic Testing –

A test methodology that assumes no knowledge of the internal structure and implementation detail of the assessment object. Also known as black box testing.

SOURCE: SP 800-53A

Bastion Host –

A special-purpose computer on a network specifically designed and configured to withstand attacks.

SOURCE: CNSSI-4009

Behavioral Outcome –	What an individual who has completed the specific training module is expected to be able to accomplish in terms of IT security-related job performance.
	SOURCE: SP 800-16
Benign Environment –	A non-hostile location protected from external hostile elements by physical, personnel, and procedural security countermeasures.
	SOURCE: CNSSI-4009
Binding –	Process of associating two related elements of information.
	SOURCE: SP 800-32
	An acknowledgement by a trusted third party that associates an entity's identity with its public key. This may take place through (1) a certification authority's generation of a public key certificate, (2) a security officer's verification of an entity's credentials and placement of the entity's public key and identifier in a secure database, or (3) an analogous method.
	SOURCE: SP 800-21
	Process of associating a specific communications terminal with a specific cryptographic key or associating two related elements of information.
	SOURCE: CNSSI-4009
Biometric –	A physical or behavioral characteristic of a human being.
	SOURCE: SP 800-32
	A measurable physical characteristic or personal behavioral trait used to recognize the identity, or verify the claimed identity, of an applicant. Facial images, fingerprints, and iris scan samples are all examples of biometrics.
	SOURCE: FIPS 201
Biometric Information –	The stored electronic information pertaining to a biometric. This information can be in terms of raw or compressed pixels or in terms of some characteristic (e.g., patterns.)
	SOURCE: FIPS 201

Biometric System –	An automated system capable of: 1) capturing a biometric sample from an end user; 2) extracting biometric data from that sample; 3) comparing the extracted biometric data with data contained in one or more references; 4) deciding how well they match; and 5) indicating whether or not an identification or verification of identity has been achieved. SOURCE: FIPS 201
Biometrics –	Measurable physical characteristics or personal behavioral traits used to identify, or verify the claimed identity, of an individual. Facial images, fingerprints, and handwriting samples are all examples of biometrics. SOURCE: CNSSI-4009
Bit –	A contraction of the term Binary Digit. The smallest unit of information in a binary system of notation. SOURCE: CNSSI-4009 A binary digit having a value of 0 or 1. SOURCE: FIPS 180-4
Bit Error Rate –	Ratio between the number of bits incorrectly received and the total number of bits transmitted in a telecommunications system. SOURCE: CNSSI-4009
BLACK –	Designation applied to encrypted information and the information systems, the associated areas, circuits, components, and equipment processing that information. See also RED. SOURCE: CNSSI-4009
Black Box Testing –	See Basic Testing.
Black Core –	A communication network architecture in which user data traversing a global Internet Protocol (IP) network is end-to-end encrypted at the IP layer. Related to striped core. SOURCE: CNSSI-4009
Blacklist –	A list of email senders who have previously sent span to a user. SOURCE: SP 800-114 A list of discrete entities, such as hosts or applications, that have been previously determined to be associated with malicious activity. SOURCE: SP 800-94

Blacklisting –

The process of the system invalidating a user ID based on the user's inappropriate actions. A blacklisted user ID cannot be used to log on to the system, even with the correct authenticator. Blacklisting and lifting of a blacklisting are both security-relevant events. Blacklisting also applies to blocks placed against IP addresses to prevent inappropriate or unauthorized use of Internet resources.

SOURCE: CNSSI-4009

Blended Attack –

A hostile action to spread malicious code via multiple methods.

SOURCE: CNSSI-4009

Blinding –

Generating network traffic that is likely to trigger many alerts in a short period of time, to conceal alerts triggered by a "real" attack performed simultaneously.

SOURCE: SP 800-94

Block –

Sequence of binary bits that comprise the input, output, State, and Round Key. The length of a sequence is the number of bits it contains. Blocks are also interpreted as arrays of bytes.

SOURCE: FIPS 197

Block Cipher –

A symmetric key cryptographic algorithm that transforms a block of information at a time using a cryptographic key. For a block cipher algorithm, the length of the input block is the same as the length of the output block.

SOURCE: SP 800-90

Block Cipher Algorithm –

A family of functions and their inverses that is parameterized by a cryptographic key; the function maps bit strings of a fixed length to bit strings of the same length.

SOURCE: SP 800-67

Blue Team –

1. The group responsible for defending an enterprise's use of information systems by maintaining its security posture against a group of mock attackers (i.e., the Red Team). Typically the Blue Team and its supporters must defend against real or simulated attacks 1) over a significant period of time, 2) in a representative operational context (e.g., as part of an operational exercise), and 3) according to rules established and monitored with the help of a neutral group refereeing the simulation or exercise (i.e., the White Team).

2. The term Blue Team is also used for defining a group of individuals that conduct operational network vulnerability evaluations and provide mitigation techniques to customers who have a need for an independent technical review of their network security posture. The Blue Team identifies security threats and risks in the operating environment, and in cooperation with the customer, analyzes the network environment and its current state of security readiness. Based on the Blue Team findings and expertise, they provide recommendations that integrate into an overall community security solution to increase the customer's cyber security readiness posture. Often times a Blue Team is employed by itself or prior to a Red Team employment to ensure that the customer's networks are as secure as possible before having the Red Team test the systems.

SOURCE: CNSSI-4009

Body of Evidence (BoE) –

The set of data that documents the information system's adherence to the security controls applied. The BoE will include a Requirements Verification Traceability Matrix (RVTM) delineating where the selected security controls are met and evidence to that fact can be found. The BoE content required by an Authorizing Official will be adjusted according to the impact levels selected.

SOURCE: CNSSI-4009

Boundary –

Physical or logical perimeter of a system.

SOURCE: CNSSI-4009

Boundary Protection –

Monitoring and control of communications at the external boundary of an information system to prevent and detect malicious and other unauthorized communication, through the use of boundary protection devices (e.g., proxies, gateways, routers, firewalls, guards, encrypted tunnels).

SOURCE: SP 800-53; CNSSI-4009

Boundary Protection Device –

A device with appropriate mechanisms that: (i) facilitates the adjudication of different interconnected system security policies (e.g., controlling the flow of information into or out of an interconnected system); and/or (ii) provides information system boundary protection.

SOURCE: SP 800-53

A device with appropriate mechanisms that facilitates the adjudication of different security policies for interconnected systems.

SOURCE: CNSSI-4009

Browsing –

Act of searching through information system storage or active content to locate or acquire information, without necessarily knowing the existence or format of information being sought.

SOURCE: CNSSI-4009

Brute Force Password Attack –

A method of accessing an obstructed device through attempting multiple combinations of numeric and/or alphanumeric passwords.

SOURCE: SP 800-72

Buffer Overflow –

A condition at an interface under which more input can be placed into a buffer or data holding area than the capacity allocated, overwriting other information. Attackers exploit such a condition to crash a system or to insert specially crafted code that allows them to gain control of the system.

SOURCE: SP 800-28; CNSSI-4009

Buffer Overflow Attack –

A method of overloading a predefined amount of space in a buffer, which can potentially overwrite and corrupt data in memory.

SOURCE: SP 800-72

Bulk Encryption –

Simultaneous encryption of all channels of a multichannel telecommunications link.

SOURCE: CNSSI-4009

Business Continuity Plan (BCP) –

The documentation of a predetermined set of instructions or procedures that describe how an organization's mission/business functions will be sustained during and after a significant disruption.

SOURCE: SP 800-34

The documentation of a predetermined set of instructions or procedures that describe how an organization's business functions will be sustained during and after a significant disruption.

SOURCE: CNSSI-4009

Business Impact Analysis (BIA) –	An analysis of an information system's requirements, functions, and interdependencies used to characterize system contingency requirements and priorities in the event of a significant disruption. SOURCE: SP 800-34 An analysis of an enterprise's requirements, processes, and interdependencies used to characterize information system contingency requirements and priorities in the event of a significant disruption. SOURCE: CNSSI-4009
Call Back –	Procedure for identifying and authenticating a remote information system terminal, whereby the host system disconnects the terminal and reestablishes contact. SOURCE: CNSSI-4009
Canister –	Type of protective package used to contain and dispense keying material in punched or printed tape form. SOURCE: CNSSI-4009
Capstone Policies –	Those policies that are developed by governing or coordinating institutions of Health Information Exchanges (HIEs). They provide overall requirements and guidance for protecting health information within those HIEs. Capstone Policies must address the requirements imposed by: (1) all laws, regulations, and guidelines at the federal, state, and local levels; (2) business needs; and (3) policies at the institutional and HIE levels. SOURCE: NISTIR-7497
Capture –	The method of taking a biometric sample from an end user. Source: FIPS 201
Cardholder –	An individual possessing an issued Personal Identity Verification (PIV) card. Source: FIPS 201
Cascading –	Downward flow of information through a range of security levels greater than the accreditation range of a system, network, or component. SOURCE: CNSSI-4009
Category –	Restrictive label applied to classified or unclassified information to limit access. SOURCE: CNSSI-4009

| CBC/MAC – | See Cipher Block Chaining-Message Authentication Code. |

CCM – See Counter with Cipher-Block Chaining-Message Authentication Code.

Central Office of Record (COR) – Office of a federal department or agency that keeps records of accountable COMSEC material held by elements subject to its oversight

SOURCE: CNSSI-4009

Central Services Node (CSN) – The Key Management Infrastructure core node that provides central security management and data management services.

SOURCE: CNSSI-4009

Certificate – A digital representation of information which at least
1) identifies the certification authority issuing it,
2) names or identifies its subscriber,
3) contains the subscriber's public key,
4) identifies its operational period, and
5) is digitally signed by the certification authority issuing it.

SOURCE: SP 800-32

A set of data that uniquely identifies an entity, contains the entity's public key and possibly other information, and is digitally signed by a trusted party, thereby binding the public key to the entity. Additional information in the certificate could specify how the key is used and its cryptoperiod.

SOURCE: SP 800-21

A digitally signed representation of information that 1) identifies the authority issuing it, 2) identifies the subscriber, 3) identifies its valid operational period (date issued / expiration date). In the information assurance (IA) community, certificate usually implies public key certificate and can have the following types:

cross certificate – a certificate issued from a CA that signs the public key of another CA not within its trust hierarchy that establishes a trust relationship between the two CAs.

encryption certificate – a certificate containing a public key that can encrypt or decrypt electronic messages, files, documents, or data transmissions, or establish or exchange a session key for these same purposes. Key management sometimes refers to the process of storing, protecting, and escrowing the private component of the key pair associated with the encryption certificate.

identity certificate – a certificate that provides authentication of the identity claimed. Within the National Security Systems (NSS) PKI, identity certificates may be used only for authentication or may be used for both authentication and digital signatures.

SOURCE: CNSSI-4009

A set of data that uniquely identifies a key pair and an owner that is authorized to use the key pair. The certificate contains the owner's public key and possibly other information, and is digitally signed by a Certification Authority (i.e., a trusted party), thereby binding the public key to the owner.

SOURCE: FIPS 186

Certificate Management –

Process whereby certificates (as defined above) are generated, stored, protected, transferred, loaded, used, and destroyed.

SOURCE: CNSSI-4009

Certificate Management Authority – (CMA)

A Certification Authority (CA) or a Registration Authority (RA).

SOURCE: SP 800-32

Certificate Policy (CP) –

A specialized form of administrative policy tuned to electronic transactions performed during certificate management. A Certificate Policy addresses all aspects associated with the generation, production, distribution, accounting, compromise recovery, and administration of digital certificates. Indirectly, a certificate policy can also govern the transactions conducted using a communications system protected by a certificate-based security system. By controlling critical certificate extensions, such policies and associated enforcement technology can support provision of the security services required by particular applications.

SOURCE: CNSSI-4009; SP 800-32

Certificate-Related Information – Information, such as a subscriber's postal address, that is not included in a certificate. May be used by a Certification Authority (CA) managing certificates.

SOURCE: SP 800-32

Data, such as a subscriber's postal address that is not included in a certificate. May be used by a Certification Authority (CA) managing certificates.

SOURCE: CNSSI-4009

Certificate Revocation List (CRL) – A list of revoked public key certificates created and digitally signed by a Certification Authority.

SOURCE: SP 800-63; FIPS 201

A list of revoked but un-expired certificates issued by a CA.

SOURCE: SP 800-21

A list of revoked public key certificates created and digitally signed by a Certification Authority.

SOURCE: CNSSI-4009

Certificate Status Authority – A trusted entity that provides online verification to a Relying Party of a subject certificate's trustworthiness, and may also provide additional attribute information for the subject certificate.

SOURCE: SP 800-32; CNSSI-4009

Certification – A comprehensive assessment of the management, operational, and technical security controls in an information system, made in support of security accreditation, to determine the extent to which the controls are implemented correctly, operating as intended, and producing the desired outcome with respect to meeting the security requirements for the system.

SOURCE: FIPS 200

The process of verifying the correctness of a statement or claim and issuing a certificate as to its correctness.

SOURCE: FIPS 201

Comprehensive evaluation of the technical and nontechnical security safeguards of an information system to support the accreditation process that establishes the extent to which a particular design and implementation meets a set of specified security requirements. See Security Control Assessment.

SOURCE: CNSSI-4009

Certification Analyst –	The independent technical liaison for all stakeholders involved in the C&A process responsible for objectively and independently evaluating a system as part of the risk management process. Based on the security requirements documented in the security plan, performs a technical and non-technical review of potential vulnerabilities in the system and determines if the security controls (management, operational, and technical) are correctly implemented and effective. SOURCE: CNSSI-4009
Certification Authority (CA) –	A trusted entity that issues and revokes public key certificates. SOURCE: FIPS 201 The entity in a public key infrastructure (PKI) that is responsible for issuing certificates and exacting compliance to a PKI policy. SOURCE: SP 800-21; FIPS 186 1. For Certification and Accreditation (C&A) (C&A Assessment): Official responsible for performing the comprehensive evaluation of the security features of an information system and determining the degree to which it meets its security requirements 2. For Public Key Infrastructure (PKI): A trusted third party that issues digital certificates and verifies the identity of the holder of the digital certificate. SOURCE: CNSSI-4009
Certification Authority Facility –	The collection of equipment, personnel, procedures and structures that are used by a Certification Authority to perform certificate issuance and revocation. SOURCE: SP 800-32
Certification Authority Workstation (CAW) –	Commercial off-the-shelf (COTS) workstation with a trusted operating system and special-purpose application software that is used to issue certificates SOURCE: CNSSI-4009
Certification Package –	Product of the certification effort documenting the detailed results of the certification activities. SOURCE: CNSSI-4009

Certification Practice Statement – (CPS)	A statement of the practices that a Certification Authority employs in issuing, suspending, revoking, and renewing certificates and providing access to them, in accordance with specific requirements (i.e., requirements specified in this Certificate Policy, or requirements specified in a contract for services). SOURCE: SP 800-32; CNSSI-4009
Certification Test and Evaluation – (CT&E)	Software and hardware security tests conducted during development of an information system. SOURCE: CNSSI-4009
Certified TEMPEST Technical Authority (CTTA) –	An experienced, technically qualified U.S. government employee who has met established certification requirements in accordance with CNSS-approved criteria and has been appointed by a U.S. government department or agency to fulfill CTTA responsibilities. SOURCE: CNSSI-4009
Certifier –	Individual responsible for making a technical judgment of the system's compliance with stated requirements, identifying and assessing the risks associated with operating the system, coordinating the certification activities, and consolidating the final certification and accreditation packages. SOURCE: CNSSI-4009
Chain of Custody –	A process that tracks the movement of evidence through its collection, safeguarding, and analysis lifecycle by documenting each person who handled the evidence, the date/time it was collected or transferred, and the purpose for the transfer. SOURCE: SP 800-72; CNSSI-4009
Chain of Evidence –	A process and record that shows who obtained the evidence; where and when the evidence was obtained; who secured the evidence; and who had control or possession of the evidence. The "sequencing" of the chain of evidence follows this order: collection and identification; analysis; storage; preservation; presentation in court; return to owner. SOURCE: CNSSI-4009
Challenge and Reply Authentication –	Prearranged procedure in which a subject requests authentication of another and the latter establishes validity with a correct reply. SOURCE: CNSSI-4009

Challenge-Response Protocol –	An authentication protocol where the verifier sends the claimant a challenge (usually a random value or a nonce) that the claimant combines with a secret (often by hashing the challenge and a shared secret together, or by applying a private key operation to the challenge) to generate a response that is sent to the verifier. The verifier can independently verify the response generated by the Claimant (such as by re-computing the hash of the challenge and the shared secret and comparing to the response, or performing a public key operation on the response) and establish that the Claimant possesses and controls the secret. SOURCE: SP 800-63
Check Word –	Cipher text generated by cryptographic logic to detect failures in cryptography. SOURCE: CNSSI-4009
Checksum –	Value computed on data to detect error or manipulation. SOURCE: CNSSI-4009

Chief Information Officer (CIO) –

Agency official responsible for:
1) Providing advice and other assistance to the head of the executive agency and other senior management personnel of the agency to ensure that information technology is acquired and information resources are managed in a manner that is consistent with laws, Executive Orders, directives, policies, regulations, and priorities established by the head of the agency;
2) Developing, maintaining, and facilitating the implementation of a sound and integrated information technology architecture for the agency; and
3) Promoting the effective and efficient design and operation of all major information resources management processes for the agency, including improvements to work processes of the agency.

SOURCE: FIPS 200; Public Law 104-106, Sec. 5125(b)

Agency official responsible for: 1) providing advice and other assistance to the head of the executive agency and other senior management personnel of the agency to ensure that information systems are acquired and information resources are managed in a manner that is consistent with laws, Executive Orders, directives, policies, regulations, and priorities established by the head of the agency; 2) developing, maintaining, and facilitating the implementation of a sound and integrated information system architecture for the agency; and 3) promoting the effective and efficient design and operation of all major information resources management processes for the agency, including improvements to work processes of the agency.

Note: Organizations subordinate to federal agencies may use the term Chief Information Officer to denote individuals filling positions with similar security responsibilities to agency-level Chief Information Officers.

SOURCE: CNSSI-4009; SP 800-53

Chief Information Security Officer – (CISO)

See Senior Agency Information Security Officer.

Cipher –

Series of transformations that converts plaintext to ciphertext using the Cipher Key.

SOURCE: FIPS 197

Any cryptographic system in which arbitrary symbols or groups of symbols, represent units of plain text, or in which units of plain text are rearranged, or both.

SOURCE: CNSSI-4009

Cipher Block Chaining-Message Authentication Code – (CBC-MAC)	A secret-key block-cipher algorithm used to encrypt data and to generate a Message Authentication Code (MAC) to provide assurance that the payload and the associated data are authentic. SOURCE: SP 800-38C
Cipher Suite –	Negotiated algorithm identifiers. Cipher suites are identified in human-readable form using a pneumonic code. SOURCE: SP 800-52
Cipher Text Auto-Key (CTAK) –	Cryptographic logic that uses previous cipher text to generate a key stream. SOURCE: CNSSI-4009
Ciphertext –	Data output from the Cipher or input to the Inverse Cipher. SOURCE: FIPS 197 Data in its enciphered form. SOURCE: SP 800-56B
Ciphertext/Cipher Text –	Data in its encrypted form. SOURCE: SP 800-21; CNSSI-4009
Ciphony –	Process of enciphering audio information, resulting in encrypted speech. SOURCE: CNSSI-4009
Claimant –	A party whose identity is to be verified using an authentication protocol. SOURCE: SP 800-63; FIPS 201 An entity which is or represents a principal for the purposes of authentication, together with the functions involved in an authentication exchange on behalf of that entity. A claimant acting on behalf of a principal must include the functions necessary for engaging in an authentication exchange. (e.g., a smartcard [claimant] can act on behalf of a human user [principal]) SOURCE: FIPS 196 An entity (user, device or process) whose assertion is to be verified using an authentication protocol. SOURCE: CNSSI-4009

Classified Information –	Information that has been determined pursuant to Executive Order (E.O.) 13292 or any predecessor order to require protection against unauthorized disclosure and is marked to indicate its classified status when in documentary form.
	SOURCE: SP 800-60; E.O. 13292
	See Classified National Security Information.
	SOURCE: CNSSI-4009
	Information that has been determined: (i) pursuant to Executive Order 12958 as amended by Executive Order 13292, or any predecessor Order, to be classified national security information; or (ii) pursuant to the Atomic Energy Act of 1954, as amended, to be Restricted Data (RD).
	SOURCE: SP 800-53
Classified Information Spillage –	Security incident that occurs whenever classified data is spilled either onto an unclassified information system or to an information system with a lower level of classification.
	SOURCE: CNSSI-4009
Classified National Security Information –	Information that has been determined pursuant to Executive Order 13526 or any predecessor order to require protection against unauthorized disclosure and is marked to indicate its classified status when in documentary form.
	SOURCE: CNSSI-4009
Clear –	To use software or hardware products to overwrite storage space on the media with nonsensitive data. This process may include overwriting not only the logical storage location of a file(s) (e.g., file allocation table) but also may include all addressable locations. See comments on Clear/Purge Convergence.
	SOURCE: SP 800-88
Clear Text –	Information that is not encrypted.
	SOURCE: SP 800-82
Clearance –	Formal certification of authorization to have access to classified information other than that protected in a special access program (including SCI). Clearances are of three types: confidential, secret, and top secret. A top secret clearance permits access to top secret, secret, and confidential material; a secret clearance, to secret and confidential material; and a confidential clearance, to confidential material.
	SOURCE: CNSSI-4009

Clearing –	Removal of data from an information system, its storage devices, and other peripheral devices with storage capacity, in such a way that the data may not be reconstructed using common system capabilities (i.e., through the keyboard); however, the data may be reconstructed using laboratory methods. SOURCE: CNSSI-4009
Client –	Individual or process acting on behalf of an individual who makes requests of a guard or dedicated server. The client's requests to the guard or dedicated server can involve data transfer to, from, or through the guard or dedicated server. SOURCE: CNSSI-4009
Client (Application) –	A system entity, usually a computer process acting on behalf of a human user, that makes use of a service provided by a server. SOURCE: SP 800-32
Clinger-Cohen Act of 1996 –	Also known as Information Technology Management Reform Act. A statute that substantially revised the way that IT resources are managed and procured, including a requirement that each agency design and implement a process for maximizing the value and assessing and managing the risks of IT investments. SOURCE: SP 800-64
Closed Security Environment –	Environment providing sufficient assurance that applications and equipment are protected against the introduction of malicious logic during an information system life cycle. Closed security is based upon a system's developers, operators, and maintenance personnel having sufficient clearances, authorization, and configuration control. SOURCE: CNSSI-4009
Closed Storage –	Storage of classified information within an accredited facility, in General Services Administration-approved secure containers, while the facility is unoccupied by authorized personnel. SOURCE: CNSSI-4009

Cloud Computing –

A model for enabling on-demand network access to a shared pool of configurable IT capabilities/ resources (e.g., networks, servers, storage, applications, and services) that can be rapidly provisioned and released with minimal management effort or service provider interaction. It allows users to access technology-based services from the network cloud without knowledge of, expertise with, or control over the technology infrastructure that supports them. This cloud model is composed of five essential characteristics (on-demand self-service, ubiquitous network access, location independent resource pooling, rapid elasticity, and measured service); three service delivery models (Cloud Software as a Service [SaaS], Cloud Platform as a Service [PaaS], and Cloud Infrastructure as a Service [IaaS]); and four models for enterprise access (Private cloud, Community cloud, Public cloud, and Hybrid cloud).

Note: Both the user's data and essential security services may reside in and be managed within the network cloud.

SOURCE: CNSSI-4009

Code –

System of communication in which arbitrary groups of letters, numbers, or symbols represent units of plain text of varying length.

SOURCE: CNSSI-4009

Code Book –

Document containing plain text and code equivalents in a systematic arrangement, or a technique of machine encryption using a word substitution technique.

SOURCE: CNSSI-4009

Code Group –

Group of letters, numbers, or both in a code system used to represent a plain text word, phrase, or sentence.

SOURCE: CNSSI-4009

Code Vocabulary –

Set of plain text words, numerals, phrases, or sentences for which code equivalents are assigned in a code system.

SOURCE: CNSSI-4009

Cold Site –

Backup site that can be up and operational in a relatively short time span, such as a day or two. Provision of services, such as telephone lines and power, is taken care of, and the basic office furniture might be in place, but there is unlikely to be any computer equipment, even though the building might well have a network infrastructure and a room ready to act as a server room. In most cases, cold sites provide the physical location and basic services.

SOURCE: CNSSI-4009

A backup facility that has the necessary electrical and physical components of a computer facility, but does not have the computer equipment in place. The site is ready to receive the necessary replacement computer equipment in the event that the user has to move from their main computing location to an alternate site.

SOURCE: SP 800-34

Cold Start –

Procedure for initially keying crypto-equipment.

SOURCE: CNSSI-4009

Collision –

Two or more distinct inputs produce the same output. Also see Hash Function.

SOURCE: SP 800-57 Part 1

Command Authority –

Individual responsible for the appointment of user representatives for a department, agency, or organization and their key ordering privileges.

SOURCE: CNSSI-4009

Commercial COMSEC Evaluation Program (CCEP) –

Relationship between NSA and industry in which NSA provides the COMSEC expertise (i.e., standards, algorithms, evaluations, and guidance) and industry provides design, development, and production capabilities to produce a type 1 or type 2 product. Products developed under the CCEP may include modules, subsystems, equipment, systems, and ancillary devices.

SOURCE: CNSSI-4009

Commodity Service –

An information system service (e.g., telecommunications service) provided by a commercial service provider typically to a large and diverse set of consumers. The organization acquiring and/or receiving the commodity service possesses limited visibility into the management structure and operations of the provider, and while the organization may be able to negotiate service-level agreements, the organization is typically not in a position to require that the provider implement specific security controls.

SOURCE: SP 800-53

Common Access Card (CAC) –

Standard identification/smart card issued by the Department of Defense that has an embedded integrated chip storing public key infrastructure (PKI) certificates.

SOURCE: CNSSI-4009

Common Carrier –	In a telecommunications context, a telecommunications company that holds itself out to the public for hire to provide communications transmission services. Note: In the United States, such companies are usually subject to regulation by federal and state regulatory commissions.
	SOURCE: SP 800-53
Common Configuration Enumeration (CCE) –	A SCAP specification that provides unique, common identifiers for configuration settings found in a wide variety of hardware and software products.
	SOURCE: SP 800-128
Common Configuration Scoring System (CCSS) –	A set of measures of the severity of software security configuration issues.
	SOURCE: NISTIR 7502
	A SCAP specification for measuring the severity of software security configuration issues.
	SOURCE: SP 800-128
Common Control –	A security control that is inherited by one or more organizational information systems. See Security Control Inheritance.
	SOURCE: SP 800-53; SP 800-53A; SP 800-37; CNSSI-4009
Common Control Provider –	An organizational official responsible for the development, implementation, assessment, and monitoring of common controls (i.e., security controls inherited by information systems).
	SOURCE: SP 800-37; SP 800-53A
Common Criteria –	Governing document that provides a comprehensive, rigorous method for specifying security function and assurance requirements for products and systems.
	SOURCE: CNSSI-4009
Common Fill Device –	One of a family of devices developed to read-in, transfer, or store key.
	SOURCE: CNSSI-4009
Common Misuse Scoring System – (CMSS)	A set of measures of the severity of software feature misuse vulnerabilities. A software feature is a functional capability provided by software. A software feature misuse vulnerability is a vulnerability in which the feature also provides an avenue to compromise the security of a system.
	SOURCE: NISTIR 7864

Common Platform Enumeration – (CPE)

A SCAP specification that provides a standard naming convention for operating systems, hardware, and applications for the purpose of providing consistent, easily parsed names that can be shared by multiple parties and solutions to refer to the same specific platform type.

SOURCE: SP 800-128

Common Vulnerabilities and Exposures (CVE) –

A dictionary of common names for publicly known information system vulnerabilities.

SOURCE: SP 800-51; CNSSI-4009

An SCAP specification that provides unique, common names for publicly known information system vulnerabilities.

SOURCE: SP 800-128

Common Vulnerability Scoring System (CVSS) –

An SCAP specification for communicating the characteristics of vulnerabilities and measuring their relative severity.

SOURCE: SP 800-128

Communications Cover –

Concealing or altering of characteristic communications patterns to hide information that could be of value to an adversary.

SOURCE: CNSSI-4009

Communications Deception –

Deliberate transmission, retransmission, or alteration of communications to mislead an adversary's interpretation of the communications.

SOURCE: CNSSI-4009

Communications Profile –

Analytic model of communications associated with an organization or activity. The model is prepared from a systematic examination of communications content and patterns, the functions they reflect, and the communications security measures applied.

SOURCE: CNSSI-4009

Communications Security – (COMSEC)

A component of Information Assurance that deals with measures and controls taken to deny unauthorized persons information derived from telecommunications and to ensure the authenticity of such telecommunications. COMSEC includes crypto security, transmission security, emissions security, and physical security of COMSEC material.

SOURCE: CNSSI-4009

Community of Interest (COI) –

A collaborative group of users who exchange information in pursuit of their shared goals, interests, missions, or business processes, and who therefore must have a shared vocabulary for the information they exchange. The group exchanges information within and between systems to include security domains.

SOURCE: CNSSI-4009

Community Risk –

Probability that a particular vulnerability will be exploited within an interacting population and adversely impact some members of that population.

SOURCE: CNSSI-4009

Comparison –

The process of comparing a biometric with a previously stored reference.

SOURCE: FIPS 201

Compartmentalization –

A nonhierarchical grouping of sensitive information used to control access to data more finely than with hierarchical security classification alone.

SOURCE: CNSSI-4009

Compartmented Mode –

Mode of operation wherein each user with direct or indirect access to a system, its peripherals, remote terminals, or remote hosts has all of the following: (1) valid security clearance for the most restricted information processed in the system; (2) formal access approval and signed nondisclosure agreements for that information which a user is to have access; and (3) valid need-to-know for information which a user is to have access.

SOURCE: CNSSI-4009

Compensating Security Control –

A management, operational, and/or technical control (i.e., safeguard or countermeasure) employed by an organization in lieu of a recommended security control in the low, moderate, or high baselines that provides equivalent or comparable protection for an information system.

NIST SP 800-53: A management, operational, and technical control (i.e., safeguard or countermeasure) employed by an organization in lieu of the recommended control in the baselines described in NIST Special Publication 800-53 or in CNSS Instruction 1253, that provide equivalent or comparable protection for an information system.

SOURCE: CNSSI-4009

Compensating Security Controls –

The management, operational, and technical controls (i.e., safeguards or countermeasures) employed by an organization in lieu of the recommended controls in the low, moderate, or high baselines described in NIST Special Publication 800-53, that provide equivalent or comparable protection for an information system.

SOURCE: SP 800-37

The management, operational, and technical controls (i.e., safeguards or countermeasures) employed by an organization in lieu of the recommended controls in the baselines described in NIST Special Publication 800-53 and CNSS Instruction 1253, that provide equivalent or comparable protection for an information system.

SOURCE: SP 800-53A; SP 800-53

Comprehensive Testing –

A test methodology that assumes explicit and substantial knowledge of the internal structure and implementation detail of the assessment object. Also known as white box testing.

SOURCE: SP 800-53A

Compromise –

Disclosure of information to unauthorized persons, or a violation of the security policy of a system in which unauthorized intentional or unintentional disclosure, modification, destruction, or loss of an object may have occurred.

SOURCE: SP 800-32

The unauthorized disclosure, modification, substitution, or use of sensitive data (including plaintext cryptographic keys and other CSPs).

SOURCE: FIPS 140-2

Disclosure of information to unauthorized persons, or a violation of the security policy of a system in which unauthorized intentional or unintentional disclosure, modification, destruction, or loss of an object may have occurred.

SOURCE: CNSSI-4009

Compromising Emanations –

Unintentional signals that, if intercepted and analyzed, would disclose the information transmitted, received, handled, or otherwise processed by information systems equipment. See TEMPEST.

SOURCE: CNSSI-4009

Computer Abuse –

Intentional or reckless misuse, alteration, disruption, or destruction of information processing resources.

SOURCE: CNSSI-4009

Computer Cryptography –	Use of a crypto-algorithm program by a computer to authenticate or encrypt/decrypt information. SOURCE: CNSSI-4009
Computer Forensics –	The practice of gathering, retaining, and analyzing computer-related data for investigative purposes in a manner that maintains the integrity of the data. SOURCE: CNSSI-4009
Computer Incident Response Team – (CIRT)	Group of individuals usually consisting of Security Analysts organized to develop, recommend, and coordinate immediate mitigation actions for containment, eradication, and recovery resulting from computer security incidents. Also called a Computer Security Incident Response Team (CSIRT) or a CIRC (Computer Incident Response Center, Computer Incident Response Capability, or Cyber Incident Response Team). SOURCE: CNSSI-4009
Computer Network Attack (CNA) –	Actions taken through the use of computer networks to disrupt, deny, degrade, or destroy information resident in computers and computer networks, or the computers and networks themselves. SOURCE: CNSSI-4009
Computer Network Defense(CND) –	Actions taken to defend against unauthorized activity within computer networks. CND includes monitoring, detection, analysis (such as trend and pattern analysis), and response and restoration activities. SOURCE: CNSSI-4009
Computer Network Exploitation – (CNE)	Enabling operations and intelligence collection capabilities conducted through the use of computer networks to gather data from target or adversary information systems or networks. SOURCE: CNSSI-4009
Computer Network Operations – (CNO)	Comprised of computer network attack, computer network defense, and related computer network exploitation enabling operations. SOURCE: CNSSI-4009
Computer Security (COMPUSEC) –	Measures and controls that ensure confidentiality, integrity, and availability of information system assets including hardware, software, firmware, and information being processed, stored, and communicated. SOURCE: CNSSI-4009
Computer Security Incident –	See Incident.

Computer Security Incident Response Team (CSIRT) –	A capability set up for the purpose of assisting in responding to computer security-related incidents; also called a Computer Incident Response Team (CIRT) or a CIRC (Computer Incident Response Center, Computer Incident Response Capability).
	SOURCE: SP 800-61
Computer Security Object (CSO) –	A resource, tool, or mechanism used to maintain a condition of security in a computerized environment. These objects are defined in terms of attributes they possess, operations they perform or are performed on them, and their relationship with other objects.
	SOURCE: FIPS 188; CNSSI-4009
Computer Security Objects Register –	A collection of Computer Security Object names and definitions kept by a registration authority.
	SOURCE: FIPS 188; CNSSI-4009
Computer Security Subsystem –	Hardware/software designed to provide computer security features in a larger system environment.
	SOURCE: CNSSI-4009
Computer Virus –	See Virus.
Computing Environment –	Workstation or server (host) and its operating system, peripherals, and applications.
	SOURCE: CNSSI-4009
COMSEC –	Communications Security.
	SOURCE: CNSSI-4009
COMSEC Account –	Administrative entity, identified by an account number, used to maintain accountability, custody, and control of COMSEC material.
	SOURCE: CNSSI-4009
COMSEC Account Audit –	Examination of the holdings, records, and procedures of a COMSEC account ensuring all accountable COMSEC material is properly handled and safeguarded.
	SOURCE: CNSSI-4009
COMSEC Aid	COMSEC material that assists in securing telecommunications and is required in the production, operation, or maintenance of COMSEC systems and their components. COMSEC keying material, callsign/frequency systems, and supporting documentation, such as operating and maintenance manuals, are examples of COMSEC aids.
	SOURCE: CNSSI-4009

COMSEC Assembly –	Group of parts, elements, subassemblies, or circuits that are removable items of COMSEC equipment.
	SOURCE: CNSSI-4009
COMSEC Boundary –	Definable perimeter encompassing all hardware, firmware, and software components performing critical COMSEC functions, such as key generation, handling, and storage.
	SOURCE: CNSSI-4009
COMSEC Chip Set –	Collection of NSA-approved microchips.
	SOURCE: CNSSI-4009
COMSEC Control Program –	Computer instructions or routines controlling or affecting the externally performed functions of key generation, key distribution, message encryption/decryption, or authentication.
	SOURCE: CNSSI-4009
COMSEC Custodian –	Individual designated by proper authority to be responsible for the receipt, transfer, accounting, safeguarding, and destruction of COMSEC material assigned to a COMSEC account.
	SOURCE: CNSSI-4009
COMSEC Demilitarization –	Process of preparing COMSEC equipment for disposal by extracting all CCI, classified, or cryptographic (CRYPTO) marked components for their secure destruction, as well as defacing and disposing of the remaining equipment hulk.
	SOURCE: CNSSI-4009
COMSEC Element –	Removable item of COMSEC equipment, assembly, or subassembly; normally consisting of a single piece or group of replaceable parts.
	SOURCE: CNSSI-4009
COMSEC End-item –	Equipment or combination of components ready for use in a COMSEC application.
	SOURCE: CNSSI-4009
COMSEC Equipment –	Equipment designed to provide security to telecommunications by converting information to a form unintelligible to an unauthorized interceptor and, subsequently, by reconverting such information to its original form for authorized recipients; also, equipment designed specifically to aid in, or as an essential element of, the conversion process. COMSEC equipment includes crypto-equipment, crypto-ancillary equipment, cryptographic production equipment, and authentication equipment.
	SOURCE: CNSSI-4009

COMSEC Facility –	Authorized and approved space used for generating, storing, repairing, or using COMSEC material. SOURCE: CNSSI-4009
COMSEC Incident –	Occurrence that potentially jeopardizes the security of COMSEC material or the secure electrical transmission of national security information or information governed by 10 U.S.C. Section 2315. SOURCE: CNSSI-4009
COMSEC Insecurity –	COMSEC incident that has been investigated, evaluated, and determined to jeopardize the security of COMSEC material or the secure transmission of information. SOURCE: CNSSI-4009
COMSEC Manager –	Individual who manages the COMSEC resources of an organization. SOURCE: CNSSI-4009
COMSEC Material –	Item designed to secure or authenticate telecommunications. COMSEC material includes, but is not limited to key, equipment, devices, documents, firmware, or software that embodies or describes cryptographic logic and other items that perform COMSEC functions. SOURCE: CNSSI-4009
COMSEC Material Control System (CMCS) –	Logistics and accounting system through which COMSEC material marked "CRYPTO" is distributed, controlled, and safeguarded. Included are the COMSEC central offices of record, crypto logistic depots, and COMSEC accounts. COMSEC material other than key may be handled through the CMCS. SOURCE: CNSSI-4009
COMSEC Modification –	See Information Systems Security Equipment Modification. SOURCE: CNSSI-4009
COMSEC Module –	Removable component that performs COMSEC functions in a telecommunications equipment or system. SOURCE: CNSSI-4009
COMSEC Monitoring –	Act of listening to, copying, or recording transmissions of one's own official telecommunications to analyze the degree of security. SOURCE: CNSSI-4009
COMSEC Profile –	Statement of COMSEC measures and materials used to protect a given operation, system, or organization. SOURCE: CNSSI-4009

COMSEC Survey –	Organized collection of COMSEC and communications information relative to a given operation, system, or organization.
	SOURCE: CNSSI-4009
COMSEC System Data –	Information required by a COMSEC equipment or system to enable it to properly handle and control key.
	SOURCE: CNSSI-4009
COMSEC Training –	Teaching of skills relating to COMSEC accounting, use of COMSEC aids, or installation, use, maintenance, and repair of COMSEC equipment.
	SOURCE: CNSSI-4009
Concept of Operations (CONOP) –	See Security Concept of Operations.
	SOURCE: CNSSI-4009
Confidentiality –	Preserving authorized restrictions on information access and disclosure, including means for protecting personal privacy and proprietary information.
	SOURCE: SP 800-53; SP 800-53A; SP 800-18; SP 800-27; SP 800-60; SP 800-37; FIPS 200; FIPS 199; 44 U.S.C., Sec. 3542
	The property that sensitive information is not disclosed to unauthorized individuals, entities, or processes.
	SOURCE: FIPS 140-2
	The property that information is not disclosed to system entities (users, processes, devices) unless they have been authorized to access the information.
	SOURCE: CNSSI-4009
Configuration Control –	Process of controlling modifications to hardware, firmware, software, and documentation to protect the information system against improper modification prior to, during, and after system implementation.
	SOURCE: CNSSI-4009; SP 800-37; SP 800-53
Configuration Control Board – (CCB)	A group of qualified people with responsibility for the process of regulating and approving changes to hardware, firmware, software, and documentation throughout the development and operational life cycle of an information system.
	SOURCE: CNSSI-4009
Confinement Channel –	See Covert Channel.
	SOURCE: CNSSI-4009

Container –

The file used by a virtual disk encryption technology to encompass and protect other files.

SOURCE: SP 800-111

Contamination –

Type of incident involving the introduction of data of one security classification or security category into data of a lower security classification or different security category.

SOURCE: CNSSI-4009

Content Filtering –

The process of monitoring communications such as email and Web pages, analyzing them for suspicious content, and preventing the delivery of suspicious content to users.

SOURCE: SP 800-114

Contingency Key –

Key held for use under specific operational conditions or in support of specific contingency plans. See Reserve Keying Material.

SOURCE: CNSSI-4009

Contingency Plan –

Management policy and procedures used to guide an enterprise response to a perceived loss of mission capability. The Contingency Plan is the first plan used by the enterprise risk managers to determine what happened, why, and what to do. It may point to the Continuity of Operations Plan (COOP) or Disaster Recovery Plan for major disruptions.

SOURCE: CNSSI-4009

See also Information System Contingency Plan.

Continuity of Government (COG) –

A coordinated effort within the federal government's executive branch to ensure that national essential functions continue to be performed during a catastrophic emergency.

SOURCE: CNSSI-4009

Continuity of Operations Plan – (COOP)

A predetermined set of instructions or procedures that describe how an organization's mission-essential functions will be sustained within 12 hours and for up to 30 days as a result of a disaster event before returning to normal operations.

SOURCE: SP 800-34

Management policy and procedures used to guide an enterprise response to a major loss of enterprise capability or damage to its facilities. The COOP is the third plan needed by the enterprise risk managers and is used when the enterprise must recover (often at an alternate site) for a specified period of time. Defines the activities of individual departments and agencies and their sub-components to ensure that their essential functions are performed. This includes plans and procedures that delineate essential functions; specifies succession to office and the emergency delegation of authority; provide for the safekeeping of vital records and databases; identify alternate operating facilities; provide for interoperable communications, and validate the capability through tests, training, and exercises. See also Disaster Recovery Plan and Contingency Plan.

SOURCE: CNSSI-4009

Continuous Monitoring –

The process implemented to maintain a current security status for one or more information systems or for the entire suite of information systems on which the operational mission of the enterprise depends. The process includes: 1) The development of a strategy to regularly evaluate selected IA controls/metrics, 2) Recording and evaluating IA relevant events and the effectiveness of the enterprise in dealing with those events, 3) Recording changes to IA controls, or changes that affect IA risks, and 4) Publishing the current security status to enable information-sharing decisions involving the enterprise.

SOURCE: CNSSI-4009

Maintaining ongoing awareness to support organizational risk decisions.

SOURCE: SP 800-137

Control Information –

Information that is entered into a cryptographic module for the purposes of directing the operation of the module.

SOURCE: FIPS 140-2

Controlled Access Area –

Physical area (e.g., building, room, etc.) to which only authorized personnel are granted unrestricted access. All other personnel are either escorted by authorized personnel or are under continuous surveillance.

SOURCE: CNSSI-4009

Controlled Access Protection –

Minimum set of security functionality that enforces access control on individual users and makes them accountable for their actions through login procedures, auditing of security-relevant events, and resource isolation.

SOURCE: CNSSI-4009

Controlled Area –	Any area or space for which the organization has confidence that the physical and procedural protections provided are sufficient to meet the requirements established for protecting the information and/or information system. SOURCE: SP 800-53
Controlled Cryptographic Item – (CCI)	Secure telecommunications or information system, or associated cryptographic component, that is unclassified and handled through the COMSEC Material Control System (CMCS), an equivalent material control system, or a combination of the two that provides accountability and visibility. Such items are marked "Controlled Cryptographic Item," or, where space is limited, "CCI". SOURCE: CNSSI-4009
Controlled Cryptographic Item (CCI) Assembly –	Device embodying a cryptographic logic or other COMSEC design that NSA has approved as a Controlled Cryptographic Item (CCI). It performs the entire COMSEC function, but depends upon the host equipment to operate. SOURCE: CNSSI-4009
Controlled Cryptographic Item (CCI) Component –	Part of a Controlled Cryptographic Item (CCI) that does not perform the entire COMSEC function but depends upon the host equipment, or assembly, to complete and operate the COMSEC function. SOURCE: CNSSI-4009
Controlled Cryptographic Item (CCI) Equipment –	Telecommunications or information handling equipment that embodies a Controlled Cryptographic Item (CCI) component or CCI assembly and performs the entire COMSEC function without dependence on host equipment to operate. SOURCE: CNSSI-4009
Controlled Interface –	A boundary with a set of mechanisms that enforces the security policies and controls the flow of information between interconnected information systems. SOURCE: CNSSI-4009; SP 800-37
Controlled Space –	Three-dimensional space surrounding information system equipment, within which unauthorized individuals are denied unrestricted access and are either escorted by authorized individuals or are under continuous physical or electronic surveillance. SOURCE: CNSSI-4009

Controlled Unclassified Information (CUI) –	A categorical designation that refers to unclassified information that does not meet the standards for National Security Classification under Executive Order 12958, as amended, but is (i) pertinent to the national interests of the United States or to the important interests of entities outside the federal government, and (ii) under law or policy requires protection from unauthorized disclosure, special handling safeguards, or prescribed limits on exchange or dissemination. Henceforth, the designation CUI replaces "Sensitive But Unclassified" (SBU). SOURCE: SP 800-53; SP 800-53A
Controlling Authority –	Official responsible for directing the operation of a cryptonet and for managing the operational use and control of keying material assigned to the cryptonet. SOURCE: CNSSI-4009
Cookie –	A piece of state information supplied by a Web server to a browser, in a response for a requested resource, for the browser to store temporarily and return to the server on any subsequent visits or requests. SOURCE: SP 800-28 Data exchanged between an HTTP server and a browser (a client of the server) to store state information on the client side and retrieve it later for server use. SOURCE: CNSSI-4009
Cooperative Key Generation –	Electronically exchanging functions of locally generated, random components, from which both terminals of a secure circuit construct traffic encryption key or key encryption key for use on that circuit. See Per-Call Key. SOURCE: CNSSI-4009
Cooperative Remote Rekeying –	Synonymous with manual remote rekeying. SOURCE: CNSSI-4009
Correctness Proof –	A mathematical proof of consistency between a specification and its implementation. SOURCE: CNSSI-4009
Counter with Cipher Block Chaining-Message Authentication Code (CCM) –	A mode of operation for a symmetric key block cipher algorithm. It combines the techniques of the Counter (CTR) mode and the Cipher Block Chaining-Message Authentication Code (CBC-MAC) algorithm to provide assurance of the confidentiality and the authenticity of computer data. SOURCE: SP 800-38C

Countermeasure –	Actions, devices, procedures, or techniques that meet or oppose (i.e., counters) a threat, a vulnerability, or an attack by eliminating or preventing it, by minimizing the harm it can cause, or by discovering and reporting it so that corrective action can be taken. SOURCE: CNSSI-4009
Countermeasures –	Actions, devices, procedures, techniques, or other measures that reduce the vulnerability of an information system. Synonymous with security controls and safeguards. SOURCE: SP 800-53; SP 800-37; FIPS 200
Cover-Coding –	A technique to reduce the risks of eavesdropping by obscuring the information that is transmitted. SOURCE: SP 800-98
Coverage –	An attribute associated with an assessment method that addresses the scope or breadth of the assessment objects included in the assessment (e.g., types of objects to be assessed and the number of objects to be assessed by type). The values for the coverage attribute, hierarchically from less coverage to more coverage, are basic, focused, and comprehensive. SOURCE: SP 800-53A
Covert Channel –	An unauthorized communication path that manipulates a communications medium in an unexpected, unconventional, or unforeseen way in order to transmit information without detection by anyone other than the entities operating the covert channel. SOURCE: CNSSI-4009
Covert Channel Analysis –	Determination of the extent to which the security policy model and subsequent lower-level program descriptions may allow unauthorized access to information. SOURCE: CNSSI-4009
Covert Storage Channel –	Covert channel involving the direct or indirect writing to a storage location by one process and the direct or indirect reading of the storage location by another process. Covert storage channels typically involve a finite resource (e.g., sectors on a disk) that is shared by two subjects at different security levels. SOURCE: CNSSI-4009
Covert Testing –	Testing performed using covert methods and without the knowledge of the organization's IT staff, but with the full knowledge and permission of upper management. SOURCE: SP 800-115

Covert Timing Channel –	Covert channel in which one process signals information to another process by modulating its own use of system resources (e.g., central processing unit time) in such a way that this manipulation affects the real response time observed by the second process. SOURCE: CNSSI-4009
Credential –	An object or data structure that authoritatively binds an identity (and optionally, additional attributes) to a token possessed and controlled by a Subscriber. SOURCE: SP 800-63 Evidence attesting to one's right to credit or authority. SOURCE: FIPS 201 Evidence or testimonials that support a claim of identity or assertion of an attribute and usually are intended to be used more than once. SOURCE: CNSSI-4009
Credential Service Provider – (CSP)	A trusted entity that issues or registers Subscriber tokens and issues electronic credentials to Subscribers. The CSP may encompass Registration Authorities (RAs) and Verifiers that it operates. A CSP may be an independent third party, or may issue credentials for its own use. SOURCE: SP 800-63
Critical Infrastructure –	System and assets, whether physical or virtual, so vital to the U.S. that the incapacity or destruction of such systems and assets would have a debilitating impact on security, national economic security, national public health or safety, or any combination of those matters. [Critical Infrastructures Protection Act of 2001, 42 U.S.C. 5195c(e)] SOURCE: CNSSI-4009
Critical Security Parameter (CSP) –	Security-related information (e.g., secret and private cryptographic keys, and authentication data such as passwords and Personal Identification Numbers [PINs]) whose disclosure or modification can compromise the security of a cryptographic module. SOURCE: FIPS 140-2; CNSSI-4009
Criticality –	A measure of the degree to which an organization depends on the information or information system for the success of a mission or of a business function. SOURCE: SP 800-60

Criticality Level –	Refers to the (consequences of) incorrect behavior of a system. The more serious the expected direct and indirect effects of incorrect behavior, the higher the criticality level. SOURCE: CNSSI-4009
Cross Site Scripting (XSS) –	A vulnerability that allows attackers to inject malicious code into an otherwise benign website. These scripts acquire the permissions of scripts generated by the target website and can therefore compromise the confidentiality and integrity of data transfers between the website and client. Websites are vulnerable if they display user supplied data from requests or forms without sanitizing the data so that it is not executable. SOURCE: SP 800-63
Cross-Certificate –	A certificate used to establish a trust relationship between two Certification Authorities. SOURCE: SP 800-32; CNSSI-4009
Cross-Domain Capabilities –	The set of functions that enable the transfer of information between security domains in accordance with the policies of the security domains involved. SOURCE: CNSSI-4009
Cross-Domain Solution (CDS) –	A form of controlled interface that provides the ability to manually and/or automatically access and/or transfer information between different security domains. SOURCE: CNSSI-4009; SP 800-37
Cryptanalysis –	1) Operations performed in defeating cryptographic protection without an initial knowledge of the key employed in providing the protection. 2) The study of mathematical techniques for attempting to defeat cryptographic techniques and information system security. This includes the process of looking for errors or weaknesses in the implementation of an algorithm or of the algorithm itself. SOURCE: SP 800-57 Part 1; CNSSI-4009
Crypto Officer –	An operator or process (subject), acting on behalf of the operator, performing cryptographic initialization or management functions. SOURCE: FIPS 140-2
Cryptographic –	Pertaining to, or concerned with, cryptography. SOURCE: CNSSI-4009

Cryptographic Alarm –	Circuit or device that detects failures or aberrations in the logic or operation of crypto-equipment. Crypto-alarm may inhibit transmission or may provide a visible and/or audible alarm. SOURCE: CNSSI-4009
Cryptographic Algorithm –	A well-defined computational procedure that takes variable inputs, including a cryptographic key, and produces an output. SOURCE: SP 800-21; CNSSI-4009
Cryptographic Ancillary Equipment –	Equipment designed specifically to facilitate efficient or reliable operation of cryptographic equipment, without performing cryptographic functions itself. SOURCE: CNSSI-4009
Cryptographic Binding –	Associating two or more related elements of information using cryptographic techniques. SOURCE: CNSSI-4009
Cryptographic Boundary –	An explicitly defined continuous perimeter that establishes the physical bounds of a cryptographic module and contains all the hardware, software, and/or firmware components of a cryptographic module. SOURCE: FIPS 140-2
Cryptographic Component –	Hardware or firmware embodiment of the cryptographic logic. A cryptographic component may be a modular assembly, a printed wiring assembly, a microcircuit, or a combination of these items. SOURCE: CNSSI-4009
Cryptographic Equipment –	Equipment that embodies a cryptographic logic. SOURCE: CNSSI-4009
Cryptographic Hash Function –	A function that maps a bit string of arbitrary length to a fixed length bit string. Approved hash functions satisfy the following properties: 1) (One-way) It is computationally infeasible to find any input which maps to any pre-specified output, and 2) (Collision resistant) It is computationally infeasible to find any two distinct inputs that map to the same output. SOURCE: SP 800-21
Cryptographic Ignition Key (CIK) –	Device or electronic key used to unlock the secure mode of crypto-equipment. SOURCE: CNSSI-4009

Cryptographic Initialization –	Function used to set the state of a cryptographic logic prior to key generation, encryption, or other operating mode. SOURCE: CNSSI-4009
Cryptographic Key –	A value used to control cryptographic operations, such as decryption, encryption, signature generation, or signature verification. SOURCE: SP 800-63 A binary string used as a secret parameter by a cryptographic algorithm. SOURCE: SP 800-108 A parameter used in conjunction with a cryptographic algorithm that determines the specific operation of that algorithm. SOURCE: FIPS 201; FIPS 198 A parameter used in conjunction with a cryptographic algorithm that determines • the transformation of plaintext data into ciphertext data, • the transformation of ciphertext data into plaintext data, • a digital signature computed from data, • the verification of a digital signature computed from data, • an authentication code computed from data, or • an exchange agreement of a shared secret. SOURCE: FIPS 140-2
Cryptographic Logic –	The embodiment of one (or more) cryptographic algorithm(s) along with alarms, checks, and other processes essential to effective and secure performance of the cryptographic process(es). SOURCE: CNSSI-4009
Cryptographic Material – (slang CRYPTO)	COMSEC material used to secure or authenticate information. SOURCE: CNSSI-4009
Cryptographic Module –	The set of hardware, software, firmware, or some combination thereof that implements cryptographic logic or processes, including cryptographic algorithms, and is contained within the cryptographic boundary of the module. SOURCE: SP 800-32; FIPS 196 The set of hardware, software, and/or firmware that implements Approved security functions (including cryptographic algorithms and key generation) and is contained within the cryptographic boundary. SOURCE: FIPS 140-2

Cryptographic Module Security Policy –	A precise specification of the security rules under which a cryptographic module will operate, including the rules derived from the requirements of this standard (FIPS 140-2) and additional rules imposed by the vendor. SOURCE: FIPS 140-2
Cryptographic Module Validation Program (CMVP) –	Validates cryptographic modules to Federal Information Processing Standard (FIPS) 140-2 and other cryptography-based standards. The CMVP is a joint effort between National Institute of Standards and Technology (NIST) and the Communications Security Establishment (CSE) of the government of Canada. Products validated as conforming to FIPS 140-2 are accepted by the federal agencies of both countries for the protection of sensitive information (United States) or Designated Information (Canada). The goal of the CMVP is to promote the use of validated cryptographic modules and provide federal agencies with a security metric to use in procuring equipment containing validated cryptographic modules. SOURCE: FIPS 140-2
Cryptographic Net –	Stations holding a common key. SOURCE: CNSSI-4009
Cryptographic Period –	Time span during which each key setting remains in effect. SOURCE: CNSSI-4009
Cryptographic Product –	A cryptographic key (public, private, or shared) or public key certificate, used for encryption, decryption, digital signature, or signature verification; and other items, such as compromised key lists (CKL) and certificate revocation lists (CRL), obtained by trusted means from the same source which validate the authenticity of keys or certificates. Protected software which generates or regenerates keys or certificates may also be considered a cryptographic product. SOURCE: CNSSI-4009
Cryptographic Randomization –	Function that randomly determines the transmit state of a cryptographic logic. SOURCE: CNSSI-4009
Cryptographic Security –	Component of COMSEC resulting from the provision of technically sound cryptographic systems and their proper use. SOURCE: CNSSI-4009
Cryptographic Strength –	A measure of the expected number of operations required to defeat a cryptographic mechanism. SOURCE: SP 800-63

Cryptographic Synchronization –	Process by which a receiving decrypting cryptographic logic attains the same internal state as the transmitting encrypting logic. SOURCE: CNSSI-4009
Cryptographic System –	Associated information assurance items interacting to provide a single means of encryption or decryption. SOURCE: CNSSI-4009
Cryptographic System Analysis –	Process of establishing the exploitability of a cryptographic system, normally by reviewing transmitted traffic protected or secured by the system under study. SOURCE: CNSSI-4009
Cryptographic System Evaluation –	Process of determining vulnerabilities of a cryptographic system and recommending countermeasures. SOURCE: CNSSI-4009
Cryptographic System Review –	Examination of a cryptographic system by the controlling authority ensuring its adequacy of design and content, continued need, and proper distribution. SOURCE: CNSSI-4009
Cryptographic System Survey –	Management technique in which actual holders of a cryptographic system express opinions on the system's suitability and provide usage information for technical evaluations. SOURCE: CNSSI-4009
Cryptographic Token –	A token where the secret is a cryptographic key. SOURCE: SP 800-63 A portable, user-controlled physical device (e.g., smart card or PCMCIA card) used to store cryptographic information and possibly also perform cryptographic functions. SOURCE: CNSSI-4009
Cryptography –	The discipline that embodies the principles, means, and methods for the transformation of data in order to hide their semantic content, prevent their unauthorized use, or prevent their undetected modification. SOURCE: SP 800-59 The discipline that embodies principles, means, and methods for providing information security, including confidentiality, data integrity, non-repudiation, and authenticity. SOURCE: SP 800-21

Is categorized as either secret key or public key. Secret key cryptography is based on the use of a single cryptographic key shared between two parties. The same key is used to encrypt and decrypt data. This key is kept secret by the two parties. Public key cryptography is a form of cryptography which makes use of two keys: a public key and a private key. The two keys are related but have the property that, given the public key, it is computationally infeasible to derive the private key [FIPS 140-1]. In a public key cryptosystem, each party has its own public/private key pair. The public key can be known by anyone; the private key is kept secret.

SOURCE: FIPS 191

Art or science concerning the principles, means, and methods for rendering plain information unintelligible and for restoring encrypted information to intelligible form.

SOURCE: CNSSI-4009

Cryptology –

The science that deals with hidden, disguised, or encrypted communications. It includes communications security and communications intelligence.

SOURCE: SP 800-60

The mathematical science that deals with cryptanalysis and cryptography.

SOURCE: CNSSI-4009

CVE –

See Common Vulnerabilities and Exposures.

Cyber Attack –

An attack, via cyberspace, targeting an enterprise's use of cyberspace for the purpose of disrupting, disabling, destroying, or maliciously controlling a computing environment/infrastructure; or destroying the integrity of the data or stealing controlled information.

SOURCE: CNSSI-4009

Cyber Incident –

Actions taken through the use of computer networks that result in an actual or potentially adverse effect on an information system and/or the information residing therein. See Incident.

SOURCE: CNSSI-4009

Cyber Infrastructure –	Includes electronic information and communications systems and services and the information contained in these systems and services. Information and communications systems and services are composed of all hardware and software that process, store, and communicate information, or any combination of all of these elements. Processing includes the creation, access, modification, and destruction of information. Storage includes paper, magnetic, electronic, and all other media types. Communications include sharing and distribution of information. For example: computer systems; control systems (e.g., supervisory control and data acquisition–SCADA); networks, such as the Internet; and cyber services (e.g., managed security services) are part of cyber infrastructure. SOURCE: NISTIR 7628
Cybersecurity –	The ability to protect or defend the use of cyberspace from cyber attacks. SOURCE: CNSSI-4009
Cyberspace –	A global domain within the information environment consisting of the interdependent network of information systems infrastructures including the Internet, telecommunications networks, computer systems, and embedded processors and controllers. SOURCE: CNSSI-4009
Cyclical Redundancy Check – (CRC)	A method to ensure data has not been altered after being sent through a communication channel. SOURCE: SP 800-72 Error checking mechanism that verifies data integrity by computing a polynomial algorithm based checksum. SOURCE: CNSSI-4009
Data –	A subset of information in an electronic format that allows it to be retrieved or transmitted. SOURCE: CNSSI-4009
Data Aggregation –	Compilation of individual data systems and data that could result in the totality of the information being classified, or classified at a higher level, or of beneficial use to an adversary. SOURCE: CNSSI-4009

Data Asset –	1. Any entity that is comprised of data. For example, a database is a data asset that is comprised of data records. A data asset may be a system or application output file, database, document, or Web page. A data asset also includes a service that may be provided to access data from an application. For example, a service that returns individual records from a database would be a data asset. Similarly, a Web site that returns data in response to specific queries (e.g., www.weather.com) would be a data asset.
	2. An information-based resource.
	SOURCE: CNSSI-4009
Data Element –	A basic unit of information that has a unique meaning and subcategories (data items) of distinct value. Examples of data elements include gender, race, and geographic location.
	SOURCE: SP 800-47; CNSSI-4009
Data Encryption Algorithm (DEA) –	The DEA cryptographic engine that is used by the Triple Data Encryption Algorithm (TDEA).
	SOURCE: SP 800-67
Data Encryption Standard (DES) –	Cryptographic algorithm designed for the protection of unclassified data and published by the National Institute of Standards and Technology (NIST) in Federal Information Processing Standard (FIPS) Publication 46. (FIPS 46-3 withdrawn 19 May 2005) See Triple DES.
	SOURCE: CNSSI-4009
Data Flow Control –	Synonymous with information flow control.
	SOURCE: CNSSI-4009
Data Integrity –	The property that data has not been altered in an unauthorized manner. Data integrity covers data in storage, during processing, and while in transit.
	SOURCE: SP 800-27
	The property that data has not been changed, destroyed, or lost in an unauthorized or accidental manner.
	SOURCE: CNSSI-4009
Data Loss –	The exposure of proprietary, sensitive, or classified information through either data theft or data leakage.
	SOURCE: SP 800-137

Data Origin Authentication –	The process of verifying that the source of the data is as claimed and that the data has not been modified.
	SOURCE: CNSSI-4009
Data Security –	Protection of data from unauthorized (accidental or intentional) modification, destruction, or disclosure.
	SOURCE: CNSSI-4009
Data Transfer Device (DTD) –	Fill device designed to securely store, transport, and transfer electronically both COMSEC and TRANSEC key, designed to be backward compatible with the previous generation of COMSEC common fill devices, and programmable to support modern mission systems.
	SOURCE: CNSSI-4009
Decertification –	Revocation of the certification of an information system item or equipment for cause.
	SOURCE: CNSSI-4009
Decipher –	Convert enciphered text to plain text by means of a cryptographic system.
	SOURCE: CNSSI-4009
Decode –	Convert encoded text to plain text by means of a code.
	SOURCE: CNSSI-4009
Decrypt –	Generic term encompassing decode and decipher.
	SOURCE: CNSSI-4009
Decryption –	The process of transforming ciphertext into plaintext.
	SOURCE: SP 800-67
	The process of changing ciphertext into plaintext using a cryptographic algorithm and key.
	SOURCE: SP 800-21
	Conversion of ciphertext to plaintext through the use of a cryptographic algorithm.
	SOURCE: FIPS 185

Dedicated Mode –	Information systems security mode of operation wherein each user, with direct or indirect access to the system, its peripherals, remote terminals, or remote hosts, has all of the following: 1. valid security clearance for all information within the system, 2. formal access approval and signed nondisclosure agreements for all the information stored and/or processed (including all compartments, subcompartments, and/or special access programs), and 3. valid need-to-know for all information contained within the information system. When in the dedicated security mode, a system is specifically and exclusively dedicated to and controlled for the processing of one particular type or classification of information, either for full-time operation or for a specified period of time.
	SOURCE: CNSSI-4009
Default Classification –	Classification reflecting the highest classification being processed in an information system. Default classification is included in the caution statement affixed to an object.
	SOURCE: CNSSI-4009
Defense-in-Breadth –	A planned, systematic set of multidisciplinary activities that seek to identify, manage, and reduce risk of exploitable vulnerabilities at every stage of the system, network, or sub-component life cycle (system, network, or product design and development; manufacturing; packaging; assembly; system integration; distribution; operations; maintenance; and retirement).
	SOURCE: CNSSI-4009
Defense-in-Depth –	Information security strategy integrating people, technology, and operations capabilities to establish variable barriers across multiple layers and dimensions of the organization.
	SOURCE: CNSSI-4009; SP 800-53
Degauss –	Procedure that reduces the magnetic flux to virtual zero by applying a reverse magnetizing field. Also called demagnetizing.
	SOURCE: CNSSI-4009
Delegated Development Program –	INFOSEC program in which the Director, NSA, delegates, on a case-by-case basis, the development and/or production of an entire telecommunications product, including the INFOSEC portion, to a lead department or agency.
	SOURCE: CNSSI-4009
Deleted File –	A file that has been logically, but not necessarily physically, erased from the operating system, perhaps to eliminate potentially incriminating evidence. Deleting files does not always necessarily eliminate the possibility of recovering all or part of the original data.
	SOURCE: SP 800-72

Demilitarized Zone (DMZ) –	An interface on a routing firewall that is similar to the interfaces found on the firewall's protected side. Traffic moving between the DMZ and other interfaces on the protected side of the firewall still goes through the firewall and can have firewall protection policies applied.
	SOURCE: SP 800-41
	A host or network segment inserted as a "neutral zone" between an organization's private network and the Internet.
	SOURCE: SP 800-45
	Perimeter network segment that is logically between internal and external networks. Its purpose is to enforce the internal network's Information Assurance policy for external information exchange and to provide external, untrusted sources with restricted access to releasable information while shielding the internal networks from outside attacks.
	SOURCE: CNSSI-4009
Denial of Service (DoS) –	The prevention of authorized access to resources or the delaying of time-critical operations. (Time-critical may be milliseconds or it may be hours, depending upon the service provided.)
	SOURCE: CNSSI-4009
Depth –	An attribute associated with an assessment method that addresses the rigor and level of detail associated with the application of the method. The values for the depth attribute, hierarchically from less depth to more depth, are basic, focused, and comprehensive.
	SOURCE: SP 800-53A
Descriptive Top-Level Specification (DTLS) –	A natural language descriptive of a system's security requirements, an informal design notation, or a combination of the two.
	SOURCE: CNSSI-4009
Designated Approval Authority – (DAA)	Official with the authority to formally assume responsibility for operating a system at an acceptable level of risk. This term is synonymous with authorizing official, designated accrediting authority, and delegated accrediting authority.
	SOURCE: CNSSI-4009
Designated Approving (Accrediting) Authority –	See Authorizing Official.

Deterministic Random Bit Generator (DRBG) –	A Random Bit Generator (RBG) that includes a DRBG mechanism and (at least initially) has access to a source of entropy input. The DRBG produces a sequence of bits from a secret initial value called a seed, along with other possible inputs. A DRBG is often called a Pseudorandom Number (or Bit) Generator. SOURCE: SP 800-90A
Deterministic Random Bit Generator (DRBG) Mechanism –	The portion of an RBG that includes the functions necessary to instantiate and uninstantiate the RBG, generate pseudorandom bits, (optionally) reseed the RBG and test the health of the DRBG mechanism. SOURCE: SP 800-90A
Device Distribution Profile –	An approval-based Access Control List (ACL) for a specific product that 1) names the user devices in a specific key management infrastructure (KMI) Operating Account (KOA) to which PRSNs distribute the product, and 2) states conditions of distribution for each device. SOURCE: CNSSI-4009
Device Registration Manager –	The management role that is responsible for performing activities related to registering users that are devices. SOURCE: CNSSI-4009
Dial Back –	Synonymous with call back. SOURCE: CNSSI-4009
Differential Power Analysis – (DPA)	An analysis of the variations of the electrical power consumption of a cryptographic module, using advanced statistical methods and/or other techniques, for the purpose of extracting information correlated to cryptographic keys used in a cryptographic algorithm. SOURCE: FIPS 140-2
Digital Evidence –	Electronic information stored or transferred in digital form. SOURCE: SP 800-72
Digital Forensics –	The application of science to the identification, collection, examination, and analysis of data while preserving the integrity of the information and maintaining a strict chain of custody for the data. SOURCE: SP 800-86
Digital Signature –	An asymmetric key operation where the private key is used to digitally sign data and the public key is used to verify the signature. Digital signatures provide authenticity protection, integrity protection, and non-repudiation. SOURCE: SP 800-63

A nonforgeable transformation of data that allows the proof of the source (with non-repudiation) and the verification of the integrity of that data.

SOURCE: FIPS 196

The result of a cryptographic transformation of data which, when properly implemented, provides the services of:
1. origin authentication,
2. data integrity, and
3. signer non-repudiation.

SOURCE: FIPS 140-2

The result of a cryptographic transformation of data that, when properly implemented, provides a mechanism for verifying origin authentication, data integrity, and signatory non-repudiation.

SOURCE: FIPS 186-3

The result of a cryptographic transformation of data that, when properly implemented, provides origin authentication, data integrity, and signatory non-repudiation.

SOURCE: SP 800-89

Cryptographic process used to assure data object originator authenticity, data integrity, and time stamping for prevention of replay.

SOURCE: CNSSI-4009

Digital Signature Algorithm –   Asymmetric algorithms used for digitally signing data.

SOURCE: SP 800-49

Direct Shipment –   Shipment of COMSEC material directly from NSA to user COMSEC accounts.

SOURCE: CNSSI-4009

Disaster Recovery Plan (DRP) –   A written plan for recovering one or more information systems at an alternate facility in response to a major hardware or software failure or destruction of facilities.

SOURCE: SP 800-34

Management policy and procedures used to guide an enterprise response to a major loss of enterprise capability or damage to its facilities. The DRP is the second plan needed by the enterprise risk managers and is used when the enterprise must recover (at its original facilities) from a loss of capability over a period of hours or days. See Continuity of Operations Plan and Contingency Plan.

SOURCE: CNSSI-4009

64

Disconnection –	The termination of an interconnection between two or more IT systems. A disconnection may be planned (e.g., due to changed business needs) or unplanned (i.e., due to an attack or other contingency). SOURCE: SP 800-47
Discretionary Access Control –	The basis of this kind of security is that an individual user, or program operating on the user's behalf, is allowed to specify explicitly the types of access other users (or programs executing on their behalf) may have to information under the user's control. SOURCE: FIPS 191 A means of restricting access to objects (e.g., files, data entities) based on the identity and need-to-know of subjects (e.g., users, processes) and/or groups to which the object belongs. The controls are discretionary in the sense that a subject with a certain access permission is capable of passing that permission (perhaps indirectly) on to any other subject (unless restrained by mandatory access control). SOURCE: CNSSI-4009
Disk Imaging –	Generating a bit-for-bit copy of the original media, including free space and slack space. SOURCE: SP 800-86
Disruption –	An unplanned event that causes the general system or major application to be inoperable for an unacceptable length of time (e.g., minor or extended power outage, extended unavailable network, or equipment or facility damage or destruction). SOURCE: CNSSI-4009 An unplanned event that causes an information system to be inoperable for a length of time (e.g., minor or extended power outage, extended unavailable network, or equipment or facility damage or destruction). SOURCE: SP 800-34
Distinguished Name (DN) –	A unique name or character string that unambiguously identifies an entity according to the hierarchical naming conventions of X.500 directory service. SOURCE: CNSSI-4009
Distinguishing Identifier –	Information which unambiguously distinguishes an entity in the authentication process. SOURCE: FIPS 196; CNSSI-4009

Distributed Denial of Service – (DDoS)	A Denial of Service technique that uses numerous hosts to perform the attack. SOURCE: CNSSI-4009
DMZ –	See Demilitarized Zone.
Domain –	A set of subjects, their information objects, and a common security policy. SOURCE: SP 800-27 An environment or context that includes a set of system resources and a set of system entities that have the right to access the resources as defined by a common security policy, security model, or security architecture. See Security Domain. SOURCE: CNSSI-4009; SP 800-53; SP 800-37
Drop Accountability –	Procedure under which a COMSEC account custodian initially receipts for COMSEC material, and provides no further accounting for it to its central office of record. Local accountability of the COMSEC material may continue to be required. See Accounting Legend Code. SOURCE: CNSSI-4009
Dual-Use Certificate –	A certificate that is intended for use with both digital signature and data encryption services. SOURCE: SP 800-32
Duplicate Digital Evidence –	A duplicate is an accurate digital reproduction of all data objects contained on the original physical item and associated media. SOURCE: SP 800-72
Duration –	A field within a certificate that is composed of two subfields; "date of issue" and "date of next issue." SOURCE: SP 800-32
Dynamic Subsystem –	A subsystem that is not continually present during the execution phase of an information system. Service-oriented architectures and cloud computing architectures are examples of architectures that employ dynamic subsystems. SOURCE: SP 800-37
E-Government (e-gov) –	The use by the U.S. government of Web-based Internet applications and other information technology. SOURCE: CNSSI-4009

Easter Egg –	Hidden functionality within an application program, which becomes activated when an undocumented, and often convoluted, set of commands and keystrokes are entered. Easter eggs are typically used to display the credits for the development team and are intended to be nonthreatening. SOURCE: SP 800-28
Eavesdropping Attack –	An attack in which an Attacker listens passively to the authentication protocol to capture information which can be used in a subsequent active attack to masquerade as the Claimant. SOURCE: SP 800-63
Education (Information Security) –	Education integrates all of the security skills and competencies of the various functional specialties into a common body of knowledge . . . and strives to produce IT security specialists and professionals capable of vision and proactive response. SOURCE: SP 800-50
Egress Filtering –	Filtering of outgoing network traffic. SOURCE: SP 800-41
Electronic Authentication – (E-authentication)	The process of establishing confidence in user identities electronically presented to an information system. SOURCE: SP 800-63; CNSSI-4009
Electronic Business (e-business) –	Doing business online. SOURCE: CNSSI-4009
Electronic Credentials –	Digital documents used in authentication that bind an identity or an attribute to a subscriber's token. SOURCE: CNSSI-4009
Electronic Evidence –	Information and data of investigative value that is stored on or transmitted by an electronic device. SOURCE: SP 800-72
Electronic Key Entry –	The entry of cryptographic keys into a cryptographic module using electronic methods such as a smart card or a key-loading device. (The operator of the key may have no knowledge of the value of the key being entered.) SOURCE: FIPS 140-2

Electronic Key Management System (EKMS) –	Interoperable collection of systems being developed by services and agencies of the U.S. government to automate the planning, ordering, generating, distributing, storing, filling, using, and destroying of electronic key and management of other types of COMSEC material. SOURCE: CNSSI-4009
Electronic Messaging Services –	Services providing interpersonal messaging capability; meeting specific functional, management, and technical requirements; and yielding a business-quality electronic mail service suitable for the conduct of official government business. SOURCE: CNSSI-4009
Electronic Signature –	The process of applying any mark in electronic form with the intent to sign a data object. See also Digital Signature. SOURCE: CNSSI-4009
Electronically Generated Key –	Key generated in a COMSEC device by introducing (either mechanically or electronically) a seed key into the device and then using the seed, together with a software algorithm stored in the device, to produce the desired key. SOURCE: CNSSI-4009
Emanations Security (EMSEC) –	Protection resulting from measures taken to deny unauthorized individuals information derived from intercept and analysis of compromising emissions from crypto-equipment or an information system. See TEMPEST. SOURCE: CNSSI-4009
Embedded Computer –	Computer system that is an integral part of a larger system. SOURCE: CNSSI-4009
Embedded Cryptographic System –	Cryptosystem performing or controlling a function as an integral element of a larger system or subsystem. SOURCE: CNSSI-4009
Embedded Cryptography –	Cryptography engineered into an equipment or system whose basic function is not cryptographic. SOURCE: CNSSI-4009
Encipher –	Convert plain text to cipher text by means of a cryptographic system. SOURCE: CNSSI-4009

Enclave –	Collection of information systems connected by one or more internal networks under the control of a single authority and security policy. The systems may be structured by physical proximity or by function, independent of location. SOURCE: CNSSI-4009
Enclave Boundary –	Point at which an enclave's internal network service layer connects to an external network's service layer, i.e., to another enclave or to a Wide Area Network (WAN). SOURCE: CNSSI-4009
Encode –	Convert plain text to cipher text by means of a code. SOURCE: CNSSI-4009
Encrypt –	Generic term encompassing encipher and encode. SOURCE: CNSSI-4009
Encrypted Key –	A cryptographic key that has been encrypted using an Approved security function with a key encrypting key, a PIN, or a password in order to disguise the value of the underlying plaintext key. SOURCE: FIPS 140-2
Encrypted Network –	A network on which messages are encrypted (e.g., using DES, AES, or other appropriate algorithms) to prevent reading by unauthorized parties. SOURCE: SP 800-32
Encryption –	Conversion of plaintext to ciphertext through the use of a cryptographic algorithm. SOURCE: FIPS 185 The process of changing plaintext into ciphertext for the purpose of security or privacy. SOURCE: SP 800-21; CNSSI-4009
Encryption Algorithm –	Set of mathematically expressed rules for rendering data unintelligible by executing a series of conversions controlled by a key. SOURCE: CNSSI-4009
Encryption Certificate –	A certificate containing a public key that is used to encrypt electronic messages, files, documents, or data transmissions, or to establish or exchange a session key for these same purposes. SOURCE: SP 800-32

End-Item Accounting –

Accounting for all the accountable components of a COMSEC equipment configuration by a single short title.

SOURCE: CNSSI-4009

End Cryptographic Unit (ECU) –

Device that (1) performs cryptographic functions, (2) typically is part of a larger system for which the device provides security services, and (3) from the viewpoint of a supporting security infrastructure (e.g., a key management system), is the lowest level of identifiable component with which a management transaction can be conducted.

SOURCE: CNSSI-4009

End-to-End Encryption –

Communications encryption in which data is encrypted when being passed through a network, but routing information remains visible.

SOURCE: SP 800-12

Encryption of information at its origin and decryption at its intended destination without intermediate decryption.

SOURCE: CNSSI-4009

End-to-End Security –

Safeguarding information in an information system from point of origin to point of destination.

SOURCE: CNSSI-4009

Enrollment Manager –

The management role that is responsible for assigning user identities to management and non-management roles.

SOURCE: CNSSI-4009

Enterprise –

An organization with a defined mission/goal and a defined boundary, using information systems to execute that mission, and with responsibility for managing its own risks and performance. An enterprise may consist of all or some of the following business aspects: acquisition, program management, financial management (e.g., budgets), human resources, security, and information systems, information and mission management.

SOURCE: CNSSI-4009

Enterprise Architecture (EA) –

The description of an enterprise's entire set of information systems: how they are configured, how they are integrated, how they interface to the external environment at the enterprise's boundary, how they are operated to support the enterprise mission, and how they contribute to the enterprise's overall security posture.

SOURCE: CNSSI-4009

Enterprise Risk Management –	The methods and processes used by an enterprise to manage risks to its mission and to establish the trust necessary for the enterprise to support shared missions. It involves the identification of mission dependencies on enterprise capabilities, the identification and prioritization of risks due to defined threats, the implementation of countermeasures to provide both a static risk posture and an effective dynamic response to active threats; and it assesses enterprise performance against threats and adjusts countermeasures as necessary.

SOURCE: CNSSI-4009 |
| Enterprise Service – | A set of one or more computer applications and middleware systems hosted on computer hardware that provides standard information systems capabilities to end users and hosted mission applications and services.

SOURCE: CNSSI-4009 |
| Entity – | Either a subject (an active element that operates on information or the system state) or an object (a passive element that contains or receives information).

SOURCE: SP 800-27

An active element in an open system.

SOURCE: FIPS 188

Any participant in an authentication exchange; such a participant may be human or nonhuman, and may take the role of a claimant and/or verifier.

SOURCE: FIPS 196 |
| Entrapment – | Deliberate planting of apparent flaws in an IS for the purpose of detecting attempted penetrations.

SOURCE: CNSSI-4009 |
| Entropy – | A measure of the amount of uncertainty that an Attacker faces to determine the value of a secret. Entropy is usually stated in bits.

SOURCE: SP 800-63 |
| Environment – | Aggregate of external procedures, conditions, and objects affecting the development, operation, and maintenance of an information system.

SOURCE: FIPS 200; CNSSI-4009 |

Environment of Operation –	The physical surroundings in which an information system processes, stores, and transmits information. SOURCE: SP 800-37; SP 800-53A The physical, technical, and organizational setting in which an information system operates, including but not limited to: missions/business functions; mission/business processes; threat space; vulnerabilities; enterprise and information security architectures; personnel; facilities; supply chain relationships; information technologies; organizational governance and culture; acquisition and procurement processes; organizational policies and procedures; organizational assumptions, constraints, risk tolerance, and priorities/trade-offs). SOURCE: SP 800-30
Ephemeral Key –	A cryptographic key that is generated for each execution of a key establishment process and that meets other requirements of the key type (e.g., unique to each message or session). In some cases, ephemeral keys are used more than once within a single session (e.g., broadcast applications) where the sender generates only one ephemeral key pair per message, and the private key is combined separately with each recipient's public key. SOURCE: SP 800-57 Part 1
Erasure –	Process intended to render magnetically stored information irretrievable by normal means. SOURCE: CNSSI-4009
Error Detection Code –	A code computed from data and comprised of redundant bits of information designed to detect, but not correct, unintentional changes in the data. SOURCE: FIPS 140-2; CNSSI-4009
Escrow –	Something (e.g., a document, an encryption key) that is "delivered to a third person to be given to the grantee only upon the fulfillment of a condition." SOURCE: FIPS 185
Evaluation Products List (EPL) –	List of validated products that have been successfully evaluated under the National Information Assurance Partnership (NIAP) Common Criteria Evaluation and Validation Scheme (CCEVS). SOURCE: CNSSI-4009
Evaluation Assurance Level (EAL) –	Set of assurance requirements that represent a point on the Common Criteria predefined assurance scale. SOURCE: CNSSI-4009

Event –

Any observable occurrence in a network or system.

SOURCE: SP 800-61

Any observable occurrence in a system and/or network. Events sometimes provide indication that an incident is occurring.

SOURCE: CNSSI-4009

Examination –

A technical review that makes the evidence visible and suitable for analysis; tests performed on the evidence to determine the presence or absence of specific data.

SOURCE: SP 800-72

Examine –

A type of assessment method that is characterized by the process of checking, inspecting, reviewing, observing, studying, or analyzing one or more assessment objects to facilitate understanding, achieve clarification, or obtain evidence, the results of which are used to support the determination of security control effectiveness over time.

SOURCE: SP 800-53A

Exculpatory Evidence –

Evidence that tends to decrease the likelihood of fault or guilt.

SOURCE: SP 800-72

Executive Agency –

An executive department specified in 5 United States Code (U.S.C.), Sec. 101; a military department specified in 5 U.S.C., Sec. 102; an independent establishment as defined in 5 U.S.C., Sec. 104(1); and a wholly owned government corporation fully subject to the provisions of 31 U.S.C., Chapter 91.

SOURCE: SP 800-53; SP 800-37; FIPS 200; FIPS 199; 41 U.S.C., Sec. 403; CNSSI-4009

Exercise Key –

Cryptographic key material used exclusively to safeguard communications transmitted over-the-air during military or organized civil training exercises.

SOURCE: CNSSI-4009

Expected Output –

Any data collected from monitoring and assessments as part of the Information Security Continuous Monitoring (ISCM) strategy.

SOURCE: SP 800-137

Exploit Code –

A program that allows attackers to automatically break into a system.

SOURCE: SP 800-40

Exploitable Channel –	Channel that allows the violation of the security policy governing an information system and is usable or detectable by subjects external to the trusted computing base. See Covert Channel. SOURCE: CNSSI-4009
Extensible Configuration Checklist Description Format (XCCDF) –	SCAP language for specifying checklists and reporting checklist results. SOURCE: SP 800-128
External Information System (or Component) –	An information system or component of an information system that is outside of the authorization boundary established by the organization and for which the organization typically has no direct control over the application of required security controls or the assessment of security control effectiveness. SOURCE: SP 800-37; SP 800-53; CNSSI-4009
External Information System Service –	An information system service that is implemented outside of the authorization boundary of the organizational information system (i.e., a service that is used by, but not a part of, the organizational information system) and for which the organization typically has no direct control over the application of required security controls or the assessment of security control effectiveness. SOURCE: SP 800-53; SP 800-37; CNSSI-4009
External Information System Service Provider –	A provider of external information system services to an organization through a variety of consumer-producer relationships, including but not limited to: joint ventures; business partnerships; outsourcing arrangements (i.e., through contracts, interagency agreements, lines of business arrangements); licensing agreements; and/or supply chain exchanges. SOURCE: SP 800-37; SP 800-53
External Network –	A network not controlled by the organization. SOURCE: SP 800-53; CNSSI-4009
External Security Testing –	Security testing conducted from outside the organization's security perimeter. SOURCE: SP 800-115
Extraction Resistance –	Capability of crypto-equipment or secure telecommunications equipment to resist efforts to extract key. SOURCE: CNSSI-4009

Extranet –	A private network that uses Web technology, permitting the sharing of portions of an enterprise's information or operations with suppliers, vendors, partners, customers, or other enterprises. SOURCE: CNSSI-4009
Fail Safe –	Automatic protection of programs and/or processing systems when hardware or software failure is detected. SOURCE: CNSSI-4009
Fail Soft –	Selective termination of affected nonessential processing when hardware or software failure is determined to be imminent. SOURCE: CNSSI-4009
Failover –	The capability to switch over automatically (typically without human intervention or warning) to a redundant or standby information system upon the failure or abnormal termination of the previously active system. SOURCE: SP 800-53; CNSSI-4009
Failure Access –	Type of incident in which unauthorized access to data results from hardware or software failure. SOURCE: CNSSI-4009
Failure Control –	Methodology used to detect imminent hardware or software failure and provide fail safe or fail soft recovery. SOURCE: CNSSI-4009
False Acceptance –	When a biometric system incorrectly identifies an individual or incorrectly verifies an impostor against a claimed identity SOURCE: SP 800-76 In biometrics, the instance of a security system incorrectly verifying or identifying an unauthorized person. It typically is considered the most serious of biometric security errors as it gives unauthorized users access to systems that expressly are trying to keep them out. SOURCE: CNSSI-4009
False Acceptance Rate (FAR) –	The probability that a biometric system will incorrectly identify an individual or will fail to reject an impostor. The rate given normally assumes passive impostor attempts. SOURCE: SP 800-76

The measure of the likelihood that the biometric security system will incorrectly accept an access attempt by an unauthorized user. A system's false acceptance rate typically is stated as the ratio of the number of false acceptances divided by the number of identification attempts.

SOURCE: CNSSI-4009

False Positive –

An alert that incorrectly indicates that malicious activity is occurring.

SOURCE: SP 800-61

False Rejection –

When a biometric system fails to identify an applicant or fails to verify the legitimate claimed identity of an applicant.

SOURCE: SP 800-76

In biometrics, the instance of a security system failing to verify or identify an authorized person. It does not necessarily indicate a flaw in the biometric system; for example, in a fingerprint-based system, an incorrectly aligned finger on the scanner or dirt on the scanner can result in the scanner misreading the fingerprint, causing a false rejection of the authorized user.

SOURCE: CNSSI-4009

False Rejection Rate (FRR) –

The probability that a biometric system will fail to identify an applicant, or verify the legitimate claimed identity of an applicant.

SOURCE: SP 800-76

The measure of the likelihood that the biometric security system will incorrectly reject an access attempt by an authorized user. A system's false rejection rate typically is stated as the ratio of the number of false rejections divided by the number of identification attempts.

SOURCE: CNSSI-4009

Federal Agency –

See Agency, See Executive Agency.

Federal Bridge Certification Authority (FBCA) –

The Federal Bridge Certification Authority consists of a collection of Public Key Infrastructure components (Certificate Authorities, Directories, Certificate Policies and Certificate Practice Statements) that are used to provide peer-to-peer interoperability among Agency Principal Certification Authorities.

SOURCE: SP 800-32; CNSSI-4009

Federal Bridge Certification Authority Membrane –	The Federal Bridge Certification Authority Membrane consists of a collection of Public Key Infrastructure components including a variety of Certification Authority PKI products, Databases, CA specific Directories, Border Directory, Firewalls, Routers, Randomizers, etc. SOURCE: SP 800-32
Federal Bridge Certification Authority Operational Authority –	The Federal Bridge Certification Authority Operational Authority is the organization selected by the Federal Public Key Infrastructure Policy Authority to be responsible for operating the Federal Bridge Certification Authority. SOURCE: SP 800-32
Federal Enterprise Architecture –	A business-based framework for governmentwide improvement developed by the Office of Management and Budget that is intended to facilitate efforts to transform the federal government to one that is citizen-centered, results-oriented, and market-based. SOURCE: SP 800-53; SP 800-18; SP 800-60; CNSSI-4009
Federal Information Processing Standard (FIPS) –	A standard for adoption and use by federal departments and agencies that has been developed within the Information Technology Laboratory and published by the National Institute of Standards and Technology, a part of the U.S. Department of Commerce. A FIPS covers some topic in information technology in order to achieve a common level of quality or some level of interoperability. SOURCE: FIPS 201
Federal Information Security Management Act (FISMA) –	A statute (Title III, P.L. 107-347) that requires agencies to assess risk to information systems and provide information security protections commensurate with the risk. FISMA also requires that agencies integrate information security into their capital planning and enterprise architecture processes, conduct annual information systems security reviews of all programs and systems, and report the results of those reviews to OMB. SOURCE: CNSSI-4009 Title III of the E-Government Act requiring each federal agency to develop, document, and implement an agency-wide program to provide information security for the information and information systems that support the operations and assets of the agency, including those provided or managed by another agency, contractor, or other source. SOURCE: SP 800-63

Federal Information System –	An information system used or operated by an executive agency, by a contractor of an executive agency, or by another organization on behalf of an executive agency. SOURCE: SP 800-53; FIPS 200; FIPS 199; 40 U.S.C., Sec. 11331; CNSSI-4009
Federal Information Systems Security Educators' Association – (FISSEA)	An organization whose members come from federal agencies, industry, and academic institutions devoted to improving the IT security awareness and knowledge within the federal government and its related external workforce. SOURCE: SP 800-16
Federal Public Key Infrastructure Policy Authority (FPKI PA) –	The Federal PKI Policy Authority is a federal government body responsible for setting, implementing, and administering policy decisions regarding interagency PKI interoperability that uses the FBCA. SOURCE: SP 800-32
File Encryption –	The process of encrypting individual files on a storage medium and permitting access to the encrypted data only after proper authentication is provided. SOURCE: SP 800-111
File Name Anomaly –	1. A mismatch between the internal file header and its external extension; or 2. A file name inconsistent with the content of the file (e.g., renaming a graphics file with a non-graphical extension. SOURCE: SP 800-72
File Protection –	Aggregate of processes and procedures designed to inhibit unauthorized access, contamination, elimination, modification, or destruction of a file or any of its contents. SOURCE: CNSSI-4009
File Security –	Means by which access to computer files is limited to authorized users only. SOURCE: CNSSI-4009
Fill Device –	COMSEC item used to transfer or store key in electronic form or to insert key into cryptographic equipment. SOURCE: CNSSI-4009
FIPS –	See Federal Information Processing Standard.

FIPS-Approved Security Method –	A security method (e.g., cryptographic algorithm, cryptographic key generation algorithm or key distribution technique, random number generator, authentication technique, or evaluation criteria) that is either a) specified in a FIPS, or b) adopted in a FIPS.
	SOURCE: FIPS 196
FIPS-Validated Cryptography –	A cryptographic module validated by the Cryptographic Module Validation Program (CMVP) to meet requirements specified in FIPS 140-2 (as amended). As a prerequisite to CMVP validation, the cryptographic module is required to employ a cryptographic algorithm implementation that has successfully passed validation testing by the Cryptographic Algorithm Validation Program (CAVP). See NSA-Approved Cryptography.
	SOURCE: SP 800-53
FIPS PUB –	An acronym for Federal Information Processing Standards Publication. FIPS publications (PUB) are issued by NIST after approval by the Secretary of Commerce.
	SOURCE: SP 800-64
FIREFLY –	Key management protocol based on public key cryptography.
	SOURCE: CNSSI-4009
Firewall –	A gateway that limits access between networks in accordance with local security policy.
	SOURCE: SP 800-32
	A hardware/software capability that limits access between networks and/or systems in accordance with a specific security policy.
	SOURCE: CNSSI-4009
	A device or program that controls the flow of network traffic between networks or hosts that employ differing security postures.
	SOURCE: SP 800-41
Firewall Control Proxy –	The component that controls a firewall's handling of a call. The firewall control proxy can instruct the firewall to open specific ports that are needed by a call, and direct the firewall to close these ports at call termination.
	SOURCE: SP 800-58
Firmware –	The programs and data components of a cryptographic module that are stored in hardware within the cryptographic boundary and cannot be dynamically written or modified during execution.
	SOURCE: FIPS 140-2

Computer programs and data stored in hardware - typically in read-only memory (ROM) or programmable read-only memory (PROM) - such that the programs and data cannot be dynamically written or modified during execution of the programs.

SOURCE: CNSSI-4009

FISMA –

See Federal Information Security Management Act.

Fixed COMSEC Facility –

COMSEC facility located in an immobile structure or aboard a ship.

SOURCE: CNSSI-4009

Flaw –

Error of commission, omission, or oversight in an information system that may allow protection mechanisms to be bypassed.

SOURCE: CNSSI-4009

Flaw Hypothesis Methodology –

System analysis and penetration technique in which the specification and documentation for an information system are analyzed to produce a list of hypothetical flaws. This list is prioritized on the basis of the estimated probability that a flaw exists, on the ease of exploiting it, and on the extent of control or compromise it would provide. The prioritized list is used to perform penetration testing of a system.

SOURCE: CNSSI-4009

Flooding –

An attack that attempts to cause a failure in a system by providing more input than the system can process properly.

SOURCE: CNSSI-4009

Focused Testing –

A test methodology that assumes some knowledge of the internal structure and implementation detail of the assessment object. Also known as gray box testing.

SOURCE: SP 800-53A

Forensic Copy –

An accurate bit-for-bit reproduction of the information contained on an electronic device or associated media, whose validity and integrity has been verified using an accepted algorithm.

SOURCE: SP 800-72; CNSSI-4009

Forensic Specialist –

A professional who locates, identifies, collects, analyzes, and examines data while preserving the integrity and maintaining a strict chain of custody of information discovered.

SOURCE: SP 800-72

Forensics –	The practice of gathering, retaining, and analyzing computer-related data for investigative purposes in a manner that maintains the integrity of the data. SOURCE: CNSSI-4009 See Also Computer Forensics.
Forensically Clean –	Digital media that is completely wiped of all data, including nonessential and residual data, scanned for malware, and verified before use. SOURCE: SP 800-86
Formal Access Approval –	A formalization of the security determination for authorizing access to a specific type of classified or sensitive information, based on specified access requirements, a determination of the individual's security eligibility and a determination that the individual's official duties require the individual be provided access to the information. SOURCE: CNSSI-4009
Formal Development Methodology –	Software development strategy that proves security design specifications. SOURCE: CNSSI-4009
Formal Method –	Mathematical argument which verifies that the system satisfies a mathematically-described security policy. SOURCE: CNSSI-4009
Formal Proof –	Complete and convincing mathematical argument presenting the full logical justification for each proof step and for the truth of a theorem or set of theorems. SOURCE: CNSSI-4009
Formal Security Policy –	Mathematically-precise statement of a security policy. SOURCE: CNSSI-4009
Formatting Function –	The function that transforms the payload, associated data, and nonce into a sequence of complete blocks. SOURCE: SP 800-38C
Forward Cipher –	One of the two functions of the block cipher algorithm that is determined by the choice of a cryptographic key. The term "forward cipher operation" is used for TDEA, while the term "forward transformation" is used for DEA. SOURCE: SP 800-67

Frequency Hopping –

Repeated switching of frequencies during radio transmission according to a specified algorithm, to minimize unauthorized interception or jamming of telecommunications.

SOURCE: CNSSI-4009

Full Disk Encryption (FDE) –

The process of encrypting all the data on the hard disk drive used to boot a computer, including the computer's operating system, and permitting access to the data only after successful authentication with the full disk encryption product.

SOURCE: SP 800-111

Full Maintenance –

Complete diagnostic repair, modification, and overhaul of COMSEC equipment, including repair of defective assemblies by piece part replacement. See Limited Maintenance.

SOURCE: CNSSI-4009

Functional Testing –

Segment of security testing in which advertised security mechanisms of an information system are tested under operational conditions.

SOURCE: CNSSI-4009

Gateway –

Interface providing compatibility between networks by converting transmission speeds, protocols, codes, or security measures.

SOURCE: CNSSI-4009

General Support System –

An interconnected set of information resources under the same direct management control that shares common functionality. It normally includes hardware, software, information, data, applications, communications, and people.

SOURCE: OMB Circular A-130, App. III

An interconnected set of information resources under the same direct management control which shares common functionality. A system normally includes hardware, software, information, data, applications, communications, and people. A system can be, for example, a local area network (LAN) including smart terminals that supports a branch office, an agency-wide backbone, a communications network, a departmental data processing center including its operating system and utilities, a tactical radio network, or a shared information processing service organization (IPSO).

SOURCE: CNSSI-4009

Global Information Grid (GIG) –

The globally interconnected, end-to-end set of information capabilities for collecting, processing, storing, disseminating, and managing information on demand to warfighters, policy makers, and support personnel. The GIG includes owned and leased communications and computing systems and services, software (including applications), data, security services, other associated services, and National Security Systems. Non-GIG IT includes stand-alone, self-contained, or embedded IT that is not, and will not be, connected to the enterprise network.

SOURCE: CNSSI-4009

Global Information Infrastructure – (GII)

Worldwide interconnections of the information systems of all countries, international and multinational organizations, and international commercial communications.

SOURCE: CNSSI-4009

Graduated Security –

A security system that provides several levels (e.g., low, moderate, high) of protection based on threats, risks, available technology, support services, time, human concerns, and economics.

SOURCE: FIPS 201

Gray Box Testing –

See Focused Testing.

Group Authenticator –

Used, sometimes in addition to a sign-on authenticator, to allow access to specific data or functions that may be shared by all members of a particular group.

SOURCE: CNSSI-4009

Guard (System) –

A mechanism limiting the exchange of information between information systems or subsystems.

SOURCE: CNSSI-4009

Guessing Entropy –

A measure of the difficulty that an Attacker has to guess the average password used in a system. In this document, entropy is stated in bits. When a password has n-bits of guessing entropy then an attacker has as much difficulty guessing the average password as in guessing an n-bit random quantity. The attacker is assumed to know the actual password frequency distribution.

SOURCE: SP 800-63

Hacker –

Unauthorized user who attempts to or gains access to an information system.

SOURCE: CNSSI-4009

| Handshaking Procedures – | Dialogue between two information systems for synchronizing, identifying, and authenticating themselves to one another. |
| | SOURCE: CNSSI-4009 |

| Hard Copy Key – | Physical keying material, such as printed key lists, punched or printed key tapes, or programmable, read-only memories (PROM). |
| | SOURCE: CNSSI-4009 |

| Hardening – | Configuring a host's operating systems and applications to reduce the host's security weaknesses. |
| | SOURCE: SP 800-123 |

| Hardware – | The physical components of an information system. See also Software and Firmware. |
| | SOURCE: CNSSI-4009 |

| Hardwired Key – | Permanently installed key. |
| | SOURCE: CNSSI-4009 |

Hash Function –	A function that maps a bit string of arbitrary length to a fixed length bit string. Approved hash functions satisfy the following properties: 1) One-Way. It is computationally infeasible to find any input that maps to any prespecified output. 2) Collision Resistant. It is computationally infeasible to find any two distinct inputs that map to the same output.
	SOURCE: SP 800-63; FIPS 201
	A mathematical function that maps a string of arbitrary length (up to a predetermined maximum size) to a fixed length string.
	SOURCE: FIPS 198
	A function that maps a bit string of arbitrary length to a fixed length bit string. Approved hash functions are specified in FIPS 180 and are designed to satisfy the following properties: 1. (One-way) It is computationally infeasible to find any input that maps to any new prespecified output, and 2. (Collision resistant) It is computationally infeasible to find any two distinct inputs that map to the same output.
	SOURCE: FIPS 186

| Hash Total – | Value computed on data to detect error or manipulation. See Checksum. |
| | SOURCE: CNSSI-4009 |

Hash Value –	The result of applying a cryptographic hash function to data (e.g., a message). SOURCE: SP 800-106
Hash Value/Result –	See Message Digest. SOURCE: FIPS 186; CNSSI-4009
Hash-based Message Authentication Code (HMAC) –	A message authentication code that uses a cryptographic key in conjunction with a hash function. SOURCE: FIPS 201; CNSSI-4009 A message authentication code that utilizes a keyed hash. SOURCE: FIPS 140-2
Hashing –	The process of using a mathematical algorithm against data to produce a numeric value that is representative of that data. SOURCE: SP 800-72; CNSSI-4009
Hashword –	Memory address containing hash total. SOURCE: CNSSI-4009
Health Information Exchange – (HIE)	A health information organization that brings together healthcare stakeholders within a defined geographic area and governs health information exchange among them for the purpose of improving health and care in that community. SOURCE: NISTIR-7497
High Assurance Guard (HAG) –	An enclave boundary protection device that controls access between a local area network that an enterprise system has a requirement to protect, and an external network that is outside the control of the enterprise system, with a high degree of assurance. SOURCE: SP 800-32 A guard that has two basic functional capabilities: a Message Guard and a Directory Guard. The Message Guard provides filter service for message traffic traversing the Guard between adjacent security domains. The Directory Guard provides filter service for directory access and updates traversing the Guard between adjacent security domains. SOURCE: CNSSI-4009
High Availability –	A failover feature to ensure availability during device or component interruptions. SOURCE: SP 800-113

85

High Impact –

The loss of confidentiality, integrity, or availability that could be expected to have a severe or catastrophic adverse effect on organizational operations, organizational assets, individuals, other organizations, or the national security interests of the United States; (i.e., 1) causes a severe degradation in mission capability to an extent and duration that the organization is able to perform its primary functions, but the effectiveness of the functions is significantly reduced; 2) results in major damage to organizational assets; 3) results in major financial loss; or 4) results in severe or catastrophic harm to individuals involving loss of life or serious life threatening injuries).

SOURCE: FIPS 199; CNSSI-4009

High-Impact System –

An information system in which at least one security objective (i.e., confidentiality, integrity, or availability) is assigned a FIPS 199 potential impact value of high.

SOURCE: SP 800-37; SP 800-53; SP 800-60; FIPS 200

An information system in which at least one security objective (i.e., confidentiality, integrity, or availability) is assigned a potential impact value of high.

SOURCE: CNSSI-4009

Honeypot –

A system (e.g., a Web server) or system resource (e.g., a file on a server) that is designed to be attractive to potential crackers and intruders and has no authorized users other than its administrators.

SOURCE: CNSSI-4009

Hot Site –

A fully operational offsite data processing facility equipped with hardware and software, to be used in the event of an information system disruption.

SOURCE: SP 800-34

Backup site that includes phone systems with the phone lines already connected. Networks will also be in place, with any necessary routers and switches plugged in and turned on. Desks will have desktop PCs installed and waiting, and server areas will be replete with the necessary hardware to support business-critical functions. Within a few hours, a hot site can become a fully functioning element of an organization.

SOURCE: CNSSI-4009

Hot Wash –

A debrief conducted immediately after an exercise or test with the staff and participants.

SOURCE: SP 800-84

Hybrid Security Control –	A security control that is implemented in an information system in part as a common control and in part as a system-specific control. See also Common Control and System-Specific Security Control.
	SOURCE: SP 800-37; SP 800-53; SP 800-53A; CNSSI-4009
IA Architecture –	A description of the structure and behavior for an enterprise's security processes, information security systems, personnel and organizational sub-units, showing their alignment with the enterprise's mission and strategic plans.
	SOURCE: CNSSI-4009
IA Infrastructure –	The underlying security framework that lies beyond an enterprise's defined boundary, but supports its IA and IA-enabled products, its security posture and its risk management plan.
	SOURCE: CNSSI-4009
IA Product –	Product whose primary purpose is to provide security services (e.g., confidentiality, authentication, integrity, access control, non-repudiation of data); correct known vulnerabilities; and/or provide layered defense against various categories of non-authorized or malicious penetrations of information systems or networks.
	SOURCE: CNSSI-4009
IA-Enabled Information Technology Product –	Product or technology whose primary role is not security, but which provides security services as an associated feature of its intended operating capabilities. Examples include such products as security-enabled Web browsers, screening routers, trusted operating systems, and security-enabled messaging systems.
	SOURCE: CNSSI-4009
IA-Enabled Product –	Product whose primary role is not security, but provides security services as an associated feature of its intended operating capabilities.
	Note: Examples include such products as security-enabled Web browsers, screening routers, trusted operating systems, and security enabling messaging systems.
	SOURCE: CNSSI-4009
Identification –	The process of verifying the identity of a user, process, or device, usually as a prerequisite for granting access to resources in an IT system.
	SOURCE: SP 800-47

The process of discovering the true identity (i.e., origin, initial history) of a person or item from the entire collection of similar persons or items.

SOURCE: FIPS 201

An act or process that presents an identifier to a system so that the system can recognize a system entity (e.g., user, process, or device) and distinguish that entity from all others.

SOURCE: CNSSI-4009

Identifier –

Unique data used to represent a person's identity and associated attributes. A name or a card number are examples of identifiers.

SOURCE: FIPS 201

A data object - often, a printable, non-blank character string - that definitively represents a specific identity of a system entity, distinguishing that identity from all others.

SOURCE: CNSSI-4009

Identity –

A set of attributes that uniquely describe a person within a given context.

SOURCE: SP 800-63

The set of physical and behavioral characteristics by which an individual is uniquely recognizable.

SOURCE: FIPS 201

The set of attribute values (i.e., characteristics) by which an entity is recognizable and that, within the scope of an identity manager's responsibility, is sufficient to distinguish that entity from any other entity.

SOURCE: CNSSI-4009

Identity-Based Access Control –

Access control based on the identity of the user (typically relayed as a characteristic of the process acting on behalf of that user) where access authorizations to specific objects are assigned based on user identity.

SOURCE: SP 800-53; CNSSI-4009

Identity-Based Security Policy –

A security policy based on the identities and/or attributes of the object (system resource) being accessed and of the subject (user, group of users, process, or device) requesting access.

SOURCE: SP 800-33

Identity Binding –	Binding of the vetted claimed identity to the individual (through biometrics) according to the issuing authority.
	SOURCE: FIPS 201
Identity Proofing –	The process by which a Credentials Service Provider (CSP) and a Registration Authority (RA) collect and verify information about a person for the purpose of issuing credentials to that person. SOURCE: SP 800-63
	The process of providing sufficient information (e.g., identity history, credentials, documents) to a Personal Identity Verification Registrar when attempting to establish an identity.
	SOURCE: FIPS 201
Identity Registration –	The process of making a person's identity known to the Personal Identity Verification (PIV) system, associating a unique identifier with that identity, and collecting and recording the person's relevant attributes into the system.
	SOURCE: FIPS 201; CNSSI-4009
Identity Token –	Smart card, metal key, or other physical object used to authenticate identity.
	SOURCE: CNSSI-4009
Identity Validation –	Tests enabling an information system to authenticate users or resources.
	SOURCE: CNSSI-4009
Identity Verification –	The process of confirming or denying that a claimed identity is correct by comparing the credentials (something you know, something you have, something you are) of a person requesting access with those previously proven and stored in the PIV Card of system and associated with the identity being claimed.
	SOURCE: FIPS 201
	The process of confirming or denying that a claimed identity is correct by comparing the credentials (something you know, something you have, something you are) of a person requesting access with those previously proven and stored in the PIV Card or system and associated with the identity being claimed.
	SOURCE: SP 800-79

Image –	An exact bit-stream copy of all electronic data on a device, performed in a manner that ensures that the information is not altered.
	SOURCE: SP 800-72
Imitative Communications Deception –	Introduction of deceptive messages or signals into an adversary's telecommunications signals. See also Communications Deception and Manipulative Communications Deception.
	SOURCE: CNSSI-4009
Impact –	The magnitude of harm that can be expected to result from the consequences of unauthorized disclosure of information, unauthorized modification of information, unauthorized destruction of information, or loss of information or information system availability.
	SOURCE: SP 800-60
Impact Level –	The magnitude of harm that can be expected to result from the consequences of unauthorized disclosure of information, unauthorized modification of information, unauthorized destruction of information, or loss of information or information system availability.
	SOURCE: CNSSI-4009
	High, Moderate, or Low security categories of an information system established in FIPS 199 which classify the intensity of a potential impact that may occur if the information system is jeopardized.
	SOURCE: SP 800-34
Impact Value –	The assessed potential impact resulting from a compromise of the confidentiality, integrity, or availability of an information type, expressed as a value of low, moderate, or high.
	SOURCE: SP 800-30
Implant –	Electronic device or electronic equipment modification designed to gain unauthorized interception of information-bearing emanations.
	SOURCE: CNSSI-4009
Inadvertent Disclosure –	Type of incident involving accidental exposure of information to an individual not authorized access.
	SOURCE: CNSSI-4009
Incident –	A violation or imminent threat of violation of computer security policies, acceptable use policies, or standard security practices.
	SOURCE: SP 800-61

An occurrence that actually or potentially jeopardizes the confidentiality, integrity, or availability of an information system or the information the system processes, stores, or transmits or that constitutes a violation or imminent threat of violation of security policies, security procedures, or acceptable use policies.

SOURCE: FIPS 200; SP 800-53

An assessed occurrence that actually or potentially jeopardizes the confidentiality, integrity, or availability of an information system; or the information the system processes, stores, or transmits; or that constitutes a violation or imminent threat of violation of security policies, security procedures, or acceptable use policies.

SOURCE: CNSSI-4009

Incident Handling –

The mitigation of violations of security policies and recommended practices.

SOURCE: SP 800-61

Incident Response Plan –

The documentation of a predetermined set of instructions or procedures to detect, respond to, and limit consequences of a malicious cyber attacks against an organization's information system(s).

SOURCE: SP 800-34

The documentation of a predetermined set of instructions or procedures to detect, respond to, and limit consequences of an incident against an organization's IT system(s).

SOURCE: CNSSI-4009

Incomplete Parameter Checking –

System flaw that exists when the operating system does not check all parameters fully for accuracy and consistency, thus making the system vulnerable to penetration.

SOURCE: CNSSI-4009

Inculpatory Evidence –

Evidence that tends to increase the likelihood of fault or guilt.

SOURCE: SP 800-72

Independent Validation Authority – (IVA)

Entity that reviews the soundness of independent tests and system compliance with all stated security controls and risk mitigation actions. IVAs will be designated by the Authorizing Official as needed.

SOURCE: CNSSI-4009

Independent Verification & Validation (IV&V) –	A comprehensive review, analysis, and testing (software and/or hardware) performed by an objective third party to confirm (i.e., verify) that the requirements are correctly defined, and to confirm (i.e., validate) that the system correctly implements the required functionality and security requirements. SOURCE: CNSSI-4009
Indicator –	Recognized action, specific, generalized, or theoretical, that an adversary might be expected to take in preparation for an attack. SOURCE: CNSSI-4009 A sign that an incident may have occurred or may be currently occurring. SOURCE: SP 800-61
Individual –	A citizen of the United States or an alien lawfully admitted for permanent residence. Agencies may, consistent with individual practice, choose to extend the protections of the Privacy Act and E-Government Act to businesses, sole proprietors, aliens, etc. SOURCE: SP 800-60
Individual Accountability –	Ability to associate positively the identity of a user with the time, method, and degree of access to an information system. SOURCE: CNSSI-4009
Individuals –	An assessment object that includes people applying specifications, mechanisms, or activities. SOURCE: SP 800-53A
Industrial Control System –	An information system used to control industrial processes such as manufacturing, product handling, production, and distribution. Industrial control systems include supervisory control and data acquisition systems (SCADA) used to control geographically dispersed assets, as well as distributed control systems (DCS) and smaller control systems using programmable logic controllers to control localized processes. SOURCE: SP 800-53; SP 800-53A; SP 800-39; SP 800-30
Informal Security Policy –	Natural language description, possibly supplemented by mathematical arguments, demonstrating the correspondence of the functional specification to the high-level design. SOURCE: CNSSI-4009
Information –	An instance of an information type. SOURCE: FIPS 200; FIPS 199; SP 800-60; SP 800-53; SP 800-37

	Any communication or representation of knowledge such as facts, data, or opinions in any medium or form, including textual, numerical, graphic, cartographic, narrative, or audiovisual.
	SOURCE: CNSSI-4009
Information Assurance (IA) –	Measures that protect and defend information and information systems by ensuring their availability, integrity, authentication, confidentiality, and non-repudiation. These measures include providing for restoration of information systems by incorporating protection, detection, and reaction capabilities.
	SOURCE: SP 800-59; CNSSI-4009
Information Assurance Component – (IAC)	An application (hardware and/or software) that provides one or more Information Assurance capabilities in support of the overall security and operational objectives of a system.
	SOURCE: CNSSI-4009
Information Assurance Manager – (IAM)	See Information Systems Security Manager.
	SOURCE: CNSSI-4009
Information Assurance Officer – (IAO)	See Information Systems Security Officer.
	SOURCE: CNSSI-4009
Information Assurance (IA) Professional –	Individual who works IA issues and has real-world experience plus appropriate IA training and education commensurate with their level of IA responsibility.
	SOURCE: CNSSI-4009
Information Assurance Vulnerability Alert (IAVA) –	Notification that is generated when an Information Assurance vulnerability may result in an immediate and potentially severe threat to DoD systems and information; this alert requires corrective action because of the severity of the vulnerability risk.
	SOURCE: CNSSI-4009
Information Domain –	A three-part concept for information sharing, independent of, and across information systems and security domains that 1) identifies information sharing participants as individual members, 2) contains shared information objects, and 3) provides a security policy that identifies the roles and privileges of the members and the protections required for the information objects.
	SOURCE: CNSSI-4009
Information Environment –	Aggregate of individuals, organizations, and/or systems that collect, process, or disseminate information, also included is the information itself.
	SOURCE: CNSSI-4009

Information Flow Control –	Procedure to ensure that information transfers within an information system are not made in violation of the security policy. SOURCE: CNSSI-4009
Information Management –	The planning, budgeting, manipulating, and controlling of information throughout its life cycle. SOURCE: CNSSI-4009
Information Operations (IO) –	The integrated employment of the core capabilities of electronic warfare, computer network operations, psychological operations, military deception, and operations security, in concert with specified supporting and related capabilities, to influence, disrupt, corrupt, or usurp adversarial human and automated decision-making process, information, and information systems while protecting our own. SOURCE: CNSSI-4009
Information Owner –	Official with statutory or operational authority for specified information and responsibility for establishing the controls for its generation, collection, processing, dissemination, and disposal. See Information Steward. SOURCE: FIPS 200; SP 800-37; SP 800-53; SP 800-60; SP 800-18 Official with statutory or operational authority for specified information and responsibility for establishing the controls for its generation, classification, collection, processing, dissemination, and disposal. SOURCE: CNSSI-4009
Information Resources –	Information and related resources, such as personnel, equipment, funds, and information technology. SOURCE: FIPS 200; FIPS 199; SP 800-53; SP 800-18; SP 800-60; 44 U.S.C., Sec. 3502; CNSSI-4009
Information Resources Management (IRM) –	The planning, budgeting, organizing, directing, training, controlling, and management activities associated with the burden, collection, creation, use, and dissemination of information by agencies. SOURCE: CNSSI-4009
Information Security –	The protection of information and information systems from unauthorized access, use, disclosure, disruption, modification, or destruction in order to provide confidentiality, integrity, and availability. SOURCE: SP 800-37; SP 800-53; SP 800-53A; SP 800-18; SP 800-60; CNSSI-4009; FIPS 200; FIPS 199; 44 U.S.C., Sec. 3542

Protecting information and information systems from unauthorized access, use, disclosure, disruption, modification, or destruction in order to provide—

1) integrity, which means guarding against improper information modification or destruction, and includes ensuring information nonrepudiation and authenticity;

2) confidentiality, which means preserving authorized restrictions on access and disclosure, including means for protecting personal privacy and proprietary information; and

3) availability, which means ensuring timely and reliable access to and use of information.

SOURCE: SP 800-66; 44 U.S.C., Sec 3541

Information Security Architect –

Individual, group, or organization responsible for ensuring that the information security requirements necessary to protect the organization's core missions and business processes are adequately addressed in all aspects of enterprise architecture including reference models, segment and solution architectures, and the resulting information systems supporting those missions and business processes.

SOURCE: SP 800-37

Information Security Architecture –

An embedded, integral part of the enterprise architecture that describes the structure and behavior for an enterprise's security processes, information security systems, personnel and organizational sub-units, showing their alignment with the enterprise's mission and strategic plans.

SOURCE: SP 800-39

Information Security Continuous Monitoring (ISCM) –

Maintaining ongoing awareness of information security, vulnerabilities, and threats to support organizational risk management decisions.

[Note: The terms "continuous" and "ongoing" in this context mean that security controls and organizational risks are assessed and analyzed at a frequency sufficient to support risk-based security decisions to adequately protect organization information.]

SOURCE: SP 800-137

Information Security Continuous Monitoring (ISCM) Process –

A process to:
• Define an ISCM strategy;
• Establish an ISCM program;
• Implement an ISCM program;
• Analyze data and Report findings;
• Respond to findings; and
• Review and Update the ISCM strategy and program.

SOURCE: SP 800-137

Information Security Continuous Monitoring (ISCM) Program –	A program established to collect information in accordance with pre-established metrics, utilizing information readily available in part through implemented security controls. SOURCE: SP 800-137
Information Security Policy –	Aggregate of directives, regulations, rules, and practices that prescribes how an organization manages, protects, and distributes information. SOURCE: SP 800-53; SP 800-37; SP 800-18; CNSSI-4009
Information Security Program Plan –	Formal document that provides an overview of the security requirements for an organization-wide information security program and describes the program management controls and common controls in place or planned for meeting those requirements. SOURCE: SP 800-37; SP 800-53; SP 800-53A
Information Security Risk –	The risk to organizational operations (including mission, functions, image, reputation), organizational assets, individuals, other organizations, and the Nation due to the potential for unauthorized access, use, disclosure, disruption, modification, or destruction of information and/or information systems. See Risk. SOURCE: SP 800-30
Information Sharing –	The requirements for information sharing by an IT system with one or more other IT systems or applications, for information sharing to support multiple internal or external organizations, missions, or public programs. SOURCE: SP 800-16
Information Sharing Environment –	1. An approach that facilitates the sharing of terrorism and homeland security information; or 2. ISE in its broader application enables those in a trusted partnership to share, discover, and access controlled information. SOURCE: CNSSI-4009
Information Steward –	An agency official with statutory or operational authority for specified information and responsibility for establishing the controls for its generation, collection, processing, dissemination, and disposal. SOURCE: CNSSI-4009

Individual or group that helps to ensure the careful and responsible management of federal information belonging to the Nation as a whole, regardless of the entity or source that may have originated, created, or compiled the information. Information stewards provide maximum access to federal information to elements of the federal government and its customers, balanced by the obligation to protect the information in accordance with the provisions of FISMA and any associated security-related federal policies, directives, regulations, standards, and guidance.

SOURCE: SP 800-37

Information System –

A discrete set of information resources organized for the collection, processing, maintenance, use, sharing, dissemination, or disposition of information.

SOURCE: FIPS 200; FIPS 199; SP 800-53A; SP 800-37; SP 800-60; SP 800-18; 44 U.S.C., Sec. 3502; OMB Circular A-130, App. III

A discrete set of information resources organized for the collection, processing, maintenance, use, sharing, dissemination, or disposition of information.

[Note: Information systems also include specialized systems such as industrial/process controls systems, telephone switching and private branch exchange (PBX) systems, and environmental control systems.]

SOURCE: SP 800-53; CNSSI-4009

Information System Boundary –

See Authorization Boundary.

Information System Contingency Plan (ISCP) –

Management policy and procedures designed to maintain or restore business operations, including computer operations, possibly at an alternate location, in the event of emergencies, system failures, or disasters.

SOURCE: SP 800-34

Information System Life Cycle –

The phases through which an information system passes, typically characterized as initiation, development, operation, and termination (i.e., sanitization, disposal and/or destruction).

SOURCE: CNSSI-4009

Information System Owner (or Program Manager) –

Official responsible for the overall procurement, development, integration, modification, or operation and maintenance of an information system.

SOURCE: SP 800-53; SP 800-53A; SP 800-18; SP 800-60

Information System Owner –

Official responsible for the overall procurement, development, integration, modification, or operation and maintenance of an information system.

SOURCE: FIPS 200

Information System Resilience –

The ability of an information system to continue to operate while under attack, even if in a degraded or debilitated state, and to rapidly recover operational capabilities for essential functions after a successful attack.

SOURCE: SP 800-30

The ability of an information system to continue to: (i) operate under adverse conditions or stress, even if in a degraded or debilitated state, while maintaining essential operational capabilities; and (ii) recover to an effective operational posture in a time frame consistent with mission needs.

SOURCE: SP 800-39

Information System Security Officer (ISSO) –

Individual with assigned responsibility for maintaining the appropriate operational security posture for an information system or program.

SOURCE: SP 800-37; SP 800-53

Individual assigned responsibility by the senior agency information security officer, authorizing official, management official, or information system owner for maintaining the appropriate operational security posture for an information system or program.

SOURCE: SP 800-53A; SP 800-60

Individual assigned responsibility by the senior agency information security officer, authorizing official, management official, or information system owner for ensuring that the appropriate operational security posture is maintained for an information system or program.

SOURCE: SP 800-18

Information System-Related Security Risks –

Information system-related security risks are those risks that arise through the loss of confidentiality, integrity, or availability of information or information systems and consider impacts to the organization (including assets, mission, functions, image, or reputation), individuals, other organizations, and the Nation.

See Risk.

SOURCE: SP 800-37; SP 800-53A

Information Systems Security – (INFOSEC)	Protection of information systems against unauthorized access to or modification of information, whether in storage, processing, or transit, and against the denial of service to authorized users, including those measures necessary to detect, document, and counter such threats. SOURCE: CNSSI-4009
Information Systems Security Engineer (ISSE) –	Individual assigned responsibility for conducting information system security engineering activities. SOURCE: SP 800-37; CNSSI-4009
Information Systems Security Engineering (ISSE) –	Process of capturing and refining information protection requirements to ensure their integration into information systems acquisition and information systems development through purposeful security design or configuration. SOURCE: CNSSI-4009 Process that captures and refines information security requirements and ensures their integration into information technology component products and information systems through purposeful security design or configuration. SOURCE: SP 800-37
Information Systems Security Equipment Modification –	Modification of any fielded hardware, firmware, software, or portion thereof, under NSA configuration control. There are three classes of modifications: mandatory (to include human safety); optional/special mission modifications; and repair actions. These classes apply to elements, subassemblies, equipment, systems, and software packages performing functions such as key generation, key distribution, message encryption, decryption, authentication, or those mechanisms necessary to satisfy security policy, labeling, identification, or accountability. SOURCE: CNSSI-4009
Information Systems Security Manager (ISSM) –	Individual responsible for the information assurance of a program, organization, system, or enclave. SOURCE: CNSSI-4009
Information Systems Security Officer (ISSO) –	Individual assigned responsibility for maintaining the appropriate operational security posture for an information system or program. SOURCE: CNSSI-4009

Individual assigned responsibility by the senior agency information security officer, authorizing official, management official, or information system owner for maintaining the appropriate operational security posture for an information system or program.

SOURCE: SP 800-39

Information Systems Security Product –	Item (chip, module, assembly, or equipment), technique, or service that performs or relates to information systems security.

SOURCE: CNSSI-4009

Information Technology –	Any equipment or interconnected system or subsystem of equipment that is used in the automatic acquisition, storage, manipulation, management, movement, control, display, switching, interchange, transmission, or reception of data or information by the executive agency. For purposes of the preceding sentence, equipment is used by an executive agency if the equipment is used by the executive agency directly or is used by a contractor under a contract with the executive agency which—

1) requires the use of such equipment; or
2) requires the use, to a significant extent, of such equipment in the performance of a service or the furnishing of a product.

The term information technology includes computers, ancillary equipment, software, firmware and similar procedures, services (including support services), and related resources.

SOURCE: SP 800-53; SP 800-53A; SP 800-37; SP 800-18; SP 800-60; FIPS 200; FIPS 199; CNSSI-4009; 40 U.S.C., Sec. 11101 and Sec 1401

Information Type –	A specific category of information (e.g., privacy, medical, proprietary, financial, investigative, contractor sensitive, security management), defined by an organization or in some instances, by a specific law, Executive Order, directive, policy, or regulation.

SOURCE: SP 800-53; SP 800-53A; SP 800-37; SP 800-18; SP 800-60; FIPS 200; FIPS 199; CNSSI-4009

Information Value –	A qualitative measure of the importance of the information based upon factors such as: level of robustness of the Information Assurance controls allocated to the protection of information based upon: mission criticality, the sensitivity (e.g., classification and compartmentalization) of the information, releasability to other countries, perishability/longevity of the information (e.g., short life data versus long life intelligence source data), and potential impact of loss of confidentiality and integrity and/or availability of the information.

SOURCE: CNSSI-4009

Inheritance –	See Security Control Inheritance.

Initialization Vector (IV) –	A vector used in defining the starting point of an encryption process within a cryptographic algorithm. SOURCE: FIPS 140-2
Initialize –	Setting the state of a cryptographic logic prior to key generation, encryption, or other operating mode. SOURCE: CNSSI-4009
Initiator –	The entity that initiates an authentication exchange. SOURCE: FIPS 196
Inside Threat –	An entity with authorized access that has the potential to harm an information system through destruction, disclosure, modification of data, and/or denial of service. SOURCE: SP 800-32
Inside(r) Threat –	An entity with authorized access (i.e., within the security domain) that has the potential to harm an information system or enterprise through destruction, disclosure, modification of data, and/or denial of service. SOURCE: CNSSI-4009
Inspectable Space –	Three dimensional space surrounding equipment that processes classified and/or sensitive information within which TEMPEST exploitation is not considered practical or where legal authority to identify and remove a potential TEMPEST exploitation exists. Synonymous with zone of control. SOURCE: CNSSI-4009
Integrity –	Guarding against improper information modification or destruction, and includes ensuring information non-repudiation and authenticity. SOURCE: SP 800-53; SP 800-53A; SP 800-18; SP 800-27; SP 800-37; SP 800-60; FIPS 200; FIPS 199; 44 U.S.C., Sec. 3542 The property that sensitive data has not been modified or deleted in an unauthorized and undetected manner. SOURCE: FIPS 140-2 The property whereby an entity has not been modified in an unauthorized manner. SOURCE: CNSSI-4009
Integrity Check Value –	Checksum capable of detecting modification of an information system. SOURCE: CNSSI-4009

Intellectual Property –

Useful artistic, technical, and/or industrial information, knowledge or ideas that convey ownership and control of tangible or virtual usage and/or representation.

SOURCE: SP 800-32

Creations of the mind such as musical, literary, and artistic works; inventions; and symbols, names, images, and designs used in commerce, including copyrights, trademarks, patents, and related rights. Under intellectual property law, the holder of one of these abstract "properties" has certain exclusive rights to the creative work, commercial symbol, or invention by which it is covered.

SOURCE: CNSSI-4009

Interconnection Security Agreement (ISA) –

An agreement established between the organizations that own and operate connected IT systems to document the technical requirements of the interconnection. The ISA also supports a Memorandum of Understanding or Agreement (MOU/A) between the organizations.

SOURCE: SP 800-47

A document that regulates security-relevant aspects of an intended connection between an agency and an external system. It regulates the security interface between any two systems operating under two different distinct authorities. It includes a variety of descriptive, technical, procedural, and planning information. It is usually preceded by a formal MOA/MOU that defines high-level roles and responsibilities in management of a cross-domain connection.

SOURCE: CNSSI-4009

Interface –

Common boundary between independent systems or modules where interactions take place.

SOURCE: CNSSI-4009

Interface Control Document –

Technical document describing interface controls and identifying the authorities and responsibilities for ensuring the operation of such controls. This document is baselined during the preliminary design review and is maintained throughout the information system life cycle.

SOURCE: CNSSI-4009

Interim Approval to Operate – (IATO)

Temporary authorization granted by a DAA for an information system to process information based on preliminary results of a security evaluation of the system. (To be replaced by ATO and POA&M)

SOURCE: CNSSI-4009

Interim Approval to Test (IATT) –	Temporary authorization to test an information system in a specified operational information environment within the time frame and under the conditions or constraints enumerated in the written authorization. SOURCE: CNSSI-4009
Intermediate Certification Authority (CA) –	A Certification Authority that is subordinate to another CA, and has a CA subordinate to itself. SOURCE: SP 800-32
Internal Network –	A network where: (i) the establishment, maintenance, and provisioning of security controls are under the direct control of organizational employees or contractors; or (ii) cryptographic encapsulation or similar security technology provides the same effect. An internal network is typically organization-owned, yet may be organization-controlled while not being organization-owned. SOURCE: SP 800-53 A network where 1) the establishment, maintenance, and provisioning of security controls are under the direct control of organizational employees or contractors; or 2) cryptographic encapsulation or similar security technology implemented between organization-controlled endpoints provides the same effect (at least with regard to confidentiality and integrity). An internal network is typically organization-owned, yet may be organization-controlled while not being organization-owned. SOURCE: CNSSI-4009
Internal Security Controls –	Hardware, firmware, or software features within an information system that restrict access to resources only to authorized subjects. SOURCE: CNSSI-4009
Internal Security Testing –	Security testing conducted from inside the organization's security perimeter. SOURCE: SP 800-115
Internet –	The Internet is the single, interconnected, worldwide system of commercial, governmental, educational, and other computer networks that share (a) the protocol suite specified by the Internet Architecture Board (IAB), and (b) the name and address spaces managed by the Internet Corporation for Assigned Names and Numbers (ICANN). SOURCE: CNSSI-4009

Internet Protocol (IP) – Standard protocol for transmission of data from source to destinations in packet-switched communications networks and interconnected systems of such networks.

SOURCE: CNSSI-4009

Interoperability – For the purposes of this standard, interoperability allows any government facility or information system, regardless of the PIV Issuer, to verify a cardholder's identity using the credentials on the PIV Card.

SOURCE: FIPS 201

Interview – A type of assessment method that is characterized by the process of conducting discussions with individuals or groups within an organization to facilitate understanding, achieve clarification, or lead to the location of evidence, the results of which are used to support the determination of security control effectiveness over time.

SOURCE: SP 800-53A

Intranet – A private network that is employed within the confines of a given enterprise (e.g., internal to a business or agency).

SOURCE: CNSSI-4009

Intrusion – Unauthorized act of bypassing the security mechanisms of a system.

SOURCE: CNSSI-4009

Intrusion Detection Systems (IDS) – Hardware or software product that gathers and analyzes information from various areas within a computer or a network to identify possible security breaches, which include both intrusions (attacks from outside the organizations) and misuse (attacks from within the organizations.)

SOURCE: CNSSI-4009

Intrusion Detection Systems (IDS) – (Host-Based) IDSs which operate on information collected from within an individual computer system. This vantage point allows host-based IDSs to determine exactly which processes and user accounts are involved in a particular attack on the Operating System. Furthermore, unlike network-based IDSs, host-based IDSs can more readily "see" the intended outcome of an attempted attack, because they can directly access and monitor the data files and system processes usually targeted by attacks.

SOURCE: SP 800-36; CNSSI-4009

Intrusion Detection Systems (IDS) – (Network-Based)	IDSs which detect attacks by capturing and analyzing network packets. Listening on a network segment or switch, one network-based IDS can monitor the network traffic affecting multiple hosts that are connected to the network segment. SOURCE: SP 800-36; CNSSI-4009
Intrusion Detection and Prevention System (IDPS) –	Software that automates the process of monitoring the events occurring in a computer system or network and analyzing them for signs of possible incidents and attempting to stop detected possible incidents. SOURCE: SP 800-61
Intrusion Prevention System(s) (IPS) –	System(s) which can detect an intrusive activity and can also attempt to stop the activity, ideally before it reaches its targets. SOURCE: SP 800-36; CNSSI-4009
Inverse Cipher –	Series of transformations that converts ciphertext to plaintext using the Cipher Key. SOURCE: FIPS 197
IP Security (IPsec) –	Suite of protocols for securing Internet Protocol (IP) communications at the network layer, layer 3 of the OSI model by authenticating and/or encrypting each IP packet in a data stream. IPsec also includes protocols for cryptographic key establishment. SOURCE: CNSSI-4009

IT-Related Risk –	The net mission/business impact considering
	1) the likelihood that a particular threat source will exploit, or trigger, a particular information system vulnerability, and
	2) the resulting impact if this should occur. IT-related risks arise from legal liability or mission/business loss due to, but not limited to:
	   ♦ Unauthorized (malicious, non-malicious, or accidental) disclosure, modification, or destruction of information;
	   ♦ Non-malicious errors and omissions;
	   ♦ IT disruptions due to natural or man-made disasters; or
	   ♦ Failure to exercise due care and diligence in the implementation and operation of the IT.
	
	SOURCE: SP 800-27

IT Security Architecture –	A description of security principles and an overall approach for complying with the principles that drive the system design; i.e., guidelines on the placement and implementation of specific security services within various distributed computing environments. SOURCE: SP 800-27

IT Security Awareness –	The purpose of awareness presentations is simply to focus attention on security. Awareness presentations are intended to allow individuals to recognize IT security concerns and respond accordingly.
	SOURCE: SP 800-50
IT Security Awareness and Training Program –	Explains proper rules of behavior for the use of agency IT systems and information. The program communicates IT security policies and procedures that need to be followed.
	SOURCE: SP 800-50
	Explains proper rules of behavior for the use of agency information systems and information. The program communicates IT security policies and procedures that need to be followed (i.e., NSTISSD 501, NIST SP 800-50).
	SOURCE: CNSSI-4009
IT Security Education –	IT Security Education seeks to integrate all of the security skills and competencies of the various functional specialties into a common body of knowledge, adds a multidisciplinary study of concepts, issues, and principles (technological and social), and strives to produce IT security specialists and professionals capable of vision and proactive response.
	SOURCE: SP 800-50
IT Security Investment –	An IT application or system that is solely devoted to security. For instance, intrusion detection systems (IDS) and public key infrastructure (PKI) are examples of IT security investments.
	SOURCE: SP 800-65
IT Security Metrics –	Metrics based on IT security performance goals and objectives.
	SOURCE: SP 800-55

IT Security Policy –

The "documentation of IT security decisions" in an organization.

NIST SP 800-12 categorizes IT Security Policy into three basic types:
1) Program Policy—high-level policy used to create an organization's IT security program, define its scope within the organization, assign implementation responsibilities, establish strategic direction, and assign resources for implementation.
2) Issue-Specific Policies—address specific issues of concern to the organization, such as contingency planning, the use of a particular methodology for systems risk management, and implementation of new regulations or law. These policies are likely to require more frequent revision as changes in technology and related factors take place.
3) System-Specific Policies—address individual systems, such as establishing an access control list or in training users as to what system actions are permitted. These policies may vary from system to system within the same organization. In addition, policy may refer to entirely different matters, such as the specific managerial decisions setting an organization's electronic mail (email) policy or fax security policy.

SOURCE: SP 800-35

IT Security Training –

IT Security Training strives to produce relevant and needed security skills and competencies by practitioners of functional specialties other than IT security (e.g., management, systems design and development, acquisition, auditing). The most significant difference between training and awareness is that training seeks to teach skills, which allow a person to perform a specific function, while awareness seeks to focus an individual's attention on an issue or set of issues. The skills acquired during training are built upon the awareness foundation, in particular, upon the security basics and literacy material.

SOURCE: SP 800-50

Jamming –

An attack in which a device is used to emit electromagnetic energy on a wireless network's frequency to make it unusable.

SOURCE: SP 800-48

An attack that attempts to interfere with the reception of broadcast communications.

SOURCE: CNSSI-4009

Joint Authorization –

Security authorization involving multiple authorizing officials.

SOURCE: SP 800-37

Kerberos –

A widely used authentication protocol developed at the Massachusetts Institute of Technology (MIT). In "classic" Kerberos, users share a secret password with a Key Distribution Center (KDC). The user, Alice, who wishes to communicate with another user, Bob, authenticates to the KDC and is furnished a "ticket" by the KDC to use to authenticate with Bob. When Kerberos authentication is based on passwords, the protocol is known to be vulnerable to off-line dictionary attacks by eavesdroppers who capture the initial user-to-KDC exchange. Longer password length and complexity provide some mitigation to this vulnerability, although sufficiently long passwords tend to be cumbersome for users.

SOURCE: SP 800-63

A means of verifying the identities of principals on an open network. It accomplishes this without relying on the authentication, trustworthiness, or physical security of hosts while assuming all packets can be read, modified and inserted at will. It uses a trust broker model and symmetric cryptography to provide authentication and authorization of users and systems on the network.

SOURCE: SP 800-95

Key –

A value used to control cryptographic operations, such as decryption, encryption, signature generation, or signature verification.

SOURCE: SP 800-63

A numerical value used to control cryptographic operations, such as decryption, encryption, signature generation, or signature verification.

SOURCE: CNSSI-4009

A parameter used in conjunction with a cryptographic algorithm that determines its operation.

Examples applicable to this Standard include:
1. The computation of a digital signature from data, and
2. The verification of a digital signature.

SOURCE: FIPS 186

Key Bundle –

The three cryptographic keys (Key1, Key2, Key3) that are used with a Triple Data Encryption Algorithm (TDEA) mode.

SOURCE: SP 800-67

Key Distribution Center (KDC) –

COMSEC facility generating and distributing key in electronic form.

SOURCE: CNSSI-4009

Key Escrow –	A deposit of the private key of a subscriber and other pertinent information pursuant to an escrow agreement or similar contract binding upon the subscriber, the terms of which require one or more agents to hold the subscriber's private key for the benefit of the subscriber, an employer, or other party, upon provisions set forth in the agreement. SOURCE: SP 800-32 The processes of managing (e.g., generating, storing, transferring, auditing) the two components of a cryptographic key by two key component holders. SOURCE: FIPS 185 1. The processes of managing (e.g., generating, storing, transferring, auditing) the two components of a cryptographic key by two key component holders. 2. A key recovery technique for storing knowledge of a cryptographic key, or parts thereof, in the custody of one or more third parties called "escrow agents," so that the key can be recovered and used in specified circumstances. SOURCE: CNSSI-4009
Key Escrow System –	A system that entrusts the two components comprising a cryptographic key (e.g., a device unique key) to two key component holders (also called "escrow agents"). SOURCE: FIPS 185; CNSSI-4009
Key Establishment –	The process by which cryptographic keys are securely established among cryptographic modules using manual transport methods (e.g., key loaders), automated methods (e.g., key transport and/or key agreement protocols), or a combination of automated and manual methods (consists of key transport plus key agreement). SOURCE: FIPS 140-2 The process by which cryptographic keys are securely established among cryptographic modules using key transport and/or key agreement procedures. See Key Distribution. SOURCE: CNSSI-4009
Key Exchange –	The process of exchanging public keys in order to establish secure communications. SOURCE: SP 800-32 Process of exchanging public keys (and other information) in order to establish secure communications. SOURCE: CNSSI-4009

Key Expansion –

Routine used to generate a series of Round Keys from the Cipher Key.

SOURCE: FIPS 197

Key Generation Material –

Random numbers, pseudo-random numbers, and cryptographic parameters used in generating cryptographic keys.

SOURCE: SP 800-32; CNSSI-4009

Key List –

Printed series of key settings for a specific cryptonet. Key lists may be produced in list, pad, or printed tape format.

SOURCE: CNSSI-4009

Key Loader –

A self-contained unit that is capable of storing at least one plaintext or encrypted cryptographic key or key component that can be transferred, upon request, into a cryptographic module.

SOURCE: FIPS 140-2

A self-contained unit that is capable of storing at least one plaintext or encrypted cryptographic key or a component of a key that can be transferred, upon request, into a cryptographic module.

SOURCE: CNSSI-4009

Key Logger –

A program designed to record which keys are pressed on a computer keyboard used to obtain passwords or encryption keys and thus bypass other security measures.

SOURCE: SP 800-82

Key Management –

The activities involving the handling of cryptographic keys and other related security parameters (e.g., IVs and passwords) during the entire life cycle of the keys, including their generation, storage, establishment, entry and output, and zeroization.

SOURCE: FIPS 140-2; CNSSI-4009

Key Management Device –

A unit that provides for secure electronic distribution of encryption keys to authorized users.

SOURCE: CNSSI-4009

Key Management Infrastructure – (KMI)

All parts – computer hardware, firmware, software, and other equipment and its documentation; facilities that house the equipment and related functions; and companion standards, policies, procedures, and doctrine that form the system that manages and supports the ordering and delivery of cryptographic material and related information products and services to users.

SOURCE: CNSSI-4009

Key Pair –	Two mathematically related keys having the properties that (1) one key can be used to encrypt a message that can only be decrypted using the other key, and 2) even knowing one key, it is computationally infeasible to discover the other key.
	SOURCE: SP 800-32
	A public key and its corresponding private key; a key pair is used with a public key algorithm.
	SOURCE: SP 800-21; CNSSI-4009
Key Production Key (KPK) –	Key used to initialize a keystream generator for the production of other electronically generated key.
	SOURCE: CNSSI-4009
Key Recovery –	Mechanisms and processes that allow authorized parties to retrieve the cryptographic key used for data confidentiality.
	SOURCE: CNSSI-4009
Key Stream –	Sequence of symbols (or their electrical or mechanical equivalents) produced in a machine or auto-manual cryptosystem to combine with plain text to produce cipher text, control transmission security processes, or produce key.
	SOURCE: CNSSI-4009
Key Tag –	Identification information associated with certain types of electronic key.
	SOURCE: CNSSI-4009
Key Tape –	Punched or magnetic tape containing key. Printed key in tape form is referred to as a key list.
	SOURCE: CNSSI-4009
Key Transport –	The secure transport of cryptographic keys from one cryptographic module to another module.
	SOURCE: FIPS 140-2; CNSSI-4009
Key Updating –	Irreversible cryptographic process for modifying key.
	SOURCE: CNSSI-4009
Key Wrap –	A method of encrypting keying material (along with associated integrity information) that provides both confidentiality and integrity protection using a symmetric key algorithm.
	SOURCE: SP 800-56A

Key-Auto-Key (KAK) –	Cryptographic logic using previous key to produce key. SOURCE: CNSSI-4009
Key-Encryption-Key (KEK) –	Key that encrypts or decrypts other key for transmission or storage. SOURCE: CNSSI-4009
Keyed-hash based message authentication code (HMAC) –	A message authentication code that uses a cryptographic key in conjunction with a hash function. SOURCE: FIPS 198; CNSSI-4009
Keying Material –	Key, code, or authentication information in physical, electronic, or magnetic form. SOURCE: CNSSI-4009
Keystroke Monitoring –	The process used to view or record both the keystrokes entered by a computer user and the computer's response during an interactive session. Keystroke monitoring is usually considered a special case of audit trails. SOURCE: SP 800-12; CNSSI-4009
KMI Operating Account (KOA) –	A KMI business relationship that is established 1) to manage the set of user devices that are under the control of a specific KMI customer organization, and 2) to control the distribution of KMI products to those devices. SOURCE: CNSSI-4009
KMI Protected Channel (KPC) –	A KMI Communication Channel that provides 1) Information Integrity Service; 2) either Data Origin Authentication Service or Peer Entity Authentication Service, as is appropriate to the mode of communications; and 3) optionally, Information Confidentiality Service. SOURCE: CNSSI-4009
KMI-Aware Device –	A user device that has a user identity for which the registration has significance across the entire KMI (i.e., the identity's registration data is maintained in a database at the PRSN level of the system, rather than only at an MGC) and for which a product can be generated and wrapped by a PSN for distribution to the specific device. SOURCE: CNSSI-4009
KOA Agent –	A user identity that is designated by a KOA manager to access PRSN product delivery enclaves for the purpose of retrieving wrapped products that have been ordered for user devices that are assigned to that KOA. SOURCE: CNSSI-4009

KOA Manager –	The Management Role that is responsible for the operation of one or KOA's (i.e., manages distribution of KMI products to the end cryptographic units, fill devices, and ADPs that are assigned to the manager's KOA). SOURCE: CNSSI-4009
KOA Registration Manager –	The individual responsible for performing activities related to registering KOAs. SOURCE: CNSSI-4009
Label –	See Security Label.
Labeled Security Protections –	Access control protection features of a system that use security labels to make access control decisions. SOURCE: CNSSI-4009
Laboratory Attack –	Use of sophisticated signal recovery equipment in a laboratory environment to recover information from data storage media. SOURCE: SP 800-88; CNSSI-4009
Least Privilege –	The security objective of granting users only those accesses they need to perform their official duties. SOURCE: SP 800-12 The principle that a security architecture should be designed so that each entity is granted the minimum system resources and authorizations that the entity needs to perform its function. SOURCE: CNSSI-4009
Least Trust –	The principal that a security architecture should be designed in a way that minimizes 1) the number of components that require trust, and 2) the extent to which each component is trusted. SOURCE: CNSSI-4009
Level of Concern –	Rating assigned to an information system indicating the extent to which protection measures, techniques, and procedures must be applied. High, Medium, and Basic are identified levels of concern. A separate Level-of-Concern is assigned to each information system for confidentiality, integrity, and availability. SOURCE: CNSSI-4009

Level of Protection –	Extent to which protective measures, techniques, and procedures must be applied to information systems and networks based on risk, threat, vulnerability, system interconnectivity considerations, and information assurance needs. Levels of protection are: 1. Basic: information systems and networks requiring implementation of standard minimum security countermeasures. 2. Medium: information systems and networks requiring layering of additional safeguards above the standard minimum security countermeasures. 3. High: information systems and networks requiring the most stringent protection and rigorous security countermeasures. SOURCE: CNSSI-4009
Likelihood of Occurrence –	In Information Assurance risk analysis, a weighted factor based on a subjective analysis of the probability that a given threat is capable of exploiting a given vulnerability. SOURCE: CNSSI-4009
Limited Maintenance –	COMSEC maintenance restricted to fault isolation, removal, and replacement of plug-in assemblies. Soldering or unsoldering usually is prohibited in limited maintenance. See Full Maintenance. SOURCE: CNSSI-4009
Line Conditioning –	Elimination of unintentional signals or noise induced or conducted on a telecommunications or information system signal, power, control, indicator, or other external interface line. SOURCE: CNSSI-4009
Line Conduction –	Unintentional signals or noise induced or conducted on a telecommunications or information system signal, power, control, indicator, or other external interface line. SOURCE: CNSSI-4009
Line of Business –	The following OMB-defined process areas common to virtually all federal agencies: Case Management, Financial Management, Grants Management, Human Resources Management, Federal Health Architecture, Information Systems Security, Budget Formulation and Execution, Geospatial, and IT Infrastructure. SOURCE: SP 800-53

"Lines of business" or "areas of operation" describe the purpose of government in functional terms or describe the support functions that the government must conduct in order to effectively deliver services to citizens. *Lines of business* relating to the purpose of government and the mechanisms the government uses to achieve its purposes tend to be mission-based. *Lines of business* relating to support functions and resource management functions that are necessary to conduct government operations tend to be common to most agencies. The recommended information types provided in NIST SP 800-60 are established from the "business areas" and "lines of business" from OMB's Business Reference Model (BRM) section of *Federal Enterprise Architecture (FEA) Consolidated Reference Model Document Version 2.3*

SOURCE: SP 800-60

Link Encryption –

Link encryption encrypts all of the data along a communications path (e.g., a satellite link, telephone circuit, or T1 line). Since link encryption also encrypts routing data, communications nodes need to decrypt the data to continue routing.

SOURCE: SP 800-12

Encryption of information between nodes of a communications system.

SOURCE: CNSSI-4009

List-Oriented –

Information system protection in which each protected object has a list of all subjects authorized to access it.

SOURCE: CNSSI-4009

Local Access –

Access to an organizational information system by a user (or process acting on behalf of a user) communicating through a direct connection without the use of a network.

SOURCE: SP 800-53; CNSSI-4009

Local Authority –

Organization responsible for generating and signing user certificates in a PKI-enabled environment.

SOURCE: CNSSI-4009

Local Management Device/Key Processor (LMD/KP) –

EKMS platform providing automated management of COMSEC material and generating key for designated users.

SOURCE: CNSSI-4009

Local Registration Authority – (LRA)

A Registration Authority with responsibility for a local community.

SOURCE: SP 800-32

A Registration Authority with responsibility for a local community in a PKI-enabled environment.

SOURCE: CNSSI-4009

Logic Bomb –

A piece of code intentionally inserted into a software system that will set off a malicious function when specified conditions are met.

SOURCE: CNSSI-4009

Logical Completeness Measure –

Means for assessing the effectiveness and degree to which a set of security and access control mechanisms meets security specifications.

SOURCE: CNSSI-4009

Logical Perimeter –

A conceptual perimeter that extends to all intended users of the system, both directly and indirectly connected, who receive output from the system without a reliable human review by an appropriate authority. The location of such a review is commonly referred to as an "air gap."

SOURCE: CNSSI-4009

Long Title –

Descriptive title of a COMSEC item.

SOURCE: CNSSI-4009

Low Impact –

The loss of confidentiality, integrity, or availability that could be expected to have a limited adverse effect on organizational operations, organizational assets, individuals, other organizations, or the national security interests of the United States; (i.e., 1) causes a degradation in mission capability to an extent and duration that the organization is able to perform its primary functions, but the effectiveness of the functions is noticeably reduced; 2) results in minor damage to organizational assets; 3) results in minor financial loss; or 4) results in minor harm to individuals).

SOURCE: CNSSI-4009

Low-Impact System –

An information system in which all three security objectives (i.e., confidentiality, integrity, and availability) are assigned a FIPS 199 potential impact value of low.

SOURCE: SP 800-37; SP 800-53; SP 800-60; FIPS 200

An information system in which all three security properties (i.e., confidentiality, integrity, and availability) are assigned a potential impact value of low.

SOURCE: CNSSI-4009

Low Probability of Detection –

Result of measures used to hide or disguise intentional electromagnetic transmissions.

SOURCE: CNSSI-4009

Low Probability of Intercept –	Result of measures to prevent the intercept of intentional electromagnetic transmissions. The objective is to minimize an adversary's capability of receiving, processing, or replaying an electronic signal. SOURCE: CNSSI-4009
Macro Virus –	A virus that attaches itself to documents and uses the macro programming capabilities of the document's application to execute and propagate. SOURCE: CNSSI-4009
Magnetic Remanence –	Magnetic representation of residual information remaining on a magnetic medium after the medium has been cleared. See Clearing. SOURCE: CNSSI-4009
Maintenance Hook –	Special instructions (trapdoors) in software allowing easy maintenance and additional feature development. Since maintenance hooks frequently allow entry into the code without the usual checks, they are a serious security risk if they are not removed prior to live implementation. SOURCE: CNSSI-4009
Maintenance Key –	Key intended only for in-shop use. SOURCE: CNSSI-4009
Major Application –	An application that requires special attention to security due to the risk and magnitude of harm resulting from the loss, misuse, or unauthorized access to or modification of the information in the application. Note: All federal applications require some level of protection. Certain applications, because of the information in them, however, require special management oversight and should be treated as major. Adequate security for other applications should be provided by security of the systems in which they operate. SOURCE: OMB Circular A-130, App. III
Major Information System –	An information system that requires special management attention because of its importance to an agency mission; its high development, operating, or maintenance costs; or its significant role in the administration of agency programs, finances, property, or other resources. SOURCE: OMB Circular A-130, App. III
Malicious Applets –	Small application programs that are automatically downloaded and executed and that perform an unauthorized function on an information system. SOURCE: CNSSI-4009

Malicious Code –	Software or firmware intended to perform an unauthorized process that will have adverse impact on the confidentiality, integrity, or availability of an information system. A virus, worm, Trojan horse, or other code-based entity that infects a host. Spyware and some forms of adware are also examples of malicious code. SOURCE: SP 800-53; CNSSI-4009
Malicious Logic –	Hardware, firmware, or software that is intentionally included or inserted in a system for a harmful purpose. SOURCE: CNSSI-4009
Malware –	A program that is inserted into a system, usually covertly, with the intent of compromising the confidentiality, integrity, or availability of the victim's data, applications, or operating system or of otherwise annoying or disrupting the victim. SOURCE: SP 800-83 See Malicious Code. See also Malicious Applets and Malicious Logic. SOURCE: SP 800-53; CNSSI-4009 A virus, worm, Trojan horse, or other code-based malicious entity that successfully infects a host. SOURCE: SP 800-61
Man-in-the-middle Attack – (MitM)	An attack on the authentication protocol run in which the Attacker positions himself in between the Claimant and Verifier so that he can intercept and alter data traveling between them. SOURCE: SP 800-63 A form of active wiretapping attack in which the attacker intercepts and selectively modifies communicated data to masquerade as one or more of the entities involved in a communication association. SOURCE: CNSSI-4009
Management Client (MGC) –	A configuration of a client node that enables a KMI external operational manager to manage KMI products and services by either 1) accessing a PRSN, or 2) exercising locally provided capabilities. An MGC consists of a client platform and an advanced key processor (AKP). SOURCE: CNSSI-4009
Management Controls –	The security controls (i.e., safeguards or countermeasures) for an information system that focus on the management of risk and the management of information system security. SOURCE: SP 800-37; SP 800-53; SP 800-53A; FIPS 200

Actions taken to manage the development, maintenance, and use of the system, including system-specific policies, procedures and rules of behavior, individual roles and responsibilities, individual accountability, and personnel security decisions.

SOURCE: CNSSI-4009

Management Security Controls –

The security controls (i.e., safeguards or countermeasures) for an information system that focus on the management of risk and the management of information systems security.

SOURCE: CNSSI-4009

Mandatory Access Control (MAC) –

A means of restricting access to system resources based on the sensitivity (as represented by a label) of the information contained in the system resource and the formal authorization (i.e., clearance) of users to access information of such sensitivity.

SOURCE: SP 800-44

Access controls (which) are driven by the results of a comparison between the user's trust level or clearance and the sensitivity designation of the information.

SOURCE: FIPS 191

A means of restricting access to objects based on the sensitivity (as represented by a security label) of the information contained in the objects and the formal authorization (i.e., clearance, formal access approvals, and need-to-know) of subjects to access information of such sensitivity.

SOURCE: CNSSI-4009

Mandatory Modification –

Change to a COMSEC end-item that NSA requires to be completed and reported by a specified date. See Optional Modification.

SOURCE: CNSSI-4009

Manipulative Communications Deception –

Alteration or simulation of friendly telecommunications for the purpose of deception. See Communications Deception and Imitative Communications Deception.

SOURCE: CNSSI-4009

Manual Cryptosystem –

Cryptosystem in which the cryptographic processes are performed without the use of crypto-equipment or auto-manual devices.

SOURCE: CNSSI-4009

Manual Key Transport –

A non-automated means of transporting cryptographic keys by physically moving a device, document, or person containing or possessing the key or key component.

SOURCE: SP 800-57 Part 1

A nonelectronic means of transporting cryptographic keys.

SOURCE: FIPS 140-2

Manual Remote Rekeying – Procedure by which a distant crypto-equipment is rekeyed electronically, with specific actions required by the receiving terminal operator. Synonymous with cooperative remote rekeying. See also Automatic Remote Keying.

SOURCE: CNSSI-4009

Marking – See Security Marking.

Masquerading – When an unauthorized agent claims the identity of another agent, it is said to be masquerading.

SOURCE: SP 800-19

A type of threat action whereby an unauthorized entity gains access to a system or performs a malicious act by illegitimately posing as an authorized entity.

SOURCE: CNSSI-4009

Master Cryptographic Ignition Key – Key device with electronic logic and circuits providing the capability for adding more operational CIKs to a keyset.

SOURCE: CNSSI-4009

Match/matching – The process of comparing biometric information against a previously stored template(s) and scoring the level of similarity.

SOURCE: FIPS 201; CNSSI-4009

Maximum Tolerable Downtime – The amount of time mission/business processes can be disrupted without causing significant harm to the organization's mission.

SOURCE: SP 800-34

Mechanisms – An assessment object that includes specific protection-related items (e.g., hardware, software, or firmware) employed within or at the boundary of an information system.

SOURCE: SP 800-53A

Media – Physical devices or writing surfaces including but not limited to magnetic tapes, optical disks, magnetic disks, Large Scale Integration (LSI) memory chips, and printouts (but not including display media) onto which information is recorded, stored, or printed within an information system.

SOURCE: FIPS 200; SP 800-53; CNSSI-4009

Media Sanitization –	A general term referring to the actions taken to render data written on media unrecoverable by both ordinary and extraordinary means.
	SOURCE: SP 800-88
	The actions taken to render data written on media unrecoverable by both ordinary and extraordinary means.
	SOURCE: CNSSI-4009
Memorandum of Understanding/Agreement – (MOU/A)	A document established between two or more parties to define their respective responsibilities in accomplishing a particular goal or mission. In this guide, an MOU/A defines the responsibilities of two or more organizations in establishing, operating, and securing a system interconnection.
	SOURCE: SP 800-47
	A document established between two or more parties to define their respective responsibilities in accomplishing a particular goal or mission, e.g., establishing, operating, and securing a system interconnection.
	SOURCE: CNSSI-4009
Memory Scavenging –	The collection of residual information from data storage.
	SOURCE: CNSSI-4009
Message Authentication Code – (MAC)	A cryptographic checksum on data that uses a symmetric key to detect both accidental and intentional modifications of the data. MACs provide authenticity and integrity protection, but not non-repudiation protection.
	SOURCE: SP 800-63; FIPS 201
	A cryptographic checksum that results from passing data through a message authentication algorithm.
	SOURCE: FIPS 198
	1. See Checksum. 2. A specific ANSI standard for a checksum.
	SOURCE: CNSSI-4009
Message Digest –	The result of applying a hash function to a message. Also known as a "hash value" or "hash output".
	SOURCE: SP 800-107

A digital signature that uniquely identifies data and has the property that changing a single bit in the data will cause a completely different message digest to be generated.

SOURCE: SP 800-92

A cryptographic checksum, typically generated for a file that can be used to detect changes to the file. Synonymous with hash value/result.

SOURCE: CNSSI-4009

Message Externals –

Information outside of the message text, such as the header, trailer, etc.

SOURCE: CNSSI-4009

Message Indicator –

Sequence of bits transmitted over a communications system for synchronizing cryptographic equipment.

SOURCE: CNSSI-4009

Metrics –

Tools designed to facilitate decision-making and improve performance and accountability through collection, analysis, and reporting of relevant performance-related data.

SOURCE: SP 800-55

MIME –

See Multipurpose Internet Mail Extensions.

Mimicking –

See Spoofing.

Min-Entropy –

A measure of the difficulty that an Attacker has to guess the most commonly chosen password used in a system.

SOURCE: SP 800-63

Minimalist Cryptography –

Cryptography that can be implemented on devices with very limited memory and computing capabilities, such as RFID tags.

SOURCE: SP 800-98

Minor Application –

An application, other than a major application, that requires attention to security due to the risk and magnitude of harm resulting from the loss, misuse, or unauthorized access to or modification of the information in the application. Minor applications are typically included as part of a general support system.

SOURCE: SP 800-18

Misnamed Files –

A technique used to disguise a file's content by changing the file's name to something innocuous or altering its extension to a different type of file, forcing the examiner to identify the files by file signature versus file extension.

SOURCE: SP 800-72; CNSSI-4009

Mission Assurance Category – (MAC)

A Department of Defense Information Assurance Certification and Accreditation Process (DIACAP) term primarily used to determine the requirements for availability and integrity.

SOURCE: CNSSI-4009

Mission Critical –

Any telecommunications or information system that is defined as a national security system (Federal Information Security Management Act of 2002 - FISMA) or processes any information the loss, misuse, disclosure, or unauthorized access to or modification of, would have a debilitating impact on the mission of an agency.

SOURCE: SP 800-60

Mission/Business Segment –

Elements of organizations describing mission areas, common/shared business services, and organization-wide services. Mission/business segments can be identified with one or more information systems which collectively support a mission/business process.

SOURCE: SP 800-30

Mobile Code –

Software programs or parts of programs obtained from remote information systems, transmitted across a network, and executed on a local information system without explicit installation or execution by the recipient.

SOURCE: SP 800-53; SP 800-18

A program (e.g., script, macro, or other portable instruction) that can be shipped unchanged to a heterogeneous collection of platforms and executed with identical semantics.

SOURCE: SP 800-28

Software programs or parts of programs obtained from remote information systems, transmitted across a network, and executed on a local information system without explicit installation or execution by the recipient.

Note: Some examples of software technologies that provide the mechanisms for the production and use of mobile code include Java, JavaScript, ActiveX, VBScript, etc.

SOURCE: CNSSI-4009

Mobile Code Technologies –	Software technologies that provide the mechanisms for the production and use of mobile code (e.g., Java, JavaScript, ActiveX, VBScript). SOURCE: SP 800-53; SP 800-18
Mobile Device –	Portable cartridge/disk-based, removable storage media (e.g., floppy disks, compact disks, USB flash drives, external hard drives, and other flash memory cards/drives that contain nonvolatile memory). Portable computing and communications device with information storage capability (e.g., notebook/laptop computers, personal digital assistants, cellular telephones, digital cameras, and audio recording devices). SOURCE: SP 800-53
Mobile Software Agent –	Programs that are goal-directed and capable of suspending their execution on one platform and moving to another platform where they resume execution. SOURCE: SP 800-19
Mode of Operation –	An algorithm for the cryptographic transformation of data that features a symmetric key block cipher algorithm. SOURCE: SP 800-38C Description of the conditions under which an information system operates based on the sensitivity of information processed and the clearance levels, formal access approvals, and need-to-know of its users. Four modes of operation are authorized for processing or transmitting information: dedicated mode, system high mode, compartmented/partitioned mode, and multilevel mode. SOURCE: CNSSI-4009
Moderate Impact –	The loss of confidentiality, integrity, or availability that could be expected to have a serious adverse effect on organizational operations, organizational assets, individuals, other organizations, or the national security interests of the United States; (i.e., 1) causes a significant degradation in mission capability to an extent and duration that the organization is able to perform its primary functions, but the effectiveness of the functions is significantly reduced; 2) results in significant damage to organizational assets; 3) results in significant financial loss; or 4) results in significant harm to individuals that does not involve loss of life or serious life threatening injuries). SOURCE: CNSSI-4009

Moderate-Impact System –	An information system in which at least one security objective (i.e., confidentiality, integrity, or availability) is assigned a FIPS 199 potential impact value of moderate and no security objective is assigned a FIPS 199 potential impact value of high. SOURCE: SP 800-53; SP 800-60; SP 800-37; FIPS 200 An information system in which at least one security objective (i.e., confidentiality, integrity, or availability) is assigned a potential impact value of moderate and no security objective is assigned a potential impact value of high. SOURCE: CNSSI-4009
Multi-Hop Problem –	The security risks resulting from a mobile software agent visiting several platforms. SOURCE: SP 800-19
Multi-Releasable –	A characteristic of an information domain where access control mechanisms enforce policy-based release of information to authorized users within the information domain. SOURCE: CNSSI-4009
Multifactor Authentication –	Authentication using two or more factors to achieve authentication. Factors include: (i) something you know (e.g. password/PIN); (ii) something you have (e.g., cryptographic identification device, token); or (iii) something you are (e.g., biometric). See Authenticator. SOURCE: SP 800-53
Multilevel Device –	Equipment trusted to properly maintain and separate data of different security domains. SOURCE: CNSSI-4009
Multilevel Mode –	Mode of operation wherein all the following statements are satisfied concerning the users who have direct or indirect access to the system, its peripherals, remote terminals, or remote hosts: 1) some users do not have a valid security clearance for all the information processed in the information system; 2) all users have the proper security clearance and appropriate formal access approval for that information to which they have access; and 3) all users have a valid need-to-know only for information to which they have access. SOURCE: CNSSI-4009
Multilevel Security (MLS) –	Concept of processing information with different classifications and categories that simultaneously permits access by users with different security clearances and denies access to users who lack authorization. SOURCE: CNSSI-4009

Multiple Security Levels (MSL) – Capability of an information system that is trusted to contain, and maintain separation between, resources (particularly stored data) of different security domains.

SOURCE: CNSSI-4009

Mutual Authentication – Occurs when parties at both ends of a communication activity authenticate each other.

SOURCE: SP 800-32

The process of both entities involved in a transaction verifying each other.

SOURCE: CNSSI-4009

Mutual Suspicion – Condition in which two information systems need to rely upon each other to perform a service, yet neither trusts the other to properly protect shared data.

SOURCE: CNSSI-4009

Naming Authority – An organizational entity responsible for assigning distinguished names (DNs) and for assuring that each DN is meaningful and unique within its domain.

SOURCE: SP 800-32

National Information Assurance Partnership (NIAP) – A U.S. government initiative established to promote the use of evaluated information systems products and champion the development and use of national and international standards for information technology security. NIAP was originally established as a collaboration between the National Institute of Standards and Technology (NIST) and the National Security Agency (NSA) in fulfilling their respective responsibilities under P.L. 100-235 (Computer Security Act of 1987). NIST officially withdrew from the partnership in 2007 but NSA continues to manage and operate the program. The key operational component of NIAP is the Common Criteria Evaluation and Validation Scheme (CCEVS) which is the only U.S. government-sponsored and endorsed program for conducting internationally recognized security evaluations of commercial off-the-shelf (COTS) Information Assurance (IA) and IA-enabled information technology products. NIAP employs the CCEVS to provide government oversight or "validation" to U.S. CC evaluations to ensure correct conformance to the International Common Criteria for IT Security Evaluation (ISO/IEC 15408).

SOURCE: CNSSI-4009

National Information Infrastructure –	Nationwide interconnection of communications networks, computers, databases, and consumer electronics that make vast amounts of information available to users. It includes both public and private networks, the Internet, the public switched network, and cable, wireless, and satellite communications. SOURCE: CNSSI-4009
National Security Emergency Preparedness Telecommunications Services –	Telecommunications services that are used to maintain a state of readiness or to respond to and manage any event or crisis (local, national, or international) that causes or could cause injury or harm to the population, damage to or loss of property, or degrade or threaten the national security or emergency preparedness posture of the United States. SOURCE: SP 800-53; CNSSI-4009; 47 C.F.R., Part 64, App A
National Security Information –	Information that has been determined pursuant to Executive Order 12958 as amended by Executive Order 13292, or any predecessor order, or by the Atomic Energy Act of 1954, as amended, to require protection against unauthorized disclosure and is marked to indicate its classified status. SOURCE: SP 800-53A; SP 800-60; FIPS 200
National Security Information (NSI) –	See Classified National Security Information. SOURCE: CNSSI-4009
National Security System –	Any information system (including any telecommunications system) used or operated by an agency or by a contractor of an agency, or other organization on behalf of an agency—(i) the function, operation, or use of which involves intelligence activities; involves cryptologic activities related to national security; involves command and control of military forces; involves equipment that is an integral part of a weapon or weapons system; or is critical to the direct fulfillment of military or intelligence missions (excluding a system that is to be used for routine administrative and business applications, for example, payroll, finance, logistics, and personnel management applications); or (ii) is protected at all times by procedures established for information that have been specifically authorized under criteria established by an Executive Order or an Act of Congress to be kept classified in the interest of national defense or foreign policy. [44 U.S.C., SEC. 3542] SOURCE: FIPS 200; SP 800-37; SP 800-53; SP 800-53A; SP 800-60

Any information system (including any telecommunications system) used or operated by an agency or by a contractor of any agency, or other organization on behalf of an agency, the function, operation, or use of which: I. involves intelligence activities; II. involves cryptologic activities related to national security; III. Involves command and control of military forces; IV. involves equipment that is an integral part of a weapon or weapon system; or V. subject to subparagraph (B), is critical to the direct fulfillment of military or intelligence missions; or is protected at all times by procedures established for information that have been specifically authorized under criteria established by an Executive Order or an Act of Congress to be kept classified in the interest of national defense or foreign policy.

Subparagraph (B). Does not include a system that is to be used for routine administrative and business applications (including payroll, finance, logistics, and personnel management applications). (Title 44 U.S. Code Section 3542, Federal Information Security Management Act of 2002.)

SOURCE: CNSSI-4009

National Vulnerability Database – (NVD)	The U.S. government repository of standards-based vulnerability management data. This data enables automation of vulnerability management, security measurement, and compliance (e.g., FISMA). SOURCE: http://nvd.nist.gov/
Need To Know Determination –	Decision made by an authorized holder of official information that a prospective recipient requires access to specific official information to carry out official duties. SOURCE: CNSSI-4009
Need-To-Know –	A method of isolating information resources based on a user's need to have access to that resource in order to perform their job but no more. The terms 'need-to know" and "least privilege" express the same idea. Need-to-know is generally applied to people, while least privilege is generally applied to processes. SOURCE: CNSSI-4009
Needs Assessment (IT Security Awareness and Training) –	A process that can be used to determine an organization's awareness and training needs. The results of a needs assessment can provide justification to convince management to allocate adequate resources to meet the identified awareness and training needs. SOURCE: SP 800-50

Net-centric Architecture –	A complex system of systems composed of subsystems and services that are part of a continuously evolving, complex community of people, devices, information and services interconnected by a network that enhances information sharing and collaboration. Subsystems and services may or may not be developed or owned by the same entity, and, in general, will not be continually present during the full life cycle of the system of systems. Examples of this architecture include service-oriented architectures and cloud computing architectures. SOURCE: SP 800-37
Network –	Information system(s) implemented with a collection of interconnected components. Such components may include routers, hubs, cabling, telecommunications controllers, key distribution centers, and technical control devices. SOURCE: SP 800-53; CNSSI-4009
Network Access –	Access to an organizational information system by a user (or a process acting on behalf of a user) communicating through a network (e.g., local area network, wide area network, Internet). SOURCE: SP 800-53; CNSSI-4009
Network Access Control (NAC) –	A feature provided by some firewalls that allows access based on a user's credentials and the results of health checks performed on the telework client device. SOURCE: SP 800-41
Network Address Translation (NAT) –	A routing technology used by many firewalls to hide internal system addresses from an external network through use of an addressing schema. SOURCE: SP 800-41
Network Front-End –	Device implementing protocols that allow attachment of a computer system to a network. SOURCE: CNSSI-4009
Network Reference Monitor –	See Reference Monitor.
Network Resilience –	A computing infrastructure that provides continuous business operation (i.e., highly resistant to disruption and able to operate in a degraded mode if damaged), rapid recovery if failure does occur, and the ability to scale to meet rapid or unpredictable demands. SOURCE: CNSSI-4009
Network Security –	See Information Assurance.
Network Security Officer –	See Information Systems Security Officer.

Network Sniffing –	A passive technique that monitors network communication, decodes protocols, and examines headers and payloads for information of interest. It is both a review technique and a target identification and analysis technique.
	SOURCE: SP 800-115
Network Sponsor –	Individual or organization responsible for stating the security policy enforced by the network, designing the network security architecture to properly enforce that policy, and ensuring that the network is implemented in such a way that the policy is enforced.
	SOURCE: CNSSI-4009
Network System –	System implemented with a collection of interconnected components. A network system is based on a coherent security architecture and design.
	SOURCE: CNSSI-4009
Network Weaving –	Penetration technique in which different communication networks are linked to access an information system to avoid detection and trace-back.
	SOURCE: CNSSI-4009
No-Lone Zone (NLZ) –	Area, room, or space that, when staffed, must be occupied by two or more appropriately cleared individuals who remain within sight of each other. See Two-Person Integrity.
	SOURCE: CNSSI-4009
Non-deterministic Random Bit Generator (NRBG) –	An RBG that (when working properly) produces outputs that have full entropy. Contrast with a DRBG. Other names for non-deterministic RBGs are True Random Number (or Bit) Generators and, simply, Random Number (or Bit) Generators.
	SOURCE: SP 800-90A
Non-Local Maintenance –	Maintenance activities conducted by individuals communicating through a network; either an external network (e.g., the Internet) or an internal network.
	SOURCE: SP 800-53
Non-Organizational User –	A user who is not an organizational user (including public users).
	SOURCE: SP 800-53
Non-repudiation –	Assurance that the sender of information is provided with proof of delivery and the recipient is provided with proof of the sender's identity, so neither can later deny having processed the information.
	SOURCE: CNSSI-4009; SP 800-60

Protection against an individual falsely denying having performed a particular action. Provides the capability to determine whether a given individual took a particular action such as creating information, sending a message, approving information, and receiving a message.

SOURCE: SP 800-53; SP 800-18

Is the security service by which the entities involved in a communication cannot deny having participated. Specifically, the sending entity cannot deny having sent a message (non-repudiation with proof of origin), and the receiving entity cannot deny having received a message (non-repudiation with proof of delivery).

SOURCE: FIPS 191

A service that is used to provide assurance of the integrity and origin of data in such a way that the integrity and origin can be verified and validated by a third party as having originated from a specific entity in possession of the private key (i.e., the signatory).

SOURCE: FIPS 186

Nonce –

A value used in security protocols that is never repeated with the same key. For example, nonces used as challenges in challenge-response authentication protocols generally must not be repeated until authentication keys are changed. Otherwise, there is a possibility of a replay attack. Using a nonce as a challenge is a different requirement than a random challenge, because a nonce is not necessarily unpredictable.

SOURCE: SP 800-63

A random or non-repeating value that is included in data exchanged by a protocol, usually for the purpose of guaranteeing the transmittal of live data rather than replayed data, thus detecting and protecting against replay attacks.

SOURCE: CNSSI-4009

NSA-Approved Cryptography –

Cryptography that consists of: (i) an approved algorithm; (ii) an implementation that has been approved for the protection of classified information in a particular environment; and (iii) a supporting key management infrastructure.

SOURCE: SP 800-53

Null –

Dummy letter, letter symbol, or code group inserted into an encrypted message to delay or prevent its decryption or to complete encrypted groups for transmission or transmission security purposes.

SOURCE: CNSSI-4009

Object –	A passive entity that contains or receives information. SOURCE: SP 800-27 Passive information system-related entity (e.g., devices, files, records, tables, processes, programs, domains) containing or receiving information. Access to an object implies access to the information it contains. SOURCE: CNSSI-4009 Passive information system-related entity (e.g., devices, files, records, tables, processes, programs, domains) containing or receiving information. Access to an object (by a subject) implies access to the information it contains. See Subject. SOURCE: SP 800-53
Object Identifier –	A specialized formatted number that is registered with an internationally recognized standards organization. The unique alphanumeric/numeric identifier registered under the ISO registration standard to reference a specific object or object class. In the federal government PKI, they are used to uniquely identify each of the four policies and cryptographic algorithms supported. SOURCE: SP 800-32
Object Reuse –	Reassignment and reuse of a storage medium containing one or more objects after ensuring no residual data remains on the storage medium. SOURCE: CNSSI-4009
Off-Card –	Refers to data that is not stored within the PIV card or computation that is not done by the Integrated Circuit Chip (ICC) of the PIV card. SOURCE: FIPS 201
Off-line Attack –	An attack where the Attacker obtains some data (typically by eavesdropping on an authentication protocol run, or by penetrating a system and stealing security files) that he/she is able to analyze in a system of his/her own choosing. SOURCE: SP 800-63
Off-line Cryptosystem –	Cryptographic system in which encryption and decryption are performed independently of the transmission and reception functions. SOURCE: CNSSI-4009

Official Information –	All information in the custody and control of a U.S. government department or agency that was acquired by U.S. government employees as a part of their official duties or because of their official status and has not been cleared for public release.
	SOURCE: CNSSI-4009
On-Card –	Refers to data that is stored within the PIV card or computation that is done by the ICC of the PIV card.
	SOURCE: FIPS 201
Online Attack –	An attack against an authentication protocol where the Attacker either assumes the role of a Claimant with a genuine Verifier or actively alters the authentication channel. The goal of the attack may be to gain authenticated access or learn authentication secrets.
	SOURCE: SP 800-63
Online Certificate Status Protocol (OCSP) –	An online protocol used to determine the status of a public key certificate.
	SOURCE: FIPS 201
Online Cryptosystem –	Cryptographic system in which encryption and decryption are performed in association with the transmitting and receiving functions.
	SOURCE: CNSSI-4009
One-part Code –	Code in which plain text elements and their accompanying code groups are arranged in alphabetical, numerical, or other systematic order, so one listing serves for both encoding and decoding. One-part codes are normally small codes used to pass small volumes of low-sensitivity information.
	SOURCE: CNSSI-4009
One-time Cryptosystem –	Cryptosystem employing key used only once.
	SOURCE: CNSSI-4009
One-time Pad –	Manual one-time cryptosystem produced in pad form.
	SOURCE: CNSSI-4009
One-time Tape –	Punched paper tape used to provide key streams on a one-time basis in certain machine cryptosystems.
	SOURCE: CNSSI-4009

One-Way Hash Algorithm –

Hash algorithms which map arbitrarily long inputs into a fixed-size output such that it is very difficult (computationally infeasible) to find two different hash inputs that produce the same output. Such algorithms are an essential part of the process of producing fixed-size digital signatures that can both authenticate the signer and provide for data integrity checking (detection of input modification after signature).

SOURCE: SP 800-49; CNSSI-4009

Open Checklist Interactive Language (OCIL) –

SCAP language for expressing security checks that cannot be evaluated without some human interaction or feedback.

SOURCE: SP 800-128

Open Vulnerability and Assessment Language (OVAL) –

SCAP language for specifying low-level testing procedures used by checklists.

SOURCE: SP 800-128

Open Storage –

Any storage of classified national security information outside of approved containers. This includes classified information that is resident on information systems media and outside of an approved storage container, regardless of whether or not that media is in use (i.e., unattended operations).

SOURCE: CNSSI-4009

Operating System (OS) Fingerprinting –

Analyzing characteristics of packets sent by a target, such as packet headers or listening ports, to identify the operating system in use on the target.

SOURCE: SP 800-115

Operational Controls –

The security controls (i.e., safeguards or countermeasures) for an information system that primarily are implemented and executed by people (as opposed to systems).

SOURCE: SP 800-53; SP 800-37; FIPS 200

The security controls (i.e., safeguards or countermeasures) for an information system that are primarily implemented and executed by people (as opposed to systems).

SOURCE: CNSSI-4009; SP 800-53A

Operational Key –

Key intended for use over-the-air for protection of operational information or for the production or secure electrical transmission of key streams.

SOURCE: CNSSI-4009

Operational Vulnerability Information –	Information that describes the presence of an information vulnerability within a specific operational setting or network.
	SOURCE: CNSSI-4009
Operational Waiver –	Authority for continued use of unmodified COMSEC end-items pending the completion of a mandatory modification.
	SOURCE: CNSSI-4009
Operations Code –	Code composed largely of words and phrases suitable for general communications use.
	SOURCE: CNSSI-4009
Operations Security (OPSEC) –	Systematic and proven process by which potential adversaries can be denied information about capabilities and intentions by identifying, controlling, and protecting generally unclassified evidence of the planning and execution of sensitive activities. The process involves five steps: identification of critical information, analysis of threats, analysis of vulnerabilities, assessment of risks, and application of appropriate countermeasures.
	SOURCE: CNSSI-4009
Optional Modification –	NSA-approved modification not required for universal implementation by all holders of a COMSEC end-item. This class of modification requires all of the engineering/doctrinal control of mandatory modification but is usually not related to security, safety, TEMPEST, or reliability. See Mandatory Modification.
	SOURCE: CNSSI-4009
Organization –	A federal agency, or, as appropriate, any of its operational elements.
	SOURCE: FIPS 200
	An entity of any size, complexity, or positioning within an organizational structure (e.g., a federal agency, or, as appropriate, any of its operational elements).
	SOURCE: SP 800-53; SP 800-53A; SP 800-37
Organizational Information Security Continuous Monitoring –	Ongoing monitoring sufficient to ensure and assure effectiveness of security controls related to systems, networks, and cyberspace, by assessing security control implementation and organizational security status in accordance with organizational risk tolerance – and within a reporting structure designed to make real-time, data-driven risk management decisions.
	SOURCE: SP 800-137
Organizational Maintenance –	Limited maintenance performed by a user organization.
	SOURCE: CNSSI-4009

Organizational Registration Authority (ORA) –	Entity within the PKI that authenticates the identity and the organizational affiliation of the users. SOURCE: CNSSI-4009
Organizational User –	An organizational employee or an individual the organization deems to have equivalent status of an employee (e.g., contractor, guest researcher, individual detailed from another organization, individual from allied nation). SOURCE: SP 800-53
Outside Threat –	An unauthorized entity from outside the domain perimeter that has the potential to harm an Information System through destruction, disclosure, modification of data, and/or denial of service. SOURCE: SP 800-32
Outside(r) Threat –	An unauthorized entity outside the security domain that has the potential to harm an information system through destruction, disclosure, modification of data, and/or denial of service. SOURCE: CNSSI-4009
Over-The-Air Key Distribution –	Providing electronic key via over-the-air rekeying, over-the-air key transfer, or cooperative key generation. SOURCE: CNSSI-4009
Over-The-Air Key Transfer –	Electronically distributing key without changing traffic encryption key used on the secured communications path over which the transfer is accomplished. SOURCE: CNSSI-4009
Over-The-Air Rekeying (OTAR) –	Changing traffic encryption key or transmission security key in remote cryptographic equipment by sending new key directly to the remote cryptographic equipment over the communications path it secures. SOURCE: CNSSI-4009
Overt Channel –	Communications path within a computer system or network designed for the authorized transfer of data. See Covert Channel. SOURCE: CNSSI-4009
Overt Testing –	Security testing performed with the knowledge and consent of the organization's IT staff. SOURCE: SP 800-115

Overwrite Procedure –	A software process that replaces data previously stored on storage media with a predetermined set of meaningless data or random patterns. SOURCE: CNSSI-4009
Packet Filter –	A routing device that provides access control functionality for host addresses and communication sessions. SOURCE: SP 800-41
Packet Sniffer –	Software that observes and records network traffic. SOURCE: CNSSI-4009
Parity –	Bit(s) used to determine whether a block of data has been altered. SOURCE: CNSSI-4009
Partitioned Security Mode –	Information systems security mode of operation wherein all personnel have the clearance, but not necessarily formal access approval and need-to-know, for all information handled by an information system. SOURCE: CNSSI-4009
Passive Attack –	An attack against an authentication protocol where the Attacker intercepts data traveling along the network between the Claimant and Verifier, but does not alter the data (i.e., eavesdropping). SOURCE: SP 800-63 An attack that does not alter systems or data. SOURCE: CNSSI-4009
Passive Security Testing –	Security testing that does not involve any direct interaction with the targets, such as sending packets to a target. SOURCE: SP 800-115
Passive Wiretapping –	The monitoring or recording of data while it is being transmitted over a communications link, without altering or affecting the data. SOURCE: CNSSI-4009
Password –	A secret that a Claimant memorizes and uses to authenticate his or her identity. Passwords are typically character strings. SOURCE: SP 800-63 A protected character string used to authenticate the identity of a computer system user or to authorize access to system resources. SOURCE: FIPS 181

137

A string of characters (letters, numbers, and other symbols) used to authenticate an identity or to verify access authorization.

SOURCE: FIPS 140-2

A protected/private string of letters, numbers, and/or special characters used to authenticate an identity or to authorize access to data.

SOURCE: CNSSI-4009

Password Cracking –

The process of recovering secret passwords stored in a computer system or transmitted over a network.

SOURCE: SP 800-115

Password Protected –

The ability to protect a file using a password access control, protecting the data contents from being viewed with the appropriate viewer unless the proper password is entered.

SOURCE: SP 800-72

The ability to protect the contents of a file or device from being accessed until the correct password is entered.

SOURCE: SP 800-124

Patch –

An update to an operating system, application, or other software issued specifically to correct particular problems with the software.

SOURCE: SP 800-123

Patch Management –

The systematic notification, identification, deployment, installation, and verification of operating system and application software code revisions. These revisions are known as patches, hot fixes, and service packs.

SOURCE: CNSSI-4009

Path Histories –

Maintaining an authenticatable record of the prior platforms visited by a mobile software agent, so that a newly visited platform can determine whether to process the agent and what resource constraints to apply.

SOURCE: SP 800-19

Payload –

The input data to the CCM generation-encryption process that is both authenticated and encrypted.

SOURCE: SP 800-38C

Peer Entity Authentication –

The process of verifying that a peer entity in an association is as claimed.

SOURCE: CNSSI-4009

Penetration –	See Intrusion.
Penetration Testing –	A test methodology in which assessors, using all available documentation (e.g., system design, source code, manuals) and working under specific constraints, attempt to circumvent the security features of an information system. SOURCE: SP 800-53A A test methodology in which assessors, typically working under specific constraints, attempt to circumvent or defeat the security features of an information system. SOURCE: SP 800-53; CNSSI-4009 Security testing in which evaluators mimic real-world attacks in an attempt to identify ways to circumvent the security features of an application, system, or network. Penetration testing often involves issuing real attacks on real systems and data, using the same tools and techniques used by actual attackers. Most penetration tests involve looking for combinations of vulnerabilities on a single system or multiple systems that can be used to gain more access than could be achieved through a single vulnerability. SOURCE: SP 800-115
Per-Call Key –	Unique traffic encryption key generated automatically by certain secure telecommunications systems to secure single voice or data transmissions. See Cooperative Key Generation. SOURCE: CNSSI-4009
Performance Reference Model – (PRM)	Framework for performance measurement providing common output measurements throughout the federal government. It allows agencies to better manage the business of government at a strategic level by providing a means for using an agency's EA to measure the success of information systems investments and their impact on strategic outcomes. SOURCE: CNSSI-4009
Perimeter –	(C&A) Encompasses all those components of the system that are to be accredited by the DAA, and excludes separately accredited systems to which the system is connected. (Authorization) Encompasses all those components of the system or network for which a Body of Evidence is provided in support of a formal approval to operate. SOURCE: CNSSI-4009

Periods Processing –	The processing of various levels of classified and unclassified information at distinctly different times. Under the concept of periods processing, the system must be purged of all information from one processing period before transitioning to the next.
	SOURCE: CNSSI-4009
Perishable Data –	Information whose value can decrease substantially during a specified time. A significant decrease in value occurs when the operational circumstances change to the extent that the information is no longer useful.
	SOURCE: CNSSI-4009
Permuter –	Device used in cryptographic equipment to change the order in which the contents of a shift register are used in various nonlinear combining circuits.
	SOURCE: CNSSI-4009
Personal Firewall –	A utility on a computer that monitors network activity and blocks communications that are unauthorized.
	SOURCE: SP 800-69
Personal Identification Number – (PIN)	A password consisting only of decimal digits.
	SOURCE: SP 800-63
	A secret that a claimant memorizes and uses to authenticate his or her identity. PINs are generally only decimal digits.
	SOURCE: FIPS 201
	An alphanumeric code or password used to authenticate an identity.
	SOURCE: FIPS 140-2
	A short numeric code used to confirm identity.
	SOURCE: CNSSI-4009
Personal Identity Verification – (PIV)	The process of creating and using a governmentwide secure and reliable form of identification for federal employees and contractors, in support of HSPD 12, *Policy for a Common Identification Standard for Federal Employees and Contractors.*
	SOURCE: CNSSI-4009
Personal Identity Verification Accreditation –	The official management decision to authorize operation of a PIV Card Issuer after determining that the Issuer's reliability has satisfactorily been established through appropriate assessment and certification processes.
	SOURCE: CNSSI-4009

Personal Identity Verification Authorizing Official –	An individual who can act on behalf of an agency to authorize the issuance of a credential to an applicant. SOURCE: CNSSI-4009
Personal Identity Verification Card – (PIV Card)	Physical artifact (e.g., identity card, "smart" card) issued to an individual that contains stored identity credentials (e.g., photograph, cryptographic keys, digitized fingerprint representation, etc.) such that a claimed identity of the cardholder may be verified against the stored credentials by another person (human-readable and verifiable) or an automated process (computer-readable and verifiable). SOURCE: FIPS 201; CNSSI-4009
Personal Identity Verification Issuer –	An authorized identity card creator that procures FIPS-approved blank identity cards, initializes them with appropriate software and data elements for the requested identity verification and access control application, personalizes the cards with the identity credentials of the authorized subjects, and delivers the personalized card to the authorized subjects along with appropriate instructions for protection and use. SOURCE: FIPS 201
Personal Identity Verification Registrar –	An entity that establishes and vouches for the identity of an applicant to a PIV Issuer. The PIV RA authenticates the applicant's identity by checking identity source documents and identity proofing, and that ensures a proper background check has been completed, before the credential is issued. SOURCE: FIPS 201
Personal Identity Verification Sponsor –	An individual who can act on behalf of a department or agency to request a PIV Card for an applicant. SOURCE: FIPS 201
Personally Identifiable Information – (PII)	Information which can be used to distinguish or trace an individual's identity, such as their name, social security number, biometric records, etc., alone, or when combined with other personal or identifying information which is linked or linkable to a specific individual, such as date and place of birth, mother's maiden name, etc. SOURCE: CNSSI-4009 Any information about an individual maintained by an agency, including (1) any information that can be used to distinguish or trace an individual's identity, such as name, social security number, date and place of birth, mother's maiden name, or biometric records; and (2) any other information that is linked or linkable to an individual, such as medical, educational, financial, and employment information. SOURCE: SP 800-122

Personnel Registration Manager –	The management role that is responsible for registering human users, i.e., users that are people. SOURCE: CNSSI-4009
Phishing –	Tricking individuals into disclosing sensitive personal information through deceptive computer-based means. SOURCE: SP 800-83 Deceiving individuals into disclosing sensitive personal information through deceptive computer-based means. SOURCE: CNSSI-4009 A digital form of social engineering that uses authentic-looking—but bogus—emails to request information from users or direct them to a fake Web site that requests information. SOURCE: SP 800-115
Physically Isolated Network –	A network that is not connected to entities or systems outside a physically controlled space. SOURCE: SP 800-32
Piconet –	A small Bluetooth network created on an ad hoc basis that includes two or more devices. SOURCE: SP 800-121
PII Confidentiality Impact Level –	The PII confidentiality impact level—*low, moderate, or high*—indicates the potential harm that could result to the subject individuals and/or the organization if PII were inappropriately accessed, used, or disclosed. SOURCE: SP 800-122
Plaintext –	Data input to the Cipher or output from the Inverse Cipher. SOURCE: FIPS 197 Intelligible data that has meaning and can be understood without the application of decryption. SOURCE: SP 800-21 Unencrypted information. SOURCE: CNSSI-4009
Plaintext Key –	An unencrypted cryptographic key. SOURCE: FIPS 140-2

Plan of Action and Milestones – (POA&M)	A document that identifies tasks needing to be accomplished. It details resources required to accomplish the elements of the plan, any milestones in meeting the tasks, and scheduled completion dates for the milestones. SOURCE: SP 800-53; SP 800-53A; SP 800-37; SP 800-64; CNSSI-4009; OMB Memorandum 02-01
Policy Approving Authority – (PAA)	First level of the PKI Certification Management Authority that approves the security policy of each PCA. SOURCE: CNSSI-4009
Policy-Based Access Control – (PBAC)	A form of access control that uses an authorization policy that is flexible in the types of evaluated parameters (e.g., identity, role, clearance, operational need, risk, and heuristics). SOURCE: CNSSI-4009
Policy Certification Authority – (PCA)	Second level of the PKI Certification Management Authority that formulates the security policy under which it and its subordinate CAs will issue public key certificates. SOURCE: CNSSI-4009
Policy Management Authority – (PMA)	Body established to oversee the creation and update of Certificate Policies, review Certification Practice Statements, review the results of CA audits for policy compliance, evaluate non-domain policies for acceptance within the domain, and generally oversee and manage the PKI certificate policies. For the FBCA, the PMA is the Federal PKI Policy Authority. SOURCE: SP 800-32
Policy Mapping –	Recognizing that, when a CA in one domain certifies a CA in another domain, a particular certificate policy in the second domain may be considered by the authority of the first domain to be equivalent (but not necessarily identical in all respects) to a particular certificate policy in the first domain. SOURCE: SP 800-15
Port –	A physical entry or exit point of a cryptographic module that provides access to the module for physical signals, represented by logical information flows (physically separated ports do not share the same physical pin or wire). SOURCE: FIPS 140-2
Port Scanning –	Using a program to remotely determine which ports on a system are open (e.g., whether systems allow connections through those ports). SOURCE: CNSSI-4009

Portal –	A high-level remote access architecture that is based on a server that offers teleworkers access to one or more applications through a single centralized interface.
	SOURCE: SP 800-46
Portable Electronic Device (PED) –	Any nonstationary electronic apparatus with singular or multiple capabilities of recording, storing, and/or transmitting data, voice, video, or photo images. This includes but is not limited to laptops, personal digital assistants, pocket personal computers, palmtops, MP3 players, cellular telephones, thumb drives, video cameras, and pagers.
	SOURCE: CNSSI-4009
Positive Control Material –	Generic term referring to a sealed authenticator system, permissive action link, coded switch system, positive enable system, or nuclear command and control documents, material, or devices.
	SOURCE: CNSSI-4009
Potential Impact –	The loss of confidentiality, integrity, or availability could be expected to have: 1) a *limited* adverse effect (FIPS 199 low); 2) a *serious* adverse effect (FIPS 199 moderate); or 3) a *severe* or *catastrophic* adverse effect (FIPS 199 high) on organizational operations, organizational assets, or individuals.
	SOURCE: SP 800-53; SP 800-60; SP 800-37; FIPS 199
	The loss of confidentiality, integrity, or availability could be expected to have a limited adverse effect; a serious adverse effect, or a severe or catastrophic adverse effect on organizational operations, organizational assets, or individuals.
	SOURCE: FIPS 200
	The loss of confidentiality, integrity, or availability that could be expected to have a limited (low) adverse effect, a serious (moderate) adverse effect, or a severe or catastrophic (high) adverse effect on organizational operations, organizational assets, or individuals.
	SOURCE: CNSSI-4009
Practice Statement –	A formal statement of the practices followed by an authentication entity (e.g., RA, CSP, or Verifier). It usually describes the policies and practices of the parties and can become legally binding. SOURCE: SP 800-63
Precursor –	A sign that an attacker may be preparing to cause an incident.
	SOURCE: SP 800-61

A sign that an attacker may be preparing to cause an incident. See Indicator.

SOURCE: CNSSI-4009

Prediction Resistance –

Prediction resistance is provided relative to time T if there is assurance that an adversary who has knowledge of the internal state of the DRBG at some time prior to T would be unable to distinguish between observations of ideal random bitstrings and bitstrings output by the DRBG at or subsequent to time T. The complementary assurance is called Backtracking Resistance.

SOURCE: SP 800-90A

Predisposing Condition –

A condition that exists within an organization, a mission/business process, enterprise architecture, or information system including its environment of operation, which contributes to (i.e., increases or decreases) the likelihood that one or more threat events, once initiated, will result in undesirable consequences or adverse impact to organizational operations and assets, individuals, other organizations, or the Nation.

SOURCE: SP 800-30

Preproduction Model –

Version of INFOSEC equipment employing standard parts and suitable for complete evaluation of form, design, and performance. Preproduction models are often referred to as beta models.

SOURCE: CNSSI-4009

Primary Services Node (PRSN) –

A Key Management Infrastructure core node that provides the users' central point of access to KMI products, services, and information.

SOURCE: CNSSI-4009

Principal –

An entity whose identity can be authenticated.

SOURCE: FIPS 196

Principal Accrediting Authority – (PAA)

Senior official with authority and responsibility for all intelligence systems within an agency.

SOURCE: CNSSI-4009

Principal Certification Authority – (CA)

The Principal Certification Authority is a CA designated by an agency to interoperate with the FBCA. An agency may designate multiple Principal CAs to interoperate with the FBCA.

SOURCE: SP 800-32

Print Suppression –

Eliminating the display of characters in order to preserve their secrecy.

SOURCE: CNSSI-4009

Privacy –	Restricting access to subscriber or Relying Party information in accordance with federal law and agency policy.
	SOURCE: SP 800-32
Privacy Impact Assessment (PIA) –	An analysis of how information is handled: 1) to ensure handling conforms to applicable legal, regulatory, and policy requirements regarding privacy; 2) to determine the risks and effects of collecting, maintaining, and disseminating information in identifiable form in an electronic information system; and 3) to examine and evaluate protections and alternative processes for handling information to mitigate potential privacy risks.
	SOURCE: SP 800-53; SP 800-18; SP 800-122; CNSSI-4009; OMB Memorandum 03-22
Privacy System –	Commercial encryption system that affords telecommunications limited protection to deter a casual listener, but cannot withstand a technically competent cryptanalytic attack.
	SOURCE: CNSSI-4009
Private Key –	The secret part of an asymmetric key pair that is typically used to digitally sign or decrypt data.
	SOURCE: SP 800-63
	A cryptographic key, used with a public key cryptographic algorithm, that is uniquely associated with an entity and is not made public. In an asymmetric (public) cryptosystem, the private key is associated with a public key. Depending on the algorithm, the private key may be used, for example, to: 1) Compute the corresponding public key, 2) Compute a digital signature that may be verified by the corresponding public key, 3) Decrypt keys that were encrypted by the corresponding public key, or 4) Compute a shared secret during a key-agreement transaction.
	SOURCE: SP 800-57 Part 1
	A cryptographic key used with a public key cryptographic algorithm, which is uniquely associated with an entity, and not made public; it is used to generate a digital signature; this key is mathematically linked with a corresponding public key.
	SOURCE: FIPS 196
	A cryptographic key, used with a public key cryptographic algorithm, that is uniquely associated with an entity and is not made public.
	SOURCE: FIPS 140-2

	In an asymmetric cryptography scheme, the private or secret key of a key pair which must be kept confidential and is used to decrypt messages encrypted with the public key or to digitally sign messages, which can then be validated with the public key.
	SOURCE: CNSSI-4009
Privilege –	A right granted to an individual, a program, or a process.
	SOURCE: CNSSI-4009
Privilege Management –	The definition and management of policies and processes that define the ways in which the user is provided access rights to enterprise systems. It governs the management of the data that constitutes the user's privileges and other attributes, including the storage, organization and access to information in directories.
	SOURCE: NISTIR 7657
Privileged Account –	An information system account with approved authorizations of a privileged user.
	SOURCE: CNSSI-4009
	An information system account with authorizations of a privileged user.
	SOURCE: SP 800-53
Privileged Accounts –	Individuals who have access to set "access rights" for users on a given system. Sometimes referred to as system or network administrative accounts.
	SOURCE: SP 800-12
Privileged Command –	A human-initiated command executed on an information system involving the control, monitoring, or administration of the system including security functions and associated security-relevant information.
	SOURCE: SP 800-53; CNSSI-4009
Privileged Process –	A computer process that is authorized (and, therefore, trusted) to perform security-relevant functions that ordinary processes are not authorized to perform.
	SOURCE: CNSSI-4009
Privileged User –	A user that is authorized (and, therefore, trusted) to perform security-relevant functions that ordinary users are not authorized to perform.
	SOURCE: SP 800-53; CNSSI-4009
Probability of Occurrence –	See Likelihood of Occurrence.

Probe –

A technique that attempts to access a system to learn something about the system.

SOURCE: CNSSI-4009

Product Source Node (PSN) –

The Key Management Infrastructure core node that provides central generation of cryptographic key material.

SOURCE: CNSSI-4009

Production Model –

INFOSEC equipment in its final mechanical and electrical form.

SOURCE: CNSSI-4009

Profiling –

Measuring the characteristics of expected activity so that changes to it can be more easily identified.

SOURCE: SP 800-61; CNSSI-4009

Promiscuous Mode –

A configuration setting for a network interface card that causes it to accept all incoming packets that it sees, regardless of their intended destinations.

SOURCE: SP 800-94

Proprietary Information (PROPIN) –

Material and information relating to or associated with a company's products, business, or activities, including but not limited to financial information; data or statements; trade secrets; product research and development; existing and future product designs and performance specifications; marketing plans or techniques; schematics; client lists; computer programs; processes; and know-how that has been clearly identified and properly marked by the company as proprietary information, trade secrets, or company confidential information. The information must have been developed by the company and not be available to the government or to the public without restriction from another source.

SOURCE: CNSSI-4009

Protected Distribution System (PDS) –

Wire line or fiber optic system that includes adequate safeguards and/or countermeasures (e.g., acoustic, electric, electromagnetic, and physical) to permit its use for the transmission of unencrypted information through an area of lesser classification or control.

SOURCE: CNSSI-4009

Protection Philosophy –

Informal description of the overall design of an information system delineating each of the protection mechanisms employed. Combination of formal and informal techniques, appropriate to the evaluation class, used to show the mechanisms are adequate to enforce the security policy.

SOURCE: CNSSI-4009

Protection Profile –	Common Criteria specification that represents an implementation-independent set of security requirements for a category of Target of Evaluations (TOE) that meets specific consumer needs. SOURCE: CNSSI-4009
Protective Distribution System –	Wire line or fiber optic system that includes adequate safeguards and/or countermeasures (e.g., acoustic, electric, electromagnetic, and physical) to permit its use for the transmission of unencrypted information. SOURCE: SP 800-53
Protective Packaging –	Packaging techniques for COMSEC material that discourage penetration, reveal a penetration has occurred or was attempted, or inhibit viewing or copying of keying material prior to the time it is exposed for use. SOURCE: CNSSI-4009
Protective Technologies –	Special tamper-evident features and materials employed for the purpose of detecting tampering and deterring attempts to compromise, modify, penetrate, extract, or substitute information processing equipment and keying material. SOURCE: CNSSI-4009
Protocol –	Set of rules and formats, semantic and syntactic, permitting information systems to exchange information. SOURCE: CNSSI-4009
Protocol Data Unit –	A unit of data specified in a protocol and consisting of protocol information and, possibly, user data. SOURCE: FIPS 188
Protocol Entity –	Entity that follows a set of rules and formats (semantic and syntactic) that determines the communication behavior of other entities. SOURCE: FIPS 188
Proxy –	A proxy is an application that "breaks" the connection between client and server. The proxy accepts certain types of traffic entering or leaving a network and processes it and forwards it. This effectively closes the straight path between the internal and external networks making it more difficult for an attacker to obtain internal addresses and other details of the organization's internal network. Proxy servers are available for common Internet services; for example, a Hyper Text Transfer Protocol (HTTP) proxy used for Web access, and a Simple Mail Transfer Protocol (SMTP) proxy used for email. SOURCE: SP 800-44

An application that "breaks" the connection between client and server. The proxy accepts certain types of traffic entering or leaving a network and processes it and forwards it.

Note: This effectively closes the straight path between the internal and external networks, making it more difficult for an attacker to obtain internal addresses and other details of the organization's internal network. Proxy servers are available for common Internet services; for example, a Hyper Text Transfer Protocol (HTTP) proxy used for Web access, and a Simple Mail Transfer Protocol (SMTP) proxy used for email.

SOURCE: CNSSI-4009

Proxy Agent –

A software application running on a firewall or on a dedicated proxy server that is capable of filtering a protocol and routing it between the interfaces of the device.

SOURCE: CNSSI-4009

Proxy Server –

A server that services the requests of its clients by forwarding those requests to other servers.

SOURCE: CNSSI-4009

Pseudorandom number generator – (PRNG)

An algorithm that produces a sequence of bits that are uniquely determined from an initial value called a seed. The output of the PRNG "appears" to be random, i.e., the output is statistically indistinguishable from random values. A cryptographic PRNG has the additional property that the output is unpredictable, given that the seed is not known.

SOURCE: CNSSI-4009

Pseudonym –

A false name.

SOURCE: SP 800-63

1. A subscriber name that has been chosen by the subscriber that is not verified as meaningful by identity proofing.
2. An assigned identity that is used to protect an individual's true identity.

SOURCE: CNSSI-4009

Public Domain Software –

Software not protected by copyright laws of any nation that may be freely used without permission of, or payment to, the creator, and that carries no warranties from, or liabilities to the creator.

SOURCE: CNSSI-4009

Public Key –

The public part of an asymmetric key pair that is typically used to verify signatures or encrypt data.

SOURCE: FIPS 201; SP 800-63

A cryptographic key, used with a public key cryptographic algorithm, that is uniquely associated with an entity and may be made public. In an asymmetric (public) cryptosystem, the public key is associated with a private key. The public key may be known by anyone and, depending on the algorithm, may be used, for example, to:
1) Verify a digital signature that is signed by the corresponding private key,
2) Encrypt keys that can be decrypted by the corresponding private key, or
3) Compute a shared secret during a key-agreement transaction.

SOURCE: SP 800-57 Part 1

A cryptographic key used with a public key cryptographic algorithm, uniquely associated with an entity, and which may be made public; it is used to verify a digital signature; this key is mathematically linked with a corresponding private key.

SOURCE: FIPS 196

A cryptographic key used with a public key cryptographic algorithm that is uniquely associated with an entity and that may be made public.

SOURCE: FIPS 140-2

A cryptographic key that may be widely published and is used to enable the operation of an asymmetric cryptography scheme. This key is mathematically linked with a corresponding private key. Typically, a public key can be used to encrypt, but not decrypt, or to validate a signature, but not to sign.

SOURCE: CNSSI-4009

Public Key Certificate –

A digital document issued and digitally signed by the private key of a Certificate authority that binds the name of a Subscriber to a public key. The certificate indicates that the Subscriber identified in the certificate has sole control and access to the private key.

SOURCE: SP 800-63

A set of data that unambiguously identifies an entity, contains the entity's public key, and is digitally signed by a trusted third party (certification authority).

SOURCE: FIPS 196

A set of data that uniquely identifies an entity, contains the entity's public key, and is digitally signed by a trusted party, thereby binding the public key to the entity.

SOURCE: FIPS 140-2

See Also Certificate.

Public Key (Asymmetric) Cryptographic Algorithm –

A cryptographic algorithm that uses two related keys, a public key and a private key. The two keys have the property that deriving the private key from the public key is computationally infeasible.

SOURCE: FIPS 140-2

Public Key Cryptography –

Encryption system that uses a public-private key pair for encryption and/or digital signature.

SOURCE: CNSSI-4009

Public Key Enabling (PKE) –

The incorporation of the use of certificates for security services such as authentication, confidentiality, data integrity, and non-repudiation.

SOURCE: CNSSI-4009

Public Key Infrastructure (PKI) –

A set of policies, processes, server platforms, software, and workstations used for the purpose of administering certificates and public-private key pairs, including the ability to issue, maintain, and revoke public key certificates.

SOURCE: SP 800-32; SP 800-63

An architecture which is used to bind public keys to entities, enable other entities to verify public key bindings, revoke such bindings, and provide other services critical to managing public keys.

SOURCE: FIPS 196

A Framework that is established to issue, maintain, and revoke public key certificates.

SOURCE: FIPS 186

A support service to the PIV system that provides the cryptographic keys needed to perform digital signature-based identity verification and to protect communications and storage of sensitive verification system data within identity cards and the verification system.

SOURCE: FIPS 201

The framework and services that provide for the generation, production, distribution, control, accounting, and destruction of public key certificates. Components include the personnel, policies, processes, server platforms, software, and workstations used for the purpose of administering certificates and public-private key pairs, including the ability to issue, maintain, recover, and revoke public key certificates.

SOURCE: CNSSI-4009

Public Seed –

A starting value for a pseudorandom number generator. The value produced by the random number generator may be made public. The public seed is often called a "salt."

SOURCE: CNSSI-4009

Purge –

Rendering sanitized data unrecoverable by laboratory attack methods.

SOURCE: SP 800-88; CNSSI-4009

Quadrant –

Short name referring to technology that provides tamper-resistant protection to cryptographic equipment.

SOURCE: CNSSI-4009

Qualitative Assessment –

Use of a set of methods, principles, or rules for assessing risk based on nonnumeric categories or levels.

SOURCE: SP 800-30

Quality of Service –

The measurable end-to-end performance properties of a network service, which can be guaranteed in advance by a Service-Level Agreement between a user and a service provider, so as to satisfy specific customer application requirements. Note: These properties may include throughput (bandwidth), transit delay (latency), error rates, priority, security, packet loss, packet jitter, etc.

SOURCE: CNSSI-4009

Quantitative Assessment –

Use of a set of methods, principles, or rules for assessing risks based on the use of numbers where the meanings and proportionality of values are maintained inside and outside the context of the assessment.

SOURCE: SP 800-30

Quarantine –

Store files containing malware in isolation for future disinfection or examination.

SOURCE: SP 800-69

Radio Frequency Identification – (RFID)	A form of automatic identification and data capture (AIDC) that uses electric or magnetic fields at radio frequencies to transmit information. SOURCE: SP 800-98
Random Bit Generator (RBG) –	A device or algorithm that outputs a sequence of binary bits that appears to be statistically independent and unbiased. An RBG is either a DRBG or an NRBG. SOURCE: SP 800-90A
Random Number Generator – (RNG)	A process used to generate an unpredictable series of numbers. Each individual value is called random if each of the values in the total population of values has an equal probability of being selected. SOURCE: CNSSI-4009 Random Number Generators (RNGs) used for cryptographic applications typically produce a sequence of zero and one bits that may be combined into sub-sequences or blocks of random numbers. There are two basic classes: deterministic and nondeterministic. A deterministic RNG consists of an algorithm that produces a sequence of bits from an initial value called a seed. A nondeterministic RNG produces output that is dependent on some unpredictable physical source that is outside human control. SOURCE: FIPS 140-2
Randomizer –	Analog or digital source of unpredictable, unbiased, and usually independent bits. Randomizers can be used for several different functions, including key generation or to provide a starting state for a key generator. SOURCE: CNSSI-4009
RBAC –	See Role-Based Access Control.
Read –	Fundamental operation in an information system that results only in the flow of information from an object to a subject. SOURCE: CNSSI-4009
Read Access –	Permission to read information in an information system. SOURCE: CNSSI-4009
Real-Time Reaction –	Immediate response to a penetration attempt that is detected and diagnosed in time to prevent access. SOURCE: CNSSI-4009

Recipient Usage Period –	The period of time during the cryptoperiod of a symmetric key when protected information is processed. SOURCE: SP 800-57 Part 1
Reciprocity –	Mutual agreement among participating enterprises to accept each other's security assessments in order to reuse information system resources and/or to accept each other's assessed security posture in order to share information. SOURCE: CNSSI-4009 Mutual agreement among participating organizations to accept each other's security assessments in order to reuse information system resources and/or to accept each other's assessed security posture in order to share information. SOURCE: SP 800-37; SP 800-53; SP 800-53A; SP 800-39
Records –	The recordings (automated and/or manual) of evidence of activities performed or results achieved (e.g., forms, reports, test results), which serve as a basis for verifying that the organization and the information system are performing as intended. Also used to refer to units of related data fields (i.e., groups of data fields that can be accessed by a program and that contain the complete set of information on particular items). SOURCE: SP 800-53; SP 800-53A; CNSSI-4009 All books, papers, maps, photographs, machine-readable materials, or other documentary materials, regardless of physical form or characteristics, made or received by an agency of the United States government under federal law or in connection with the transaction of public business and preserved or appropriate for preservation by that agency or its legitimate successor as evidence of the organization, functions, policies, decisions, procedures, operations, or other activities of the government or because of the informational value of the data in them. [44 U.S.C. SEC. 3301] SOURCE: FIPS 200
Records Management –	The process for tagging information for records-keeping requirements as mandated in the Federal Records Act and the National Archival and Records Requirements. SOURCE: CNSSI-4009
Recovery Point Objective –	The point in time to which data must be recovered after an outage. SOURCE: SP 800-34

Recovery Time Objective –	The overall length of time an information system's components can be in the recovery phase before negatively impacting the organization's mission or mission/business functions. SOURCE: SP 800-34
Recovery Procedures –	Actions necessary to restore data files of an information system and computational capability after a system failure. SOURCE: CNSSI-4009
RED –	In cryptographic systems, refers to information or messages that contain sensitive or classified information that is not encrypted. See also BLACK. SOURCE: CNSSI-4009
Red Signal –	Any electronic emission (e.g., plain text, key, key stream, subkey stream, initial fill, or control signal) that would divulge national security information if recovered. SOURCE: CNSSI-4009
Red Team –	A group of people authorized and organized to emulate a potential adversary's attack or exploitation capabilities against an enterprise's security posture. The Red Team's objective is to improve enterprise Information Assurance by demonstrating the impacts of successful attacks and by demonstrating what works for the defenders (i.e., the Blue Team) in an operational environment. SOURCE: CNSSI-4009
Red Team Exercise –	An exercise, reflecting real-world conditions, that is conducted as a simulated adversarial attempt to compromise organizational missions and/or business processes to provide a comprehensive assessment of the security capability of the information system and organization. SOURCE: SP 800-53
Red/Black Concept –	Separation of electrical and electronic circuits, components, equipment, and systems that handle unencrypted information (Red), in electrical form, from those that handle encrypted information (Black) in the same form. SOURCE: CNSSI-4009
Reference Monitor –	The security engineering term for IT functionality that— 1) controls all access, 2) cannot be bypassed, 3) is tamper-resistant, and 4) provides confidence that the other three items are true. SOURCE: SP 800-33

	Concept of an abstract machine that enforces Target of Evaluation (TOE) access control policies.
	SOURCE: CNSSI-4009
Registration –	The process through which a party applies to become a subscriber of a Credentials Service Provider (CSP) and a Registration Authority validates the identity of that party on behalf of the CSP.
	SOURCE: CNSSI-4009
	The process through which an Applicant applies to become a Subscriber of a CSP and an RA validates the identity of the Applicant on behalf of the CSP.
	SOURCE: SP 800-63
Registration Authority (RA) –	A trusted entity that establishes and vouches for the identity of a Subscriber to a CSP. The RA may be an integral part of a CSP, or it may be independent of a CSP, but it has a relationship to the CSP(s).
	SOURCE: SP 800-63; CNSSI-4009
	Organization responsible for assignment of unique identifiers to registered objects.
	SOURCE: FIPS 188
Rekey –	To change the value of a cryptographic key that is being used in a cryptographic system/application.
	SOURCE: CNSSI-4009
Rekey (a certificate) –	To change the value of a cryptographic key that is being used in a cryptographic system application; this normally entails issuing a new certificate on the new public key.
	SOURCE: SP 800-32
Release Prefix –	Prefix appended to the short title of U.S.-produced keying material to indicate its foreign releasability. "A" designates material that is releasable to specific allied nations, and "U.S." designates material intended exclusively for U. S. use.
	SOURCE: CNSSI-4009
Relying Party –	An entity that relies upon the subscriber's credentials, typically to process a transaction or grant access to information or a system.
	SOURCE: CNSSI-4009

An entity that relies upon the Subscriber's token and credentials or a Verifier's assertion of a Claimant's identity, typically to process a transaction or grant access to information or a system.

SOURCE: SP 800-63

Remanence –

Residual information remaining on storage media after clearing. See Magnetic Remanence and Clearing.

SOURCE: CNSSI-4009

Remediation –

The act of correcting a vulnerability or eliminating a threat. Three possible types of remediation are installing a patch, adjusting configuration settings, or uninstalling a software application.

SOURCE: SP 800-40

The act of mitigating a vulnerability or a threat.

SOURCE: CNSSI-4009

Remediation Plan –

A plan to perform the remediation of one or more threats or vulnerabilities facing an organization's systems. The plan typically includes options to remove threats and vulnerabilities and priorities for performing the remediation.

SOURCE: SP 800-40

Remote Access –

Access to an organizational information system by a user (or an information system acting on behalf of a user) communicating through an external network (e.g., the Internet).

SOURCE: SP 800-53

Access by users (or information systems) communicating external to an information system security perimeter.

SOURCE: SP 800-18

The ability for an organization's users to access its nonpublic computing resources from external locations other than the organization's facilities.

SOURCE: SP 800-46

Access to an organization's nonpublic information system by an authorized user (or an information system) communicating through an external, non-organization-controlled network (e.g., the Internet).

SOURCE: CNSSI-4009

Remote Diagnostics/Maintenance –

Maintenance activities conducted by authorized individuals communicating through an external network (e.g., the Internet).

SOURCE: CNSSI-4009

Remote Maintenance –	Maintenance activities conducted by individuals communicating external to an information system security perimeter. SOURCE: SP 800-18 Maintenance activities conducted by individuals communicating through an external network (e.g., the Internet). SOURCE: SP 800-53
Remote Rekeying –	Procedure by which a distant crypto-equipment is rekeyed electrically. See Automatic Remote Rekeying and Manual Remote Rekeying. SOURCE: CNSSI-4009
Removable Media –	Portable electronic storage media such as magnetic, optical, and solid-state devices, which can be inserted into and removed from a computing device, and that is used to store text, video, audio, and image information. Such devices have no independent processing capabilities. Examples include hard disks, floppy disks, zip drives, compact disks (CDs), thumb drives, pen drives, and similar USB storage devices. SOURCE: CNSSI-4009 Portable electronic storage media such as magnetic, optical, and Solid-state devices, which can be inserted into and removed from a computing device, and that is used to store text, video, audio, and image information. Examples include hard disks, floppy disks, zip drives, compact disks, thumb drives, pen drives, and similar USB storage devices. SOURCE: SP 800-53
Renew (a certificate) –	The act or process of extending the validity of the data binding asserted by a public key certificate by issuing a new certificate. SOURCE: SP 800-32
Repair Action –	NSA-approved change to a COMSEC end-item that does not affect the original characteristics of the end-item and is provided for optional application by holders. Repair actions are limited to minor electrical and/or mechanical improvements to enhance operation, maintenance, or reliability. They do not require an identification label, marking, or control but must be fully documented by changes to the maintenance manual. SOURCE: CNSSI-4009

Replay Attacks –	An attack that involves the capture of transmitted authentication or access control information and its subsequent retransmission with the intent of producing an unauthorized effect or gaining unauthorized access. SOURCE: CNSSI-4009
Repository –	A database containing information and data relating to certificates as specified in a CP; may also be referred to as a directory. SOURCE: SP 800-32
Reserve Keying Material –	Key held to satisfy unplanned needs. See Contingency Key. SOURCE: CNSSI-4009
Residual Risk –	The remaining potential risk after all IT security measures are applied. There is a residual risk associated with each threat. SOURCE: SP 800-33 Portion of risk remaining after security measures have been applied. SOURCE: CNSSI-4009; SP 800-30
Residue –	Data left in storage after information-processing operations are complete, but before degaussing or overwriting has taken place. SOURCE: CNSSI-4009
Resilience –	The ability to quickly adapt and recover from any known or unknown changes to the environment through holistic implementation of risk management, contingency, and continuity planning. SOURCE: SP 800-34 The ability to continue to: (i) operate under adverse conditions or stress, even if in a degraded or debilitated state, while maintaining essential operational capabilities; and (ii) recover to an effective operational posture in a time frame consistent with mission needs. SOURCE: SP 800-137
Resource Encapsulation –	Method by which the reference monitor mediates accesses to an information system resource. Resource is protected and not directly accessible by a subject. Satisfies requirement for accurate auditing of resource usage. SOURCE: CNSSI-4009
Responder –	The entity that responds to the initiator of the authentication exchange. SOURCE: FIPS 196

Responsible Individual –

A trustworthy person designated by a sponsoring organization to authenticate individual applicants seeking certificates on the basis of their affiliation with the sponsor.

SOURCE: SP 800-32

Responsibility to Provide –

An information distribution approach whereby relevant essential information is made readily available and discoverable to the broadest possible pool of potential users.

SOURCE: CNSSI-4009

Restricted Data –

All data concerning (i) design, manufacture, or utilization of atomic weapons; (ii) the production of special nuclear material; or (iii) the use of special nuclear material in the production of energy, but shall not include data declassified or removed from the Restricted Data category pursuant to Section 142 [of the Atomic Energy Act of 1954].

SOURCE: SP 800-53; Atomic Energy Act of 1954

Revoke a Certificate –

To prematurely end the operational period of a certificate effective at a specific date and time.

SOURCE: SP 800-32

RFID –

See Radio Frequency Identification.

Rijndael –

Cryptographic algorithm specified in the Advanced Encryption Standard (AES).

SOURCE: FIPS 197

Risk –

The level of impact on organizational operations (including mission, functions, image, or reputation), organizational assets, or individuals resulting from the operation of an information system given the potential impact of a threat and the likelihood of that threat occurring.

SOURCE: FIPS 200

The level of impact on organizational operations (including mission, functions, image, or reputation), organizational assets, individuals, other organizations, or the Nation resulting from the operation of an information system given the potential impact of a threat and the likelihood of that threat occurring.

SOURCE: SP 800-60

A measure of the extent to which an entity is threatened by a potential circumstance or event, and typically a function of: (i) the adverse impacts that would arise if the circumstance or event occurs; and (ii) the likelihood of occurrence.

Note: Information system-related security risks are those risks that arise from the loss of confidentiality, integrity, or availability of information or information systems and consider the adverse impacts to organizational operations (including mission, functions, image, or reputation), organizational assets, individuals, other organizations, and the Nation.

SOURCE: SP 800-53

A measure of the extent to which an entity is threatened by a potential circumstance or event, and typically a function of: (1) the adverse impacts that would arise if the circumstance or event occurs; and (2) the likelihood of occurrence.

Note: Information system-related security risks are those risks that arise from the loss of confidentiality, integrity, or availability of information or information systems and reflect the potential adverse impacts to organizational operations (including mission, functions, image, or reputation), organizational assets, individuals, other organizations, and the Nation.

SOURCE: CNSSI-4009

A measure of the extent to which an entity is threatened by a potential circumstance or event, and typically a function of: (i) the adverse impacts that would arise if the circumstance or event occurs; and (ii) the likelihood of occurrence.

[Note: Information system-related security risks are those risks that arise from the loss of confidentiality, integrity, or availability of information or information systems and reflect the potential adverse impacts to organizational operations (including mission, functions, image, or reputation), organizational assets, individuals, other organizations, and the Nation. Adverse impacts to the Nation include, for example, compromises to information systems that support critical infrastructure applications or are paramount to government continuity of operations as defined by the Department of Homeland Security.]

SOURCE: SP 800-37; SP 800-53A

Risk-Adaptable Access Control – (RAdAC)

A form of access control that uses an authorization policy that takes into account operational need, risk, and heuristics.

SOURCE: CNSSI-4009

Risk Analysis –

The process of identifying the risks to system security and determining the likelihood of occurrence, the resulting impact, and the additional safeguards that mitigate this impact. Part of risk management and synonymous with risk assessment.

SOURCE: SP 800-27

	Examination of information to identify the risk to an information system. See Risk Assessment.

SOURCE: CNSSI-4009

Risk Assessment –

The process of identifying risks to organizational operations (including mission, functions, image, or reputation), organizational assets, individuals, other organizations, and the Nation, arising through the operation of an information system.

Part of risk management, incorporates threat and vulnerability analyses and considers mitigations provided by security controls planned or in place. Synonymous with risk analysis.

SOURCE: SP 800-53; SP 800-53A; SP 800-37

The process of identifying, prioritizing, and estimating risks. This includes determining the extent to which adverse circumstances or events could impact an enterprise. Uses the results of threat and vulnerability assessments to identify risk to organizational operations and evaluates those risks in terms of likelihood of occurrence and impacts if they occur. The product of a risk assessment is a list of estimated potential impacts and unmitigated vulnerabilities. Risk assessment is part of risk management and is conducted throughout the Risk Management Framework (RMF).

SOURCE: CNSSI-4009

Risk Assessment Methodology –

A risk assessment process, together with a risk model, assessment approach, and analysis approach.

SOURCE: SP 800-30

Risk Assessment Report –

The report which contains the results of performing a risk assessment or the formal output from the process of assessing risk.

SOURCE: SP 800-30

Risk Assessor –

The individual, group, or organization responsible for conducting a risk assessment.

SOURCE: SP 800-30

Risk Executive –
(or Risk Executive Function)

An individual or group within an organization that helps to ensure that: (i) security risk-related considerations for individual information systems, to include the authorization decisions for those systems, are viewed from an organization-wide perspective with regard to the overall strategic goals and objectives of the organization in carrying out its missions and business functions; and (ii) managing risk from individual information systems is consistent across the organization, reflects organizational risk tolerance, and is considered along with other organizational risks affecting mission/business success.

SOURCE: CNSSI-4009; SP 800-53A; SP 800-37; SP 800-39

163

Risk Management –

The process of managing risks to organizational operations (including mission, functions, image, reputation), organizational assets, individuals, other organizations, and the Nation, resulting from the operation of an information system, and includes: (i) the conduct of a risk assessment; (ii) the implementation of a risk mitigation strategy; and (iii) employment of techniques and procedures for the continuous monitoring of the security state of the information system.

SOURCE: SP 800-53; SP 800-53A; SP 800-37

The process of managing risks to organizational operations (including mission, functions, image, or reputation), organizational assets, or individuals resulting from the operation of an information system, and includes:
1) the conduct of a risk assessment;
2) the implementation of a risk mitigation strategy; and
3) employment of techniques and procedures for the continuous monitoring of the security state of the information system.

SOURCE: FIPS 200

The process of managing risks to agency operations (including mission, functions, image, or reputation), agency assets, or individuals resulting from the operation of an information system. It includes risk assessment; cost-benefit analysis; the selection, implementation, and assessment of security controls; and the formal authorization to operate the system. The process considers effectiveness, efficiency, and constraints due to laws, directives, policies, or regulations.

SOURCE: SP 800-82; SP 800-34

The process of managing risks to organizational operations (including mission, functions, image, or reputation), organizational assets, individuals, other organizations, or the nation resulting from the operation or use of an information system, and includes: (1) the conduct of a risk assessment; (2) the implementation of a risk mitigation strategy; (3) employment of techniques and procedures for the continuous monitoring of the security state of the information system; and (4) documenting the overall risk management program.

SOURCE: CNSSI-4009

The program and supporting processes to manage information security risk to organizational operations (including mission, functions, image, reputation), organizational assets, individuals, other organizations, and the Nation, and includes: (i) establishing the context for risk-related activities; (ii) assessing risk; (iii) responding to risk once determined; and (iv) monitoring risk over time.

SOURCE: SP 800-39

Risk Management Framework –	A structured approach used to oversee and manage risk for an enterprise. SOURCE: CNSSI-4009
Risk Mitigation –	Prioritizing, evaluating, and implementing the appropriate risk-reducing controls/countermeasures recommended from the risk management process. SOURCE: CNSSI-4009; SP 800-30; SP 800-39
Risk Model –	A key component of a risk assessment methodology (in addition to assessment approach and analysis approach) that defines key terms and assessable risk factors. SOURCE: SP 800-30
Risk Monitoring –	Maintaining ongoing awareness of an organization's risk environment, risk management program, and associated activities to support risk decisions. SOURCE: SP 800-30; SP 800-39
Risk Response –	Accepting, avoiding, mitigating, sharing, or transferring risk to organizational operations (i.e., mission, functions, image, or reputation), organizational assets, individuals, other organizations, or the Nation. SOURCE: SP 800-30; SP 800-39
Risk Response Measure –	A specific action taken to respond to an identified risk. SOURCE: SP 800-39
Risk Tolerance –	The level of risk an entity is willing to assume in order to achieve a potential desired result. SOURCE: SP 800-32 The defined impacts to an enterprise's information systems that an entity is willing to accept. SOURCE: CNSSI-4009
Robust Security Network (RSN) –	A wireless security network that only allows the creation of Robust Security Network Associations (RSNAs). SOURCE: SP 800-48

Robust Security Network Association (RSNA) –	A logical connection between communicating IEEE 802.11 entities established through the IEEE 802.11i key management scheme, also known as the four-way handshake. SOURCE: SP 800-48
Robustness –	The ability of an Information Assurance entity to operate correctly and reliably across a wide range of operational conditions, and to fail gracefully outside of that operational range. SOURCE: CNSSI-4009
Rogue Device –	An unauthorized node on a network. SOURCE: SP 800-115
Role –	A group attribute that ties membership to function. When an entity assumes a role, the entity is given certain rights that belong to that role. When the entity leaves the role, those rights are removed. The rights given are consistent with the functionality that the entity needs to perform the expected tasks. SOURCE: CNSSI-4009
Role-Based Access Control – (RBAC)	A model for controlling access to resources where permitted actions on resources are identified with roles rather than with individual subject identities. SOURCE: SP 800-95 Access control based on user roles (i.e., a collection of access authorizations a user receives based on an explicit or implicit assumption of a given role). Role permissions may be inherited through a role hierarchy and typically reflect the permissions needed to perform defined functions within an organization. A given role may apply to a single individual or to several individuals. SOURCE: SP 800-53; CNSSI-4009
Root Cause Analysis –	A principle-based, systems approach for the identification of underlying causes associated with a particular set of risks. SOURCE: SP 800-30; SP 800-39
Root Certification Authority –	In a hierarchical Public Key Infrastructure, the Certification Authority whose public key serves as the most trusted datum (i.e., the beginning of trust paths) for a security domain. SOURCE: SP 800-32; CNSSI-4009

Rootkit –	A set of tools used by an attacker after gaining root-level access to a host to conceal the attacker's activities on the host and permit the attacker to maintain root-level access to the host through covert means. SOURCE: CNSSI-4009
Round Key –	Round keys are values derived from the Cipher Key using the Key Expansion routine; they are applied to the State in the Cipher and Inverse Cipher. SOURCE: FIPS 197
Rule-Based Security Policy –	A security policy based on global rules imposed for all subjects. These rules usually rely on a comparison of the sensitivity of the objects being accessed and the possession of corresponding attributes by the subjects requesting access. SOURCE: SP 800-33 A security policy based on global rules imposed for all subjects. These rules usually rely on a comparison of the sensitivity of the objects being accessed and the possession of corresponding attributes by the subjects requesting access. Also known as discretionary access control (DAC). SOURCE: CNSSI-4009
Rules of Engagement (ROE) –	Detailed guidelines and constraints regarding the execution of information security testing. The ROE is established before the start of a security test, and gives the test team authority to conduct defined activities without the need for additional permissions. SOURCE: SP 800-115
Ruleset –	A table of instructions used by a controlled interface to determine what data is allowable and how the data is handled between interconnected systems. SOURCE: SP 800-115; CNSSI-4009 A set of directives that govern the access control functionality of a firewall. The firewall uses these directives to determine how packets should be routed between its interfaces. SOURCE: SP 800-41
S-box –	Nonlinear substitution table used in several byte substitution transformations and in the Key Expansion routine to perform a one-for-one substitution of a byte value. SOURCE: FIPS 197

S/MIME –

A set of specifications for securing electronic mail. Secure/ Multipurpose Internet Mail Extensions (S/MIME) is based upon the widely used MIME standard and describes a protocol for adding cryptographic security services through MIME encapsulation of digitally signed and encrypted objects. The basic security services offered by S/MIME are authentication, non-repudiation of origin, message integrity, and message privacy. Optional security services include signed receipts, security labels, secure mailing lists, and an extended method of identifying the signer's certificate(s).

SOURCE: SP 800-49

Safeguards –

Protective measures prescribed to meet the security requirements (i.e., confidentiality, integrity, and availability) specified for an information system. Safeguards may include security features, management constraints, personnel security, and security of physical structures, areas, and devices. Synonymous with security controls and countermeasures.

SOURCE: SP 800-53; SP 800-37; FIPS 200; CNSSI-4009

Safeguarding Statement –

Statement affixed to a computer output or printout that states the highest classification being processed at the time the product was produced and requires control of the product, at that level, until determination of the true classification by an authorized individual. Synonymous with banner.

SOURCE: CNSSI-4009

Salt –

A non-secret value that is used in a cryptographic process, usually to ensure that the results of computations for one instance cannot be reused by an Attacker.

SOURCE: SP 800-63; CNSSI-4009

Sandboxing –

A method of isolating application modules into distinct fault domains enforced by software. The technique allows untrusted programs written in an unsafe language, such as C, to be executed safely within the single virtual address space of an application. Untrusted machine interpretable code modules are transformed so that all memory accesses are confined to code and data segments within their fault domain. Access to system resources can also be controlled through a unique identifier associated with each domain.

SOURCE: SP 800-19

A restricted, controlled execution environment that prevents potentially malicious software, such as mobile code, from accessing any system resources except those for which the software is authorized.

SOURCE: CNSSI-4009

Sanitization –	Process to remove information from media such that information recovery is not possible. It includes removing all labels, markings, and activity logs. SOURCE: FIPS 200 A general term referring to the actions taken to render data written on media unrecoverable by both ordinary and, for some forms of sanitization, extraordinary means. SOURCE: SP 800-53; CNSSI-4009
SCADA –	See Supervisory Control and Data Acquisition.
Scanning –	Sending packets or requests to another system to gain information to be used in a subsequent attack. SOURCE: CNSSI-4009
Scatternet –	A chain of piconets created by allowing one or more Bluetooth devices to each be a slave in one piconet and act as the master for another piconet simultaneously. A scatternet allows several devices to be networked over an extended distance. SOURCE: SP 800-121
Scavenging –	Searching through object residue to acquire data. SOURCE: CNSSI-4009
Scoping Guidance –	A part of tailoring guidance providing organizations with specific policy/regulatory-related, technology-related, system component allocation-related, operational/environmental-related, physical infrastructure-related, public access-related, scalability-related, common control-related, and security objective-related considerations on the applicability and implementation of individual security controls in the security control baseline. SOURCE: SP 800-53 Specific factors related to technology, infrastructure, public access, scalability, common security controls, and risk that can be considered by organizations in the applicability and implementation of individual security controls in the security control baseline. SOURCE: FIPS 200; CNSSI-4009
Secret Key –	A cryptographic key that is used with a secret-key (symmetric) cryptographic algorithm that is uniquely associated with one or more entities and is not made public. The use of the term "secret" in this context does not imply a classification level, but rather implies the need to protect the key from disclosure. SOURCE: SP 800-57 Part 1

A cryptographic key that is used with a symmetric cryptographic algorithm that is uniquely associated with one or more entities and is not made public. The use of the term "secret" in this context does not imply a classification level, but rather implies the need to protect the key from disclosure.

SOURCE: CNSSI-4009

A cryptographic key that must be protected from unauthorized disclosure to protect data encrypted with the key. The use of the term "secret" in this context does not imply a classification level; rather, the term implies the need to protect the key from disclosure or substitution.

SOURCE: FIPS 201

A cryptographic key that is uniquely associated with one or more entities. The use of the term "secret" in this context does not imply a classification level, but rather implies the need to protect the key from disclosure or substitution.

SOURCE: FIPS 198

A cryptographic key, used with a secret key cryptographic algorithm, that is uniquely associated with one or more entities and should not be made public.

SOURCE: FIPS 140-2

Secret Key (symmetric) Cryptographic Algorithm –

A cryptographic algorithm that uses a single secret key for both encryption and decryption.

SOURCE: FIPS 140-2

A cryptographic algorithm that uses a single key (i.e., a secret key) for both encryption and decryption.

SOURCE: CNSSI-4009

Secret Seed –

A secret value used to initialize a pseudorandom number generator.

SOURCE: CNSSI-4009

Secure/Multipurpose Internet Mail Extensions (S/MIME) –

A set of specifications for securing electronic mail. S/MIME is based upon the widely used MIME standard [MIME] and describes a protocol for adding cryptographic security services through MIME encapsulation of digitally signed and encrypted objects. The basic security services offered by S/MIME are authentication, non-repudiation of origin, message integrity, and message privacy. Optional security services include signed receipts, security labels, secure mailing lists, and an extended method of identifying the signer's certificate(s).

SOURCE: SP 800-49; CNSSI-4009

Secure Communication Protocol –   A communication protocol that provides the appropriate confidentiality, authentication, and content-integrity protection.

SOURCE: SP 800-57 Part 1; CNSSI-4009

Secure Communications –   Telecommunications deriving security through use of NSA-approved products and/or Protected Distribution Systems.

SOURCE: CNSSI-4009

Secure DNS (SECDNS) –   Configuring and operating DNS servers so that the security goals of data integrity and source authentication are achieved and maintained.

SOURCE: SP 800-81

Secure Erase –   An overwrite technology using firmware-based process to overwrite a hard drive. Is a drive command defined in the ANSI ATA and SCSI disk drive interface specifications, which runs inside drive hardware. It completes in about 1/8 the time of 5220 block erasure.

SOURCE: SP 800-88

Secure Hash Algorithm (SHA) –   A hash algorithm with the property that is computationally infeasible 1) to find a message that corresponds to a given message digest, or 2) to find two different messages that produce the same message digest.

SOURCE: CNSSI-4009

Secure Hash Standard –

This Standard specifies secure hash algorithms -SHA-1, SHA-224, SHA-256, SHA-384, SHA-512, SHA-512/224 and SHA-512/256 -for computing a condensed representation of electronic data (message). When a message of any length less than 2^{64} bits (for SHA-1, SHA-224 and SHA-256) or less than 2^{128} bits (for SHA-384, SHA-512, SHA-512/224 and SHA-512/256) is input to a hash algorithm, the result is an output called a message digest. The message digests range in length from 160 to 512 bits, depending on the algorithm. Secure hash algorithms are typically used with other cryptographic algorithms, such as digital signature algorithms and keyed-hash message authentication codes, or in the generation of random numbers (bits).

The hash algorithms specified in this Standard are called secure because, for a given algorithm, it is computationally infeasible 1) to find a message that corresponds to a given message digest, or 2) to find two different messages that produce the same message digest. Any change to a message will, with a very high probability, result in a different message digest. This will result in a verification failure when the secure hash algorithm is used with a digital signature algorithm or a keyed-hash message authentication algorithm.

SOURCE: FIPS 180-4

Specification for a secure hash algorithm that can generate a condensed message representation called a message digest.

SOURCE: CNSSI-4009

Secure Socket Layer (SSL) –

A protocol used for protecting private information during transmission via the Internet.

Note: SSL works by using a public key to encrypt data that's transferred over the SSL connection. Most Web browsers support SSL, and many Web sites use the protocol to obtain confidential user information, such as credit card numbers. By convention, URLs that require an SSL connection start with "https:" instead of "http:."

SOURCE: CNSSI-4009

Secure State –

Condition in which no subject can access any object in an unauthorized manner.

SOURCE: CNSSI-4009

Secure Subsystem –	Subsystem containing its own implementation of the reference monitor concept for those resources it controls. Secure subsystem must depend on other controls and the base operating system for the control of subjects and the more primitive system objects. SOURCE: CNSSI-4009
Security –	A condition that results from the establishment and maintenance of protective measures that enable an enterprise to perform its mission or critical functions despite risks posed by threats to its use of information systems. Protective measures may involve a combination of deterrence, avoidance, prevention, detection, recovery, and correction that should form part of the enterprise's risk management approach. SOURCE: CNSSI-4009
Security Assertion Markup Language (SAML) –	An XML-based security specification developed by the Organization for the Advancement of Structured Information Standards (OASIS) for exchanging authentication (and authorization) information between trusted entities over the Internet. SOURCE: SP 800-63 A framework for exchanging authentication and authorization information. Security typically involves checking the credentials presented by a party for authentication and authorization. SAML standardizes the representation of these credentials in an XML format called "assertions," enhancing the interoperability between disparate applications. SOURCE: SP 800-95 A protocol consisting of XML-based request and response message formats for exchanging security information, expressed in the form of assertions about subjects, between online business partners. SOURCE: CNSSI-4009
Security Association –	A relationship established between two or more entities to enable them to protect data they exchange. SOURCE: CNSSI-4009
Security Attribute –	A security-related quality of an object. Security attributes may be represented as hierarchical levels, bits in a bit map, or numbers. Compartments, caveats, and release markings are examples of security attributes. SOURCE: FIPS 188

An abstraction representing the basic properties or characteristics of an entity with respect to safeguarding information; typically associated with internal data structures (e.g., records, buffers, files) within the information system which are used to enable the implementation of access control and flow control policies; reflect special dissemination, handling, or distribution instructions; or support other aspects of the information security policy.

SOURCE: SP 800-53; CNSSI-4009

Security Authorization –	See Authorization.
Security Authorization – (To Operate)	See Authorization (to operate). SOURCE: CNSSI-4009
Security Authorization Boundary –	See Authorization Boundary.
Security Automation Domain –	An information security area that includes a grouping of tools, technologies, and data. SOURCE: SP 800-137
Security Banner –	A banner at the top or bottom of a computer screen that states the overall classification of the system in large, bold type. Also can refer to the opening screen that informs users of the security implications of accessing a computer resource. SOURCE: CNSSI-4009
Security Categorization –	The process of determining the security category for information or an information system. See Security Category. SOURCE: SP 800-53 The process of determining the security category for information or an information system. Security categorization methodologies are described in CNSS Instruction 1253 for national security systems and in FIPS 199 for other than national security systems. SOURCE: SP 800-37; SP 800-53A; SP 800-39
Security Category –	The characterization of information or an information system based on an assessment of the potential impact that a loss of confidentiality, integrity, or availability of such information or information system would have on organizational operations, organizational assets, or individuals. SOURCE: FIPS 200; FIPS 199; SP 800-18

The characterization of information or an information system based on an assessment of the potential impact that a loss of confidentiality, integrity, or availability of such information or information system would have on organizational operations, organizational assets, individuals, other organizations, and the Nation.

SOURCE: SP 800-53; CNSSI-4009; SP 800-60

Security Concept of Operations – (Security CONOP)

A security-focused description of an information system, its operational policies, classes of users, interactions between the system and its users, and the system's contribution to the operational mission.

SOURCE: CNSSI-4009

Security Content Automation Protocol (SCAP) –

A method for using specific standardized testing methods to enable automated vulnerability management, measurement, and policy compliance evaluation against a standardized set of security requirements.

SOURCE: CNSSI-4009

Security Control Assessment –

The testing and/or evaluation of the management, operational, and technical security controls in an information system to determine the extent to which the controls are implemented correctly, operating as intended, and producing the desired outcome with respect to meeting the security requirements for the system.

SOURCE: SP 800-37; SP 800-53; SP 800-53A

The testing and/or evaluation of the management, operational, and technical security controls to determine the extent to which the controls are implemented correctly, operating as intended, and producing the desired outcome with respect to meeting the security requirements for the system and/or enterprise.

SOURCE: CNSSI-4009

Security Control Assessor –

The individual, group, or organization responsible for conducting a security control assessment.

SOURCE: SP 800-37; SP 800-53A

Security Control Baseline –

The set of minimum security controls defined for a low-impact, moderate-impact, or high-impact information system.

SOURCE: SP 800-53; FIPS 200

One of the sets of minimum security controls defined for federal information systems in NIST Special Publication 800-53 and CNSS Instruction 1253.

SOURCE: SP 800-53A

Security Control Effectiveness –

The measure of correctness of implementation (i.e., how consistently the control implementation complies with the security plan) and how well the security plan meets organizational needs in accordance with current risk tolerance.

SOURCE: SP 800-137

Security Control Enhancements –

Statements of security capability to 1) build in additional, but related, functionality to a basic control; and/or 2) increase the strength of a basic control.

SOURCE: CNSSI-4009; SP 800-53A; SP 800-39

Statements of security capability to: (i) build in additional, but related, functionality to a security control; and/or (ii) increase the strength of the control.

SOURCE: SP 800-53; SP 800-18

Security Control Inheritance –

A situation in which an information system or application receives protection from security controls (or portions of security controls) that are developed, implemented, assessed, authorized, and monitored by entities other than those responsible for the system or application; entities either internal or external to the organization where the system or application resides.
See Common Control.

SOURCE: SP 800-37; SP 800-53; SP 800-53A; CNSSI-4009

Security Controls –

The management, operational, and technical controls (i.e., safeguards or countermeasures) prescribed for an information system to protect the confidentiality, integrity, and availability of the system and its information.

SOURCE: SP 800-53; SP 800-37; SP 800-53A; SP 800-60; FIPS 200; FIPS 199; CNSSI-4009

Security Controls Baseline –

The set of minimum security controls defined for a low-impact, moderate-impact, or high-impact information system.

SOURCE: CNSSI-4009

Security Domain –

A set of subjects, their information objects, and a common security policy.

SOURCE: SP 800-27

A collection of entities to which applies a single security policy executed by a single authority.

SOURCE: FIPS 188

	A domain that implements a security policy and is administered by a single authority.
	SOURCE: SP 800-37; SP 800-53; CNSSI-4009
Security Engineering –	An interdisciplinary approach and means to enable the realization of secure systems. It focuses on defining customer needs, security protection requirements, and required functionality early in the systems development life cycle, documenting requirements, and then proceeding with design, synthesis, and system validation while considering the complete problem.
	SOURCE: CNSSI-4009
Security Fault Analysis (SFA) –	An assessment, usually performed on information system hardware, to determine the security properties of a device when hardware fault is encountered.
	SOURCE: CNSSI-4009
Security Features Users Guide – (SFUG)	Guide or manual explaining how the security mechanisms in a specific system work.
	SOURCE: CNSSI-4009
Security Filter –	A secure subsystem of an information system that enforces security policy on the data passing through it.
	SOURCE: CNSSI-4009
Security Functions –	The hardware, software, and/or firmware of the information system responsible for enforcing the system security policy and supporting the isolation of code and data on which the protection is based.
	SOURCE: SP 800-53
Security Goals –	The five security goals are confidentiality, availability, integrity, accountability, and assurance.
	SOURCE: SP 800-27
Security Impact Analysis –	The analysis conducted by an organizational official to determine the extent to which changes to the information system have affected the security state of the system.
	SOURCE: SP 800-53; SP 800-53A; SP 800-37; CNSSI-4009
Security Incident –	See Incident.
Security Information and Event Management (SIEM) Tool –	Application that provides the ability to gather security data from information system components and present that data as actionable information via a single interface.
	SOURCE: SP 800-128

Security Inspection –

Examination of an information system to determine compliance with security policy, procedures, and practices.

SOURCE: CNSSI-4009

Security Kernel –

Hardware, firmware, and software elements of a trusted computing base implementing the reference monitor concept. Security kernel must mediate all accesses, be protected from modification, and be verifiable as correct.

SOURCE: CNSSI-4009

Security Label –

The means used to associate a set of security attributes with a specific information object as part of the data structure for that object.

SOURCE: SP 800-53

A marking bound to a resource (which may be a data unit) that names or designates the security attributes of that resource.

SOURCE: FIPS 188

Information that represents or designates the value of one or more security relevant-attributes (e.g., classification) of a system resource.

SOURCE: CNSSI-4009

Security Level –

A hierarchical indicator of the degree of sensitivity to a certain threat. It implies, according to the security policy being enforced, a specific level of protection.

SOURCE: FIPS 188

Security Management Dashboard –

A tool that consolidates and communicates information relevant to the organizational security posture in near real-time to security management stakeholders.

SOURCE: SP 800-128

Security Marking –

Human-readable information affixed to information system components, removable media, or output indicating the distribution limitations, handling caveats, and applicable security markings.

SOURCE: SP 800-53

Security Markings –

Human-readable indicators applied to a document, storage media, or hardware component to designate security classification, categorization, and/or handling restrictions applicable to the information contained therein. For intelligence information, these could include compartment and sub-compartment indicators and handling restrictions.

SOURCE: CNSSI-4009

Security Mechanism –

A device designed to provide one or more security services usually rated in terms of strength of service and assurance of the design.

SOURCE: CNSSI-4009

Security Net Control Station –

Management system overseeing and controlling implementation of network security policy.

SOURCE: CNSSI-4009

Security Objective –

Confidentiality, integrity, or availability.

SOURCE: SP 800-53; SP 800-53A; SP 800-60; SP 800-37; FIPS 200; FIPS 199

Security Perimeter –

See Authorization Boundary.

A physical or logical boundary that is defined for a system, domain, or enclave, within which a particular security policy or security architecture is applied.

SOURCE: CNSSI-4009

Security Plan –

Formal document that provides an overview of the security requirements for an information system or an information security program and describes the security controls in place or planned for meeting those requirements.

See 'System Security Plan' or 'Information Security Program Plan.'

SOURCE: SP 800-53; SP 800-53A; SP 800-37; SP 800-18

Security Policy –

The statement of required protection of the information objects.

SOURCE: SP 800-27

A set of criteria for the provision of security services. It defines and constrains the activities of a data processing facility in order to maintain a condition of security for systems and data.

SOURCE: FIPS 188

A set of criteria for the provision of security services.

SOURCE: SP 800-37; SP 800-53; CNSSI-4009

Security Posture –

The security status of an enterprise's networks, information, and systems based on IA resources (e.g., people, hardware, software, policies) and capabilities in place to manage the defense of the enterprise and to react as the situation changes.

SOURCE: CNSSI-4009

Security Program Plan –	Formal document that provides an overview of the security requirements for an organization-wide information security program and describes the program management security controls and common security controls in place or planned for meeting those requirements. SOURCE: CNSSI-4009
Security Range –	Highest and lowest security levels that are permitted in or on an information system, system component, subsystem, or network. SOURCE: CNSSI-4009
Security-Relevant Change –	Any change to a system's configuration, environment, information content, functionality, or users which has the potential to change the risk imposed upon its continued operations. SOURCE: CNSSI-4009
Security-Relevant Event –	An occurrence (e.g., an auditable event or flag) considered to have potential security implications to the system or its environment that may require further action (noting, investigating, or reacting). SOURCE: CNSSI-4009
Security-Relevant Information –	Any information within the information system that can potentially impact the operation of security functions in a manner that could result in failure to enforce the system security policy or maintain isolation of code and data. SOURCE: SP 800-53
Security Requirements –	Requirements levied on an information system that are derived from applicable laws, Executive Orders, directives, policies, standards, instructions, regulations, or procedures, or organizational mission/business case needs to ensure the confidentiality, integrity, and availability of the information being processed, stored, or transmitted. SOURCE: FIPS 200; SP 800-53; SP 800-53A; SP 800-37; CNSSI-4009
Security Requirements Baseline –	Description of the minimum requirements necessary for an information system to maintain an acceptable level of risk. SOURCE: CNSSI-4009
Security Requirements Traceability Matrix (SRTM) –	Matrix that captures all security requirements linked to potential risks and addresses all applicable C&A requirements. It is, therefore, a correlation statement of a system's security features and compliance methods for each security requirement. SOURCE: CNSSI-4009

Security Safeguards –

Protective measures and controls prescribed to meet the security requirements specified for an information system. Safeguards may include security features, management constraints, personnel security, and security of physical structures, areas, and devices.

SOURCE: CNSSI-4009

Security Service –

A capability that supports one, or many, of the security goals. Examples of security services are key management, access control, and authentication.

SOURCE: SP 800-27

A capability that supports one, or more, of the security requirements (Confidentiality, Integrity, Availability). Examples of security services are key management, access control, and authentication.

SOURCE: CNSSI-4009

Security Specification –

Detailed description of the safeguards required to protect an information system.

SOURCE: CNSSI-4009

Security Strength –

A measure of the computational complexity associated with recovering certain secret and/or security-critical information concerning a given cryptographic algorithm from known data (e.g. plaintext/ciphertext pairs for a given encryption algorithm).

SOURCE: SP 800-108

A number associated with the amount of work (that is, the number of operations) that is required to break a cryptographic algorithm or system. Sometimes referred to as a security level.

SOURCE: FIPS 186

Security Tag –

Information unit containing a representation of certain security-related information (e.g., a restrictive attribute bit map).

SOURCE: FIPS 188

Security Target –

Common Criteria specification that represents a set of security requirements to be used as the basis of an evaluation of an identified Target of Evaluation (TOE).

SOURCE: CNSSI-4009

Security Test & Evaluation – (ST&E)

Examination and analysis of the safeguards required to protect an information system, as they have been applied in an operational environment, to determine the security posture of that system.

SOURCE: CNSSI-4009

Security Testing –	Process to determine that an information system protects data and maintains functionality as intended. SOURCE: CNSSI-4009
Seed Key –	Initial key used to start an updating or key generation process. SOURCE: CNSSI-4009
Semi-Quantitative Assessment –	Use of a set of methods, principles, or rules for assessing risk based on bins, scales, or representative numbers whose values and meanings are not maintained in other contexts. SOURCE: SP 800-30
Senior Agency Information Security Officer (SAISO) –	Official responsible for carrying out the Chief Information Officer responsibilities under the Federal Information Security Management Act (FISMA) and serving as the Chief Information Officer's primary liaison to the agency's authorizing officials, information system owners, and information system security officers. SP 800-53 Note: Organizations subordinate to federal agencies may use the term Senior Information Security Officer or Chief Information Security Officer to denote individuals filling positions with similar responsibilities to Senior Agency Information Security Officers. SOURCE: SP 800-53; SP 800-53A; SP 800-37; SP 800-60; FIPS 200; CNSSI-4009; 44 U.S.C., Sec. 3544
Senior Information Security Officer –	See Senior Agency Information Security Officer.
Sensitive Compartmented Information (SCI) –	Classified information concerning or derived from intelligence sources, methods, or analytical processes, which is required to be handled within formal access control systems established by the Director of National Intelligence. SOURCE: SP 800-53; CNSSI-4009
Sensitive Compartmented Information Facility (SCIF) –	Accredited area, room, or group of rooms, buildings, or installation where SCI may be stored, used, discussed, and/or processed. SOURCE: CNSSI-4009
Sensitive Information –	Information, the loss, misuse, or unauthorized access to or modification of, that could adversely affect the national interest or the conduct of federal programs, or the privacy to which individuals are entitled under 5 U.S.C. Section 552a (the Privacy Act), but that has not been specifically authorized under criteria established by an Executive Order or an Act of Congress to be kept classified in the interest of national defense or foreign policy. SOURCE: SP 800-53

Information, the loss, misuse, or unauthorized access to or modification of, that could adversely affect the national interest or the conduct of federal programs, or the privacy to which individuals are entitled under 5 U.S.C. Section 552a (the Privacy Act), but that has not been specifically authorized under criteria established by an Executive Order or an Act of Congress to be kept classified in the interest of national defense or foreign policy. (Systems that are not national security systems, but contain sensitive information, are to be protected in accordance with the requirements of the Computer Security Act of 1987 [P.L.100-235].)

SOURCE: CNSSI-4009

Sensitivity –	A measure of the importance assigned to information by its owner, for the purpose of denoting its need for protection.

SOURCE: SP 800-60; CNSSI-4009

Sensitivity Label –	Information representing elements of the security label(s) of a subject and an object. Sensitivity labels are used by the trusted computing base (TCB) as the basis for mandatory access control decisions. See Security Label.

SOURCE: CNSSI-4009

Service-Level Agreement –	Defines the specific responsibilities of the service provider and sets the customer expectations.

SOURCE: CNSSI-4009

Shared Secret –	A secret used in authentication that is known to the Claimant and the Verifier.

SOURCE: SP 800-63

Shielded Enclosure –	Room or container designed to attenuate electromagnetic radiation, acoustic signals, or emanations.

SOURCE: CNSSI-4009

Short Title –	Identifying combination of letters and numbers assigned to certain COMSEC materials to facilitate handling, accounting, and controlling.

SOURCE: CNSSI-4009

Signature –	A recognizable, distinguishing pattern associated with an attack, such as a binary string in a virus or a particular set of keystrokes used to gain unauthorized access to a system.

SOURCE: SP 800-61

A recognizable, distinguishing pattern. See also Attack Signature or Digital Signature.

SOURCE: CNSSI-4009

Signature Certificate –

A public key certificate that contains a public key intended for verifying digital signatures rather than encrypting data or performing any other cryptographic functions.

SOURCE: SP 800-32; CNSSI-4009

Signature Generation –

Uses a digital signature algorithm and a private key to generate a digital signature on data.

SOURCE: SP 800-57 Part 1

The process of using a digital signature algorithm and a private key to generate a digital signature on data.

SOURCE: FIPS 186

Signature Validation –

The (mathematical) verification of the digital signature and obtaining the appropriate assurances (e.g., public key validity, private key possession, etc.).

SOURCE: FIPS 186

Signature Verification –

The use of a digital signature algorithm and a public key to verify a digital signature on data.

SOURCE: SP 800-57 Part 1

The process of using a digital signature algorithm and a public key to verify a digital signature on data.

SOURCE: SP 800-89; FIPS 186

Signed Data –

Data on which a digital signature is generated.

SOURCE: FIPS 196

Single Point Keying –

Means of distributing key to multiple, local crypto equipment or devices from a single fill point.

SOURCE: CNSSI-4009

Single-Hop Problem –

The security risks resulting from a mobile software agent moving from its home platform to another platform.

SOURCE: SP 800-19

Situational Awareness –	Within a volume of time and space, the perception of an enterprise's security posture and its threat environment; the comprehension/meaning of both taken together (risk); and the projection of their status into the near future. SOURCE: CNSSI-4009
Skimming –	The unauthorized use of a reader to read tags without the authorization or knowledge of the tag's owner or the individual in possession of the tag. SOURCE: SP 800-98
Smart Card –	A credit card-sized card with embedded integrated circuits that can store, process, and communicate information. SOURCE: CNSSI-4009
Sniffer –	See Packet Sniffer or Passive Wiretapping.
Social Engineering –	An attempt to trick someone into revealing information (e.g., a password) that can be used to attack systems or networks. SOURCE: SP 800-61 A general term for attackers trying to trick people into revealing sensitive information or performing certain actions, such as downloading and executing files that appear to be benign but are actually malicious. SOURCE: SP 800-114 The process of attempting to trick someone into revealing information (e.g., a password). SOURCE: SP 800-115 An attempt to trick someone into revealing information (e.g., a password) that can be used to attack an enterprise. SOURCE: CNSSI-4009
Software –	Computer programs and associated data that may be dynamically written or modified during execution. SOURCE: CNSSI-4009
Software Assurance –	Level of confidence that software is free from vulnerabilities, either intentionally designed into the software or accidentally inserted at any time during its life cycle, and that the software functions in the intended manner. SOURCE: CNSSI-4009

Software System Test and Evaluation Process –	Process that plans, develops, and documents the qualitative/quantitative demonstration of the fulfillment of all baseline functional performance, operational, and interface requirements. SOURCE: CNSSI-4009
Software-Based Fault Isolation –	A method of isolating application modules into distinct fault domains enforced by software. The technique allows untrusted programs written in an unsafe language, such as C, to be executed safely within the single virtual address space of an application. Untrusted machine interpretable code modules are transformed so that all memory accesses are confined to code and data segments within their fault domain. Access to system resources can also be controlled through a unique identifier associated with each domain. SOURCE: SP 800-19
Spam –	The abuse of electronic messaging systems to indiscriminately send unsolicited bulk messages. SOURCE: SP 800-53 Unsolicited bulk commercial email messages. SOURCE: SP 800-45 Electronic junk mail or the abuse of electronic messaging systems to indiscriminately send unsolicited bulk messages. SOURCE: CNSSI-4009
Spam Filtering Software –	A program that analyzes emails to look for characteristics of spam, and typically places messages that appear to be spam in a separate email folder. SOURCE: SP 800-69
Special Access Program (SAP) –	A program established for a specific class of classified information that imposes safeguarding and access requirements that exceed those normally required for information at the same classification level. SOURCE: SP 800-53; CNSSI-4009
Special Access Program Facility – (SAPF)	Facility formally accredited by an appropriate agency in accordance with DCID 6/9 in which SAP information may be processed. SOURCE: CNSSI-4009

Special Character –

Any non-alphanumeric character that can be rendered on a standard American-English keyboard. Use of a specific special character may be application-dependent.

The list of special characters follows:
` ~ ! @ # $ % ^ & * ( ) _ + | } { " : ? > < [ ] \ ; ' , . / - =
SOURCE: CNSSI-4009

Specification –

An assessment object that includes document-based artifacts (e.g., policies, procedures, plans, system security requirements, functional specifications, and architectural designs) associated with an information system.

SOURCE: SP 800-53A

Spillage –

Security incident that results in the transfer of classified or CUI information onto an information system not accredited (i.e., authorized) for the appropriate security level.

SOURCE: CNSSI-4009

Split Knowledge –

A procedure by which a cryptographic key is split into n multiple key components, individually providing no knowledge of the original key, which can be subsequently combined to recreate the original cryptographic key. If knowledge of k (where k is less than or equal to n) components is required to construct the original key, then knowledge of any k-1 key components provides no information about the original key other than, possibly, its length.

SOURCE: SP 800-57 Part 1

A process by which a cryptographic key is split into multiple key components, individually sharing no knowledge of the original key, that can be subsequently input into, or output from, a cryptographic module by separate entities and combined to recreate the original cryptographic key.

SOURCE: FIPS 140-2

1. Separation of data or information into two or more parts, each part constantly kept under control of separate authorized individuals or teams so that no one individual or team will know the whole data.
2. A process by which a cryptographic key is split into multiple key components, individually sharing no knowledge of the original key, which can be subsequently input into, or output from, a cryptographic module by separate entities and combined to recreate the original cryptographic key.

SOURCE: CNSSI-4009

Spoofing –	"IP spoofing" refers to sending a network packet that appears to come from a source other than its actual source. SOURCE: SP 800-48 Involves— 1) the ability to receive a message by masquerading as the legitimate receiving destination, or 2) masquerading as the sending machine and sending a message to a destination. SOURCE: FIPS 191 1. Faking the sending address of a transmission to gain illegal entry into a secure system. Impersonating, masquerading, piggybacking, and mimicking are forms of spoofing. 2. The deliberate inducement of a user or resource to take incorrect action. SOURCE: CNSSI-4009
Spread Spectrum –	Telecommunications techniques in which a signal is transmitted in a bandwidth considerably greater than the frequency content of the original information. Frequency hopping, direct sequence spreading, time scrambling, and combinations of these techniques are forms of spread spectrum. SOURCE: CNSSI-4009
Spyware –	Software that is secretly or surreptitiously installed into an information system to gather information on individuals or organizations without their knowledge; a type of malicious code. SOURCE: SP 800-53; CNSSI-4009
SSL –	See Secure Sockets Layer.
Standard –	A published statement on a topic specifying characteristics, usually measurable, that must be satisfied or achieved in order to comply with the standard. SOURCE: FIPS 201
Start-Up KEK	Key-encryption-key held in common by a group of potential communicating entities and used to establish ad hoc tactical networks. SOURCE: CNSSI-4009
State –	Intermediate Cipher result that can be pictured as a rectangular array of bytes. SOURCE: FIPS 197

Static Key –

A key that is intended for use for a relatively long period of time and is typically intended for use in many instances of a cryptographic key establish scheme

SOURCE: SP 800-57 Part 1

Status Monitoring –

Monitoring the information security metrics defined by the organization in the information security ISCM strategy.

SOURCE: SP 800-137

Steganography –

The art and science of communicating in a way that hides the existence of the communication. For example, a child pornography image can be hidden inside another graphic image file, audio file, or other file format.

SOURCE: SP 800-72; SP 800-101

The art, science, and practice of communicating in a way that hides the existence of the communication.

SOURCE: CNSSI-4009

Storage Object –

Object supporting both read and write accesses to an information system.

SOURCE: CNSSI-4009

Strength of Mechanism (SoM) –

A scale for measuring the relative strength of a security mechanism.

SOURCE: CNSSI-4009

Striped Core –

A network architecture in which user data traversing a core IP network is decrypted, filtered and re-encrypted one or more times. Note: The decryption, filtering, and re-encryption are performed within a "Red gateway"; consequently, the core is "striped" because the data path is alternately Black, Red, and Black.

SOURCE: CNSSI-4009

Strong Authentication –

The requirement to use multiple factors for authentication and advanced technology, such as dynamic passwords or digital certificates, to verify an entity's identity.

SOURCE: CNSSI-4009

Subassembly –

Major subdivision of an assembly consisting of a package of parts, elements, and circuits that perform a specific function.

SOURCE: CNSSI-4009

Subject –	Generally an individual, process, or device causing information to flow among objects or changes to the system state. See Object.
	SOURCE: SP 800-53
	An active entity (generally an individual, process, or device) that causes information to flow among objects or changes the system state. See also Object.
	SOURCE: CNSSI-4009
Subject Security Level –	Sensitivity label(s) of the objects to which the subject has both read and write access. Security level of a subject must always be dominated by the clearance level of the user associated with the subject.
	SOURCE: CNSSI-4009
Subordinate Certification Authority –	In a hierarchical PKI, a Certification Authority whose certificate signature key is certified by another CA, and whose activities are constrained by that other CA.
	SOURCE: SP 800-32; CNSSI-4009
Subscriber –	A party who receives a credential or token from a CSP (Credentials Service Provider) and becomes a claimant in an authentication protocol.
	SOURCE: CNSSI-4009
	A party who receives a credential or token from a CSP (Credentials Service Provider).
	SOURCE: SP 800-63
Subsystem –	A major subdivision or component of an information system consisting of information, information technology, and personnel that perform one or more specific functions.
	SOURCE: SP 800-53; SP 800-53A; SP 800-37
Suite A –	A specific set of classified cryptographic algorithms used for the protection of some categories of restricted mission-critical information.
	SOURCE: CNSSI-4009
Suite B –	A specific set of cryptographic algorithms suitable for protecting national security systems and information throughout the U.S. government and to support interoperability with allies and coalition partners.
	SOURCE: CNSSI-4009, as modified

Superencryption –	Process of encrypting encrypted information. Occurs when a message, encrypted off-line, is transmitted over a secured, online circuit, or when information encrypted by the originator is multiplexed onto a communications trunk, which is then bulk encrypted.
	SOURCE: CNSSI-4009
Superior Certification Authority –	In a hierarchical PKI, a Certification Authority who has certified the certificate signature key of another CA, and who constrains the activities of that CA.
	SOURCE: SP 800-32; CNSSI-4009
Supersession –	Scheduled or unscheduled replacement of COMSEC material with a different edition.
	SOURCE: CNSSI-4009
Supervisory Control and Data Acquisition (SCADA) –	A generic name for a computerized system that is capable of gathering and processing data and applying operational controls over long distances. Typical uses include power transmission and distribution and pipeline systems. SCADA was designed for the unique communication challenges (delays, data integrity, etc.) posed by the various media that must be used, such as phone lines, microwave, and satellite. Usually shared rather than dedicated.
	SOURCE: SP 800-82
	Networks or systems generally used for industrial controls or to manage infrastructure such as pipelines and power systems.
	SOURCE: CNSSI-4009
Supplementation (Assessment Procedures) –	The process of adding assessment procedures or assessment details to assessment procedures in order to adequately meet the organization's risk management needs.
	SOURCE: SP 800-53A
Supplementation (Security Controls) –	The process of adding security controls or control enhancements to a security control baseline from NIST Special Publication 800-53 or CNSS Instruction 1253 in order to adequately meet the organization's risk management needs.
	SOURCE: SP 800-53A; SP 800-39
Supply Chain –	A system of organizations, people, activities, information, and resources, possibly international in scope, that provides products or services to consumers.
	SOURCE: SP 800-53; CNSSI-4009

Supply Chain Attack –	Attacks that allow the adversary to utilize implants or other vulnerabilities inserted prior to installation in order to infiltrate data, or manipulate information technology hardware, software, operating systems, peripherals (information technology products) or services at any point during the life cycle. SOURCE: CNSSI-4009
Suppression Measure –	Action, procedure, modification, or device that reduces the level of, or inhibits the generation of, compromising emanations in an information system. SOURCE: CNSSI-4009
Surrogate Access –	See Discretionary Access Control.
Syllabary –	List of individual letters, combination of letters, or syllables, with their equivalent code groups, used for spelling out words or proper names not present in the vocabulary of a code. A syllabary may also be a spelling table. SOURCE: CNSSI-4009
Symmetric Encryption Algorithm –	Encryption algorithms using the same secret key for encryption and decryption. SOURCE: SP 800-49; CNSSI-4009
Symmetric Key –	A cryptographic key that is used to perform both the cryptographic operation and its inverse, for example to encrypt and decrypt, or create a message authentication code and to verify the code. SOURCE: SP 800-63; CNSSI-4009 A single cryptographic key that is used with a secret (symmetric) key algorithm. SOURCE: SP 800-21 [2nd Ed]
Synchronous Crypto-Operation –	Encryption algorithms using the same secret key for encryption and decryption. SOURCE: CNSSI-4009
System –	See Information System. Any organized assembly of resources and procedures united and regulated by interaction or interdependence to accomplish a set of specific functions. SOURCE: CNSSI-4009
System Administrator –	A person who manages the technical aspects of a system. SOURCE: SP 800-40

Individual responsible for the installation and maintenance of an information system, providing effective information system utilization, adequate security parameters, and sound implementation of established Information Assurance policy and procedures.

SOURCE: CNSSI-4009

System Assets –

Any software, hardware, data, administrative, physical, communications, or personnel resource within an information system.

SOURCE: CNSSI-4009

System Development Life Cycle – (SDLC)

The scope of activities associated with a system, encompassing the system's initiation, development and acquisition, implementation, operation and maintenance, and ultimately its disposal that instigates another system initiation.

SOURCE: SP 800-34; CNSSI-4009

System Development Methodologies –

Methodologies developed through software engineering to manage the complexity of system development. Development methodologies include software engineering aids and high-level design analysis tools.

SOURCE: CNSSI-4009

System High –

Highest security level supported by an information system.

SOURCE: CNSSI-4009

System High Mode –

Information systems security mode of operation wherein each user, with direct or indirect access to the information system, its peripherals, remote terminals, or remote hosts, has all of the following: a. valid security clearance for all information within an information system; b. formal access approval and signed nondisclosure agreements for all the information stored and/or processed (including all compartments, subcompartments and/or special access programs); and c. valid need-to-know for some of the information contained within the information system.

SOURCE: CNSSI-4009

System Indicator –

Symbol or group of symbols in an off-line encrypted message identifying the specific cryptosystem or key used in the encryption.

SOURCE: CNSSI-4009

System Integrity –

The quality that a system has when it performs its intended function in an unimpaired manner, free from unauthorized manipulation of the system, whether intentional or accidental.

SOURCE: SP 800-27

Attribute of an information system when it performs its intended function in an unimpaired manner, free from deliberate or inadvertent unauthorized manipulation of the system.

SOURCE: CNSSI-4009

System Interconnection –

The direct connection of two or more IT systems for the purpose of sharing data and other information resources.

SOURCE: SP 800-47; CNSSI-4009

System Low –

Lowest security level supported by an information system.

SOURCE: CNSSI-4009

System Of Records –

A group of any records under the control of any agency from which information is retrieved by the name of the individual or by some identifying number, symbol, or other identifying particular assigned to the individual.

SOURCE: SP 800-122

System Owner –

Person or organization having responsibility for the development, procurement, integration, modification, operation and maintenance, and/or final disposition of an information system.

SOURCE: CNSSI-4009

System Profile –

Detailed security description of the physical structure, equipment component, location, relationships, and general operating environment of an information system.

SOURCE: CNSSI-4009

System Security –

See Information System Security.

System Security Plan –

Formal document that provides an overview of the security requirements for the information system and describes the security controls in place or planned for meeting those requirements.

SOURCE: SP 800-37; SP 800-53; SP 800-53A; SP 800-18; FIPS 200

The formal document prepared by the information system owner (or common security controls owner for inherited controls) that provides an overview of the security requirements for the system and describes the security controls in place or planned for meeting those requirements. The plan can also contain as supporting appendices or as references, other key security-related documents such as a risk assessment, privacy impact assessment, system interconnection agreements, contingency plan, security configurations, configuration management plan, and incident response plan.

SOURCE: CNSSI-4009

System Software –	The special software within the cryptographic boundary (e.g., operating system, compilers or utility programs) designed for a specific computer system or family of computer systems to facilitate the operation and maintenance of the computer system, associated programs, and data. SOURCE: FIPS 140-2
System-Specific Security Control –	A security control for an information system that has not been designated as a common security control or the portion of a hybrid control that is to be implemented within an information system. SOURCE: SP 800-37; SP 800-53; SP 800-53A; CNSSI-4009
Systems Security Engineering –	See Information Systems Security Engineering.
Systems Security Officer –	See Information Systems Security Officer.
Tabletop Exercise –	A discussion-based exercise where personnel with roles and responsibilities in a particular IT plan meet in a classroom setting or in breakout groups to validate the content of the plan by discussing their roles during an emergency and their responses to a particular emergency situation. A facilitator initiates the discussion by presenting a scenario and asking questions based on the scenario. SOURCE: SP 800-84
Tactical Data –	Information that requires protection from disclosure and modification for a limited duration as determined by the originator or information owner. SOURCE: CNSSI-4009
Tactical Edge –	The platforms, sites, and personnel (U. S. military, allied, coalition partners, first responders) operating at lethal risk in a battle space or crisis environment characterized by 1) a dependence on information systems and connectivity for survival and mission success, 2) high threats to the operational readiness of both information systems and connectivity, and 3) users are fully engaged, highly stressed, and dependent on the availability, integrity, and transparency of their information systems. SOURCE: CNSSI-4009
Tailored Security Control Baseline –	A set of security controls resulting from the application of tailoring guidance to the security control baseline. See Tailoring. SOURCE: SP 800-37; SP 800-53; SP 800-53A

Tailoring –	The process by which a security control baseline is modified based on: (i) the application of scoping guidance; (ii) the specification of compensating security controls, if needed; and (iii) the specification of organization-defined parameters in the security controls via explicit assignment and selection statements. SOURCE: SP 800-37; SP 800-53; SP 800-53A; CNSSI-4009
Tailoring (Assessment Procedures) –	The process by which assessment procedures defined in Special Publication 800-53A are adjusted, or scoped, to match the characteristics of the information system under assessment, providing organizations with the flexibility needed to meet specific organizational requirements and to avoid overly-constrained assessment approaches. SOURCE: SP 800-53A
Tampering –	An intentional event resulting in modification of a system, its intended behavior, or data. SOURCE: CNSSI-4009
Target Of Evaluation (TOE) –	In accordance with Common Criteria, an information system, part of a system or product, and all associated documentation, that is the subject of a security evaluation. SOURCE: CNSSI-4009
Technical Controls –	The security controls (i.e., safeguards or countermeasures) for an information system that are primarily implemented and executed by the information system through mechanisms contained in the hardware, software, or firmware components of the system. SOURCE: SP 800-53; SP 800-53A; SP 800-37; FIPS 200
Technical Non-repudiation –	The contribution of public key mechanisms to the provision of technical evidence supporting a non-repudiation security service. SOURCE: SP 800-32
Technical Reference Model(TRM) –	A component-driven, technical framework that categorizes the standards and technologies to support and enable the delivery of service components and capabilities. SOURCE: CNSSI-4009
Technical Security Controls –	Security controls (i.e., safeguards or countermeasures) for an information system that are primarily implemented and executed by the information system through mechanisms contained in the hardware, software, or firmware components of the system. SOURCE: CNSSI-4009

Technical Vulnerability Information –	Detailed description of a weakness to include the implementable steps (such as code) necessary to exploit that weakness. SOURCE: CNSSI-4009
Telecommunications –	Preparation, transmission, communication, or related processing of information (writing, images, sounds, or other data) by electrical, electromagnetic, electromechanical, electro-optical, or electronic means. SOURCE: CNSSI-4009
Telework –	The ability for an organization's employees and contractors to perform work from locations other than the organization's facilities. SOURCE: SP 800-46
Tempest –	A name referring to the investigation, study, and control of unintentional compromising emanations from telecommunications and automated information systems equipment. SOURCE: FIPS 140-2
TEMPEST –	A name referring to the investigation, study, and control of compromising emanations from telecommunications and automated information systems equipment. SOURCE: CNSSI-4009
TEMPEST Test –	Laboratory or on-site test to determine the nature of compromising emanations associated with an information system. SOURCE: CNSSI-4009
TEMPEST Zone –	Designated area within a facility where equipment with appropriate TEMPEST characteristics (TEMPEST zone assignment) may be operated. SOURCE: CNSSI-4009
Test –	A type of assessment method that is characterized by the process of exercising one or more assessment objects under specified conditions to compare actual with expected behavior, the results of which are used to support the determination of security control effectiveness over time. SOURCE: SP 800-53A
Test Key –	Key intended for testing of COMSEC equipment or systems. SOURCE: CNSSI-4009

Threat –	Any circumstance or event with the potential to adversely impact organizational operations (including mission, functions, image, or reputation), organizational assets, individuals, other organizations, or the Nation through an information system via unauthorized access, destruction, disclosure, modification of information, and/or denial of service.
	SOURCE: SP 800-53; SP 800-53A; SP 800-27; SP 800-60; SP 800-37; CNSSI-4009
	The potential source of an adverse event.
	SOURCE: SP 800-61
	Any circumstance or event with the potential to adversely impact organizational operations (including mission, functions, image, or reputation), organizational assets, or individuals through an information system via unauthorized access, destruction, disclosure, modification of information, and/or denial of service. Also, the potential for a threat-source to successfully exploit a particular information system vulnerability.
	SOURCE: FIPS 200
Threat Analysis –	The examination of threat sources against system vulnerabilities to determine the threats for a particular system in a particular operational environment.
	SOURCE: SP 800-27
	See Threat Assessment.
	SOURCE: CNSSI-4009
Threat Assessment –	Formal description and evaluation of threat to an information system.
	SOURCE: SP 800-53; SP 800-18
	Process of formally evaluating the degree of threat to an information system or enterprise and describing the nature of the threat.
	SOURCE: CNSSI-4009; SP 800-53A
Threat Event –	An event or situation that has the potential for causing undesirable consequences or impact.
	SOURCE: SP 800-30
Threat Monitoring –	Analysis, assessment, and review of audit trails and other information collected for the purpose of searching out system events that may constitute violations of system security.
	SOURCE: CNSSI-4009

Threat Scenario –	A set of discrete threat events, associated with a specific threat source or multiple threat sources, partially ordered in time. SOURCE: SP 800-30
Threat Shifting –	Response from adversaries to perceived safeguards and/or countermeasures (i.e., security controls), in which the adversaries change some characteristic of their intent to do harm in order to avoid and/or overcome those safeguards/countermeasures. SOURCE: SP 800-30
Threat Source –	The intent and method targeted at the intentional exploitation of a vulnerability or a situation and method that may accidentally trigger a vulnerability. Synonymous with Threat Agent. SOURCE: FIPS 200; SP 800-53; SP 800-53A; SP 800-37 The intent and method targeted at the intentional exploitation of a vulnerability or a situation and method that may accidentally exploit a vulnerability. SOURCE: CNSSI-4009
Time Bomb –	Resident computer program that triggers an unauthorized act at a predefined time. SOURCE: CNSSI-4009
Time-Compliance Date –	Date by which a mandatory modification to a COMSEC end-item must be incorporated if the item is to remain approved for operational use. SOURCE: CNSSI-4009
Time-Dependent Password –	Password that is valid only at a certain time of day or during a specified interval of time. SOURCE: CNSSI-4009
TOE Security Functions (TSF) –	Set consisting of all hardware, software, and firmware of the TOE that must be relied upon for the correct enforcement of the TOE Security Policy (TSP). SOURCE: CNSSI-4009
TOE Security Policy (TSP) –	Set of rules that regulate how assets are managed, protected, and distributed within the TOE. SOURCE: CNSSI-4009
Token –	Something that the Claimant possesses and controls (typically a key or password) that is used to authenticate the Claimant's identity. SOURCE: SP 800-63

Something that the claimant possesses and controls (such as a key or password) that is used to authenticate a claim. See also Cryptographic Token.

SOURCE: CNSSI-4009

Total Risk –

The potential for the occurrence of an adverse event if no mitigating action is taken (i.e., the potential for any applicable threat to exploit a system vulnerability).

SOURCE: SP 800-16

Tracking Cookie –

A cookie placed on a user's computer to track the user's activity on different Web sites, creating a detailed profile of the user's behavior.

SOURCE: SP 800-83

Tradecraft Identity –

An identity used for the purpose of work-related interactions that may or may not be synonymous with an individual's true identity.

SOURCE: CNSSI-4009

Traditional INFOSEC Program –

Program in which NSA acts as the central procurement agency for the development and, in some cases, the production of INFOSEC items. This includes the Authorized Vendor Program. Modifications to the INFOSEC end-items used in products developed and/or produced under these programs must be approved by NSA.

SOURCE: CNSSI-4009

Traffic Analysis –

A form of passive attack in which an intruder observes information about calls (although not necessarily the contents of the messages) and makes inferences, e.g., from the source and destination numbers, or frequency and length of the messages.

SOURCE: SP 800-24

The analysis of patterns in communications for the purpose of gaining intelligence about a system or its users. It does not require examination of the content of the communications, which may or may not be decipherable. For example, an adversary may be able to detect a signal from a reader that could enable it to infer that a particular activity is occurring (e.g., a shipment has arrived, someone is entering a facility) without necessarily learning an identifier or associated data.

SOURCE: SP 800-98

	Gaining knowledge of information by inference from observable characteristics of a data flow, even if the information is not directly available (e.g., when the data is encrypted). These characteristics include the identities and locations of the source(s) and destination(s) of the flow, and the flow's presence, amount, frequency, and duration of occurrence. SOURCE: CNSSI-4009
Traffic Encryption Key (TEK) –	Key used to encrypt plain text or to superencrypt previously encrypted text and/or to decrypt cipher text. SOURCE: CNSSI-4009
Traffic Padding –	Generation of mock communications or data units to disguise the amount of real data units being sent. SOURCE: CNSSI-4009
Traffic-Flow Security (TFS) –	Techniques to counter Traffic Analysis. SOURCE: CNSSI-4009
Training (Information Security) –	Training strives to produce relevant and needed (information) security skills and competencies. SOURCE: SP 800-50
Training Assessment –	An evaluation of the training efforts. SOURCE: SP 800-16
Training Effectiveness –	A measurement of what a given student has learned from a specific course or training event. SOURCE: SP 800-16
Training Effectiveness Evaluation –	Information collected to assist employees and their supervisors in assessing individual students' subsequent on-the-job performance, to provide trend data to assist trainers in improving both learning and teaching, and to be used in return-on-investment statistics to enable responsible officials to allocate limited resources in a thoughtful, strategic manner among the spectrum of IT security awareness, security literacy, training, and education options for optimal results among the workforce as a whole. SOURCE: SP 800-16
Tranquility –	Property whereby the security level of an object cannot change while the object is being processed by an information system. SOURCE: CNSSI-4009

Transmission –

The state that exists when information is being electronically sent from one location to one or more other locations.

SOURCE: CNSSI-4009

Transmission Security – (TRANSEC)

Measures (security controls) applied to transmissions in order to prevent interception, disruption of reception, communications deception, and/or derivation of intelligence by analysis of transmission characteristics such as signal parameters or message externals.

Note: TRANSEC is that field of COMSEC which deals with the security of communication transmissions, rather than that of the information being communicated.

SOURCE: CNSSI-4009

Trap Door –

1. A means of reading cryptographically protected information by the use of private knowledge of weaknesses in the cryptographic algorithm used to protect the data.

2. In cryptography, one-to-one function that is easy to compute in one direction, yet believed to be difficult to invert without special information.

SOURCE: CNSSI-4009

Transport Layer Security (TLS) –

An authentication and security protocol widely implemented in browsers and Web servers.

SOURCE: SP 800-63

Triple DES –

An implementation of the Data Encryption Standard (DES) algorithm that uses three passes of the DES algorithm instead of one as used in ordinary DES applications. Triple DES provides much stronger encryption than ordinary DES but it is less secure than AES.

SOURCE: CNSSI-4009

Trojan Horse –

A computer program that appears to have a useful function, but also has a hidden and potentially malicious function that evades security mechanisms, sometimes by exploiting legitimate authorizations of a system entity that invokes the program.

SOURCE: CNSSI-4009

Trust Anchor –	A public key and the name of a certification authority that is used to validate the first certificate in a sequence of certificates. The trust anchor's public key is used to verify the signature on a certificate issued by a trust anchor certification authority. The security of the validation process depends upon the authenticity and integrity of the trust anchor. Trust anchors are often distributed as self-signed certificates. SOURCE: SP 800-57 Part 1 An established point of trust (usually based on the authority of some person, office, or organization) from which an entity begins the validation of an authorized process or authorized (signed) package. A "trust anchor" is sometimes defined as just a public key used for different purposes (e.g., validating a Certification Authority, validating a signed software package or key, validating the process [or person] loading the signed software or key). SOURCE: CNSSI-4009 A public or symmetric key that is trusted because it is directly built into hardware or software, or securely provisioned via out-of-band means, rather than because it is vouched for by another trusted entity (e.g. in a public key certificate). SOURCE: SP 800-63
Trust List –	The collection of trusted certificates used by Relying Parties to authenticate other certificates. SOURCE: SP 800-32; CNSSI-4009
Trusted Agent –	Entity authorized to act as a representative of an agency in confirming Subscriber identification during the registration process. Trusted Agents do not have automated interfaces with Certification Authorities. SOURCE: SP 800-32; CNSSI-4009
Trusted Certificate –	A certificate that is trusted by the Relying Party on the basis of secure and authenticated delivery. The public keys included in trusted certificates are used to start certification paths. Also known as a "trust anchor." SOURCE: SP 800-32; CNSSI-4009
Trusted Channel –	A channel where the endpoints are known and data integrity is protected in transit. Depending on the communications protocol used, data privacy may be protected in transit. Examples include SSL, IPSEC, and secure physical connection. SOURCE: CNSSI-4009

Trusted Computer System –	A system that employs sufficient hardware and software assurance measures to allow its use for processing simultaneously a range of sensitive or classified information. SOURCE: CNSSI-4009
Trusted Computing Base (TCB) –	Totality of protection mechanisms within a computer system, including hardware, firmware, and software, the combination responsible for enforcing a security policy. SOURCE: CNSSI-4009
Trusted Distribution –	Method for distributing trusted computing base (TCB) hardware, software, and firmware components that protects the TCB from modification during distribution. SOURCE: CNSSI-4009
Trusted Foundry –	Facility that produces integrated circuits with a higher level of integrity assurance. SOURCE: CNSSI-4009
Trusted Identification Forwarding –	Identification method used in information system networks whereby the sending host can verify an authorized user on its system is attempting a connection to another host. The sending host transmits the required user authentication information to the receiving host. SOURCE: CNSSI-4009
Trusted Path –	A mechanism by which a user (through an input device) can communicate directly with the security functions of the information system with the necessary confidence to support the system security policy. This mechanism can only be activated by the user or the security functions of the information system and cannot be imitated by untrusted software. SOURCE: SP 800-53; CNSSI-4009 A means by which an operator and a target of evaluation security function can communicate with the necessary confidence to support the target of evaluation security policy. SOURCE: FIPS 140-2
Trusted Platform Module (TPM) Chip –	A tamper-resistant integrated circuit built into some computer motherboards that can perform cryptographic operations (including key generation) and protect small amounts of sensitive information, such as passwords and cryptographic keys. SOURCE: SP 800-111
Trusted Process –	Process that has been tested and verified to operate only as intended. SOURCE: CNSSI-4009

Trusted Recovery –

Ability to ensure recovery without compromise after a system failure.

SOURCE: CNSSI-4009

Trusted Software –

Software portion of a trusted computing base (TCB).

SOURCE: CNSSI-4009

Trusted Timestamp –

A digitally signed assertion by a trusted authority that a specific digital object existed at a particular time.

SOURCE: SP 800-32; CNSSI-4009

Trustworthiness –

The attribute of a person or organization that provides confidence to others of the qualifications, capabilities, and reliability of that entity to perform specific tasks and fulfill assigned responsibilities.

SOURCE: SP 800-79

The attribute of a person or enterprise that provides confidence to others of the qualifications, capabilities, and reliability of that entity to perform specific tasks and fulfill assigned responsibilities.

SOURCE: CNSSI-4009; SP 800-39

Security decisions with respect to extended investigations to determine and confirm qualifications, and suitability to perform specific tasks and responsibilities.

SOURCE: FIPS 201

Trustworthy System –

Computer hardware, software and procedures that—
1) are reasonably secure from intrusion and misuse;
2) provide a reasonable level of availability, reliability, and correct operation;
3) are reasonably suited to performing their intended functions; and
4) adhere to generally accepted security procedures.

SOURCE: SP 800-32

TSEC –

Telecommunications Security.

SOURCE: CNSSI-4009

TSEC Nomenclature –

System for identifying the type and purpose of certain items of COMSEC material.

SOURCE: CNSSI-4009

Tunneling –

Technology enabling one network to send its data via another network's connections. Tunneling works by encapsulating a network protocol within packets carried by the second network.

SOURCE: CNSSI-4009

Two-Part Code –

Code consisting of an encoding section, in which the vocabulary items (with their associated code groups) are arranged in alphabetical or other systematic order, and a decoding section, in which the code groups (with their associated meanings) are arranged in a separate alphabetical or numeric order.

SOURCE: CNSSI-4009

Two-Person Control (TPC) –

Continuous surveillance and control of positive control material at all times by a minimum of two authorized individuals, each capable of detecting incorrect and unauthorized procedures with respect to the task being performed and each familiar with established security and safety requirements.

SOURCE: CNSSI-4009

Two-Person Integrity (TPI) –

System of storage and handling designed to prohibit individual access by requiring the presence of at least two authorized individuals, each capable of detecting incorrect or unauthorized security procedures with respect to the task being performed. See No-Lone Zone.

SOURCE: CNSSI-4009

Type 1 Key –

Generated and distributed under the auspices of NSA for use in a cryptographic device for the protection of national security information.

SOURCE: CNSSI-4009, as modified

Type 1 Product –

Cryptographic equipment, assembly or component classified or certified by NSA for encrypting and decrypting national security information when appropriately keyed. Developed using established NSA business processes and containing NSA-approved algorithms. Used to protect systems requiring the most stringent protection mechanisms.

SOURCE: CNSSI-4009, as modified

Type 2 Key –

Generated and distributed under the auspices of NSA for use in a cryptographic device for the protection of unclassified information.

SOURCE: CNSSI-4009, as modified

Type 2 Product –

Cryptographic equipment, assembly, or component certified by NSA for encrypting or decrypting sensitive information when appropriately keyed. Developed using established NSA business processes and containing NSA-approved algorithms. Used to protect systems requiring protection mechanisms exceeding best commercial practices including systems used for the protection of unclassified information.

SOURCE: CNSSI-4009, as modified

Type 3 Key –	Used in a cryptographic device for the protection of unclassified sensitive information, even if used in a Type 1 or Type 2 product.
	SOURCE: CNSSI-4009
Type 3 Product –	Unclassified cryptographic equipment, assembly, or component used, when appropriately keyed, for encrypting or decrypting unclassified sensitive U.S. government or commercial information, and to protect systems requiring protection mechanisms consistent with standard commercial practices. Developed using established commercial standards and containing NIST-approved cryptographic algorithms/modules or successfully evaluated by the National Information Assurance Partnership (NIAP).
	SOURCE: CNSSI-4009
Type 4 Key –	Used by a cryptographic device in support of its Type 4 functionality, i.e., any provision of key that lacks U.S. government endorsement or oversight.
	SOURCE: CNSSI-4009
Type 4 Product –	Unevaluated commercial cryptographic equipment, assemblies, or components that neither NSA nor NIST certify for any government usage. These products are typically delivered as part of commercial offerings and are commensurate with the vendor's commercial practices. These products may contain either vendor proprietary algorithms, algorithms registered by NIST, or algorithms registered by NIST and published in a FIPS.
	SOURCE: CNSSI-4009
Type Accreditation –	A form of accreditation that is used to authorize multiple instances of a major application or general support system for operation at approved locations with the same type of computing environment. In situations where a major application or general support system is installed at multiple locations, a type accreditation will satisfy C&A requirements only if the application or system consists of a common set of tested and approved hardware, software, and firmware.
	SOURCE: CNSSI-4009
Type Certification –	The certification acceptance of replica information systems based on the comprehensive evaluation of the technical and nontechnical security features of an information system and other safeguards, made as part of and in support of the formal approval process, to establish the extent to which a particular design and implementation meet a specified set of security requirements.
	SOURCE: CNSSI-4009

207

U.S. Person –

Federal law and Executive Order define a U.S. Person as: a citizen of the United States; an alien lawfully admitted for permanent residence; an unincorporated association with a substantial number of members who are citizens of the U.S. or are aliens lawfully admitted for permanent residence; and/or a corporation that is incorporated in the U.S.

SOURCE: CNSSI-4009

U.S.-Controlled Facility –

Base or building to which access is physically controlled by U.S. individuals who are authorized U.S. government or U.S. government contractor employees.

SOURCE: CNSSI-4009

U.S.-Controlled Space –

Room or floor within a facility that is not a U.S.-controlled facility, access to which is physically controlled by U.S. individuals who are authorized U.S. government or U.S. government contractor employees. Keys or combinations to locks controlling entrance to U.S.-controlled spaces must be under the exclusive control of U.S. individuals who are U.S. government or U.S. government contractor employees.

SOURCE: CNSSI-4009

Unauthorized Access –

Occurs when a user, legitimate or unauthorized, accesses a resource that the user is not permitted to use.

SOURCE: FIPS 191

Any access that violates the stated security policy.

SOURCE: CNSSI-4009

Unauthorized Disclosure –

An event involving the exposure of information to entities not authorized access to the information.

SOURCE: SP 800-57 Part 1; CNSSI-4009

Unsigned data –

Data included in an authentication token, in addition to a digital signature.

SOURCE: FIPS 196

Unclassified –

Information that has not been determined pursuant to E.O. 12958, as amended, or any predecessor order, to require protection against unauthorized disclosure and that is not designated as classified.

SOURCE: CNSSI-4009

United States Government Configuration Baseline – (USGCB)	The United States Government Configuration Baseline (USGCB) provides security configuration baselines for Information Technology products widely deployed across the federal agencies. The USGCB baseline evolved from the federal Desktop Core Configuration mandate. The USGCB is a Federal government-wide initiative that provides guidance to agencies on what should be done to improve and maintain an effective configuration settings focusing primarily on security.
	SOURCE: SP 800-128
Untrusted Process –	Process that has not been evaluated or examined for correctness and adherence to the security policy. It may include incorrect or malicious code that attempts to circumvent the security mechanisms.
	SOURCE: CNSSI-4009
Update (a Certificate) –	The act or process by which data items bound in an existing public key certificate, especially authorizations granted to the subject, are changed by issuing a new certificate.
	SOURCE: SP 800-32; CNSSI-4009
Update (key) –	Automatic or manual cryptographic process that irreversibly modifies the state of a COMSEC key.
	SOURCE: CNSSI-4009
US-CERT –	A partnership between the Department of Homeland Security and the public and private sectors, established to protect the nation's Internet infrastructure. US-CERT coordinates defense against and responses to cyber attacks across the nation.
	SOURCE: CNSSI-4009
User –	Individual or (system) process authorized to access an information system.
	SOURCE: FIPS 200
	Individual, or (system) process acting on behalf of an individual, authorized to access an information system.
	SOURCE: SP 800-53; SP 800-18; CNSSI-4009
	An individual or a process (subject) acting on behalf of the individual that accesses a cryptographic module in order to obtain cryptographic services.
	SOURCE: FIPS 140-2
User ID –	Unique symbol or character string used by an information system to identify a specific user.
	SOURCE: CNSSI-4009

User Initialization –	A function in the life cycle of keying material; the process whereby a user initializes its cryptographic application (e.g., installing and initializing software and hardware).
	SOURCE: SP 800-57 Part 1
User Partnership Program (UPP) –	Partnership between the NSA and a U.S. government agency to facilitate development of secure information system equipment incorporating NSA-approved cryptography. The result of this program is the authorization of the product or system to safeguard national security information in the user's specific application.
	SOURCE: CNSSI-4009
User Registration –	A function in the life cycle of keying material; a process whereby an entity becomes a member of a security domain.
	SOURCE: SP 800-57 Part 1
User Representative (COMSEC) –	Individual authorized by an organization to order COMSEC keying material and interface with the keying system, provide information to key users, and ensure the correct type of key is ordered.
	SOURCE: CNSSI-4009
User Representative (Risk Management) –	The person that defines the system's operational and functional requirements, and who is responsible for ensuring that user operational interests are met throughout the systems authorization process.
	SOURCE: CNSSI-4009
Valid Data Element –	A payload, an associated data string, or a nonce that satisfies the restrictions of the formatting function.
	SOURCE: SP 800-38C
Validation –	The process of demonstrating that the system under consideration meets in all respects the specification of that system.
	SOURCE: FIPS 201
	Confirmation (through the provision of strong, sound, objective evidence) that requirements for a specific intended use or application have been fulfilled (e.g., a trustworthy credential has been presented, or data or information has been formatted in accordance with a defined set of rules, or a specific process has demonstrated that an entity under consideration meets, in all respects, its defined attributes or requirements).
	SOURCE: CNSSI-4009

Variant –

One of two or more code symbols having the same plain text equivalent.

SOURCE: CNSSI-4009

Verification –

Confirmation, through the provision of objective evidence, that specified requirements have been fulfilled (e.g., an entity's requirements have been correctly defined, or an entity's attributes have been correctly presented; or a procedure or function performs as intended and leads to the expected outcome).

SOURCE: CNSSI-4009

See Also Identity Verification.

Verified Name –

A Subscriber name that has been verified by identity proofing.

SOURCE: SP 800-63

Verifier –

An entity that verifies the Claimant's identity by verifying the Claimant's possession and control of a token using an authentication protocol. To do this, the Verifier may also need to validate credentials that link the token and identity and check their status.

SOURCE: SP 800-63

An entity which is or represents the entity requiring an authenticated identity. A verifier includes the functions necessary for engaging in authentication exchanges.

SOURCE: FIPS 196

Verifier Impersonation Attack –

A scenario where the Attacker impersonates the Verifier in an authentication protocol, usually to capture information that can be used to masquerade as a Claimant to the real Verifier.

SOURCE: SP 800-63

Virtual Machine (VM) –

Software that allows a single host to run one or more guest operating systems.

SOURCE: SP 800-115

Virtual Private Network (VPN) –

A virtual network, built on top of existing physical networks, that provides a secure communications tunnel for data and other information transmitted between networks.

SOURCE: SP 800-46

Protected information system link utilizing tunneling, security controls (see Information Assurance), and endpoint address translation giving the impression of a dedicated line

SOURCE: CNSSI-4009

Virus –

A computer program that can copy itself and infect a computer without permission or knowledge of the user. A virus might corrupt or delete data on a computer, use email programs to spread itself to other computers, or even erase everything on a hard disk.

SOURCE: CNSSI-4009

Vulnerability –

Weakness in an information system, system security procedures, internal controls, or implementation that could be exploited or triggered by a threat source.

SOURCE: SP 800-53; SP 800-53A; SP 800-37; SP 800-60; SP 800-115; FIPS 200

A weakness in a system, application, or network that is subject to exploitation or misuse.

SOURCE: SP 800-61

Weakness in an information system, system security procedures, internal controls, or implementation that could be exploited by a threat source.

SOURCE: CNSSI-4009

Vulnerability Analysis –

See Vulnerability Assessment.

Vulnerability Assessment –

Formal description and evaluation of the vulnerabilities in an information system.

SOURCE: SP 800-53; SP 800-37

Systematic examination of an information system or product to determine the adequacy of security measures, identify security deficiencies, provide data from which to predict the effectiveness of proposed security measures, and confirm the adequacy of such measures after implementation.

SOURCE: SP 800-53A; CNSSI-4009

Warm Site –

An environmentally conditioned workspace that is partially equipped with information systems and telecommunications equipment to support relocated operations in the event of a significant disruption.

SOURCE: SP 800-34

Backup site which typically contains the data links and preconfigured equipment necessary to rapidly start operations, but does not contain live data. Thus commencing operations at a warm site will (at a minimum) require the restoration of current data.

SOURCE: CNSSI-4009

Web Bug –	A tiny image, invisible to a user, placed on Web pages in such a way to enable third parties to track use of Web servers and collect information about the user, including IP address, host name, browser type and version, operating system name and version, and cookies. SOURCE: SP 800-28 Malicious code, invisible to a user, placed on Web sites in such a way that it allows third parties to track use of Web servers and collect information about the user, including IP address, host name, browser type and version, operating system name and version, and Web browser cookie. SOURCE: CNSSI-4009
Web Content Filtering Software –	A program that prevents access to undesirable Web sites, typically by comparing a requested Web site address to a list of known bad Web sites. SOURCE: SP 800-69
Web Risk Assessment –	Processes for ensuring Web sites are in compliance with applicable policies. SOURCE: CNSSI-4009
White Team –	1. The group responsible for refereeing an engagement between a Red Team of mock attackers and a Blue Team of actual defenders of their enterprise's use of information systems. In an exercise, the White Team acts as the judges, enforces the rules of the exercise, observes the exercise, scores teams, resolves any problems that may arise, handles all requests for information or questions, and ensures that the competition runs fairly and does not cause operational problems for the defender's mission. The White Team helps to establish the rules of engagement, the metrics for assessing results and the procedures for providing operational security for the engagement. The White Team normally has responsibility for deriving lessons-learned, conducting the post engagement assessment, and promulgating results. 2. Can also refer to a small group of people who have prior knowledge of unannounced Red Team activities. The White Team acts as observers during the Red Team activity and ensures the scope of testing does not exceed a predefined threshold. SOURCE: CNSSI-4009
Whitelist –	A list of discrete entities, such as hosts or applications that are known to be benign and are approved for use within an organization and/or information system. SOURCE: SP 800-128

Wi-Fi Protected Access-2 (WPA2) –

The approved Wi-Fi Alliance interoperable implementation of the IEEE 802.11i security standard. For federal government use, the implementation must use FIPS-approved encryption, such as AES.

SOURCE: CNSSI-4009

Wiki –

Web applications or similar tools that allow identifiable users to add content (as in an Internet forum) and allow anyone to edit that content collectively.

SOURCE: CNSSI-4009

Wired Equivalent Privacy (WEP) –

A security protocol, specified in the IEEE 802.11 standard, that is designed to provide a WLAN with a level of security and privacy comparable to what is usually expected of a wired LAN. WEP is no longer considered a viable encryption mechanism due to known weaknesses.

SOURCE: SP 800-48

Wireless Access Point (WAP) –

A device that acts as a conduit to connect wireless communication devices together to allow them to communicate and create a wireless network.

SOURCE: CNSSI-4009

Wireless Application Protocol – (WAP)

A standard that defines the way in which Internet communications and other advanced services are provided on wireless mobile devices.

SOURCE: CNSSI-4009

Wireless Local Area Network – (WLAN)

A group of wireless networking devices within a limited geographic area, such as an office building, that exchange data through radio communications. The security of each WLAN is heavily dependent on how well each WLAN component—including client devices, APs, and wireless switches—is secured throughout the WLAN lifecycle, from initial WLAN design and deployment through ongoing maintenance and monitoring.

SOURCE: SP 800-153

Wireless Technology –

Technology that permits the transfer of information between separated points without physical connection.

Note: Currently wireless technologies use infrared, acoustic, radio frequency, and optical.

SOURCE: CNSSI-4009

Work Factor –

Estimate of the effort or time needed by a potential perpetrator, with specified expertise and resources, to overcome a protective measure.

SOURCE: CNSSI-4009

Workcraft Identity –	Synonymous with Tradecraft Identity. SOURCE: CNSSI-4009
Worm –	A self-replicating, self-propagating, self-contained program that uses networking mechanisms to spread itself. See Malicious Code. SOURCE: CNSSI-4009
Write –	Fundamental operation in an information system that results only in the flow of information from a subject to an object. See Access Type. SOURCE: CNSSI-4009
Write Access –	Permission to write to an object in an information system. SOURCE: CNSSI-4009
Write-Blocker –	A device that allows investigators to examine media while preventing data writes from occurring on the subject media. SOURCE: SP 800-72
X.509 Certificate –	The X.509 public-key certificate or the X.509 attribute certificate, as defined by the ISO/ITU-T X.509 standard. Most commonly (including in this document), an X.509 certificate refers to the X.509 public-key certificate. SOURCE: SP 800-57 Part 1
X.509 Public Key Certificate –	A digital certificate containing a public key for entity and a name for the entity, together with some other information that is rendered unforgeable by the digital signature of the certification authority that issued the certificate, encoded in the format defined in the ISO/ITU-T X.509 standard. SOURCE: SP 800-57 Part 1; CNSSI-4009 adapted
Zero Fill –	To fill unused storage locations in an information system with the representation of the character denoting "0." SOURCE: CNSSI-4009
Zeroization –	A method of erasing electronically stored data, cryptographic keys, and CSPs by altering or deleting the contents of the data storage to prevent recovery of the data. SOURCE: FIPS 140-2 A method of erasing electronically stored data, cryptographic keys, and Credentials Service Providers (CSPs) by altering or deleting the contents of the data storage to prevent recovery of the data. SOURCE: CNSSI-4009

Zeroize –

To remove or eliminate the key from a cryptographic equipment or fill device.

SOURCE: CNSSI-4009

Overwrite a memory location with data consisting entirely of bits with the value zero so that the data is destroyed and not recoverable. This is often contrasted with deletion methods that merely destroy reference to data within a file system rather than the data itself.

SOURCE: SP 800-63

Zombie –

A program that is installed on a system to cause it to attack other systems.

SOURCE: SP 800-83

Zone Of Control –

Three-dimensional space surrounding equipment that processes classified and/or sensitive information within which TEMPEST exploitation is not considered practical or where legal authority to identify and remove a potential TEMPEST exploitation exists.

SOURCE: CNSSI-4009

NON-NIST REFERENCES

40 U.S.C., Sec. 11101	U.S. Code, Title 40 – Public Buildings, Property, and Works, Subtitle III – Information Technology Management, Chapter 111 – General, Section 11101. Definitions.
40 U.S.C., Sec. 11331	U.S. Code, Title 40 – Public Buildings, Property, and Works, Subtitle III – Information Technology Management, Chapter 113 – Responsibility for Acquisitions of Information Technology, Subchapter III – Other Responsibilities, Section 11331. Responsibilities for federal information systems standards.
41 U.S.C., Sec. 403	Title 41 – Public Contracts, Chapter 7 – Office of Federal Procurement Policy, Section 403. Definitions.
44 U.S.C., Sec. 3502	U.S. Code, Title 44 – Public Printing and Documents, Chapter 35 – Coordination of Federal Information Policy, Subchapter I – Federal Information Policy, Section 3502. Definitions.
44 U.S.C., Sec. 3541	U.S. Code, Title 44 – Public Printing and Documents, Chapter 35 – Coordination of Federal Information Policy, Subchapter III – Information Security, Section 3541. Purposes.
44 U.S.C., Sec. 3542	U.S. Code, Title 44 – Public Printing and Documents, Chapter 35 – Coordination of Federal Information Policy, Subchapter III – Information Security, Section 3542. Definitions.
44 U.S.C., Sec. 3544	U.S. Code, Title 44 – Public Printing and Documents, Chapter 35 – Coordination of Federal Information Policy, Subchapter III – Information Security, Section 3544. Federal agency responsibilities.
47 C.F.R., Part 64, App A	Code of Federal Regulations, Title 47 – Telecommunication, Chapter I – Federal Communications Commission, Subchapter B – Common Carrier Services, Part 64 – Miscellaneous Rules Relating to Common Carriers, Appendix A to Part 64 – Telecommunications Service Priority (TSP) System for National Security Emergency Preparedness (NSEP).
Atomic Energy Act of 1954	*Definition of Restricted Data (42 U.S.C., Section 2011).*
CNSSI-4009	The Committee on National Security Systems Instruction No 4009 *"National Information Assurance Glossary."*
DCID 6/3	Director of Central Intelligence Directive 6/3 "Protecting Sensitive Compartmented Information Within Information Systems."
DCID 6/9	Director of Central Intelligence Directive 6/9 "Physical Security Standards for Sensitive Compartmented Information Facilities."

E.O. 13292   Executive Office of the President, Executive Order 13292— Further Amendment to Executive Order 12958, as Amended, Classified National Security Information, March 25, 2003.

Federal Information Security Management Act (FISMA)   P.L. 107-347, December 2002.

OMB Circular A-130, App. III   U.S. Office of Management and Budget, Circular No. A-130 Revised, (Transmittal Memorandum No. 4), Appendix III, Security of Federal Automated information Resources. November 28, 2000.

OMB Memorandum 02-01   U.S. Office of Management and Budget, Memorandum 02-01, Guidance for Preparing and Submitting Security Plans of Action and Milestones. October 17, 2001.

OMB Memorandum 03-22   U.S. Office of Management and Budget, Memorandum 03-22, OMB Guidance for Implementing the Privacy Provisions of the E-Government Act of 2002. September 29, 2003.

OMB Memorandum 04-04   U.S. Office of Management and Budget, Memorandum 04-04, OMB E-Authentication Guidance for Federal Agencies, December 16, 2003.

Public Law 104-106 Sec. 5125(b)   S. 1124, Division E [Public Law 104-106], 104th U.S. Cong., Information Technology Management Reform Act, February 10, 1996. Section 5125(b).